Dr Robin Royston, ~~~~~~~~~~~~~~~~~~~~~~~~~~~~~~ a
Consultant psychother~~~~~~~~~~~~~~~~~~~~~~~~~~~~~~~~ S
in Canterbury, and i~~~~~~~~~~~~~~~~~~~~~~~~~~~~~~~~~y
Ticehurst House. His p~~~~~~~~~~~~~~~~~~~~~~~~~~~~~~~d
the way they function in trauma patients. He is the co-
author of the critically acclaimed bestseller *Out of the
Dark* and has an extensive medico-legal practice. He lives
in Kent.

Annie Humphries was a director of Harvester Press before
becoming a freelance writer and editor. A graduate of
Trinity College, Dublin, and the University of Sussex, she
has a particular interest in nineteenth-century literature
and currently divides her time between London and
Northern Ireland.

Also by Dr Robin Royston

OUT OF THE DARK (with Linda Caine)

THE HIDDEN POWER OF DREAMS

An Essential Guide to
Interpreting Your Dreams

DR ROBIN ROYSTON
and
ANNIE HUMPHRIES

BANTAM BOOKS

LONDON • TORONTO • SYDNEY • AUCKLAND • JOHANNESBURG

THE HIDDEN POWER OF DREAMS
A BANTAM BOOK : 9780553817423

Originally published in Great Britain by Bantam Press,
a division of Transworld Publishers

PRINTING HISTORY
Bantam Press edition published 2006
Bantam edition published 2007

1 3 5 7 9 10 8 6 4 2

The authors and publishers are grateful to the following for permission to reproduce
extracts: to Houghton Mifflin for Anne Sexton, 'Old', from *All My Pretty Ones* (1962); to
Oxford University Press for 28 words from 'Lights Out', from *Collected Poems of Edward
Thomas* by E. Thomas, edited by G. Thomas (1978); to the Random House Group Ltd for
Jeanne Willis, 'Inside Our Dreams', from *Toffee Pockets* (Bodley Head, 1992); to
Katabasis for Ernesto Cardenal, one *cantiga* from *The Music of the Spheres*, bilingual text
translated by Dinah Livingstone (Katabasis, 1990); to Faber & Faber Ltd for Thom Gunn,
'The Reassurance', from *Collected Poems* (1993), for Seamus Heaney, 'Squarings', from
Seeing Things (1991), for T. S. Eliot, 'Burnt Norton' and 'The Dry Salvages', from *Four
Quartets* in *The Complete Poems and Plays of T. S. Eliot* (1969), for W. H. Auden, 'The
Dark Years', from *Collected Shorter Poems 1927–1957* (1966, 1969), and for Stephen
Spender, 'The Truly Great', from *Collected Poems 1928–1985* (1985); to Sheed & Ward
for Edwina Gateley, 'Let Your God Love You', from *Psalms of a Laywoman* (Sheed &
Ward, 2000: Sheed & Ward is now an imprint of Rowman & Littlefield Publishing, Inc.);
to Bloodaxe Books for Brendan Kennelly, 'I See You Dancing, Father', from *Familiar
Strangers: New & Selected Poems 1960–2004* (2004); to Pollinger Ltd and the proprietor
for D. H. Lawrence, 'Phoenix', in *The Complete Poems of D. H. Lawrence* (Heinemann,
1964); and to David Higham Associates for Charles Causley, 'Eden Rock', from *Collected
Poems 1951–2000* (Picador, 2000).

Set in 11/14pt Sabon by
Falcon Oast Graphic Art Ltd.

Bantam Books are published by Transworld Publishers,
61–63 Uxbridge Road, London W5 5SA,
a division of The Random House Group Ltd,
in Australia by Random House Australia (Pty) Ltd,
20 Alfred Street, Milsons Point, Sydney, NSW 2061, Australia,
in New Zealand by Random House New Zealand Ltd,
18 Poland Road, Glenfield, Auckland 10, New Zealand
and in South Africa by Random House (Pty) Ltd,
Isle of Houghton, Corner of Boundary Road & Carse O'Gowrie,
Houghton 2198, South Africa.

Printed in Great Britain by
Cox & Wyman Ltd, Reading, Berkshire.

Papers used by Transworld Publishers are natural, recyclable
products made from wood grown in sustainable forests. The
manufacturing processes conform to the environmental
regulations of the country of origin.

In memory of Tony Cassidy

'It's only the Red King snoring . . . He's dreaming now,' said Tweedledee: 'and what do you think he's dreaming about?'

Alice said, 'Nobody can guess that.'

'Why, about *you*!' Tweedledee exclaimed, clapping his hands triumphantly. 'And if he left off dreaming about you, where do you suppose you'd be?'

'Where I am now, of course,' said Alice.

'Not you!' Tweedledee retorted contemptuously. 'You'd be nowhere. Why, you're only a sort of thing in his dream!'

'If that there King was to wake,' added Tweedledum, 'you'd go out – bang! – just like a candle!'

'I shouldn't!' Alice exclaimed indignantly. 'Besides, if *I'm* only a sort of thing in his dream, what are *you*, I should like to know?'

(Lewis Carroll, *Through the Looking-Glass*, Chapter 4)

CONTENTS

ACKNOWLEDGEMENTS

This book began with the publication in 1994 of an article entitled 'The bad dreams which foretell illness' by Victoria Macdonald, Health Correspondent of the *Sunday Telegraph*. In 1997, she expanded on the subject in her article 'How nightmares can predict illness', which was followed by a piece for *The Times* later that year by Ian Murray. Catherine O'Brien in the *Today* newspaper was among many other journalists who took up the theme.

Louise Orpin was the lightning conductor, always making the right contact at the right time. Without her enthusiasm this book would not have appeared. I must also thank Margaret Cudmore for her support.

Mark Lucas set the ball rolling with suggestions on how to present the material, for which many thanks.

Rebecca Winfield not only saw how to turn it into a book, but also had the inspired idea of a collaboration with Annie Humphries. It has been a joy to work with Annie.

I also owe an enormous debt to Brenda Kimber, who commissioned, edited and spent many an hour honing the material.

Over the years I have had many secretaries, who have helped with the correspondence. Most important among these has been Karen Clarke, who worked long and hard and provided many ideas of her own. Also Pat Young, Sue Baynham and Vivienne Knowles.

My thanks to Di for telling me the story of David Paladin.

Finally, I am hugely grateful to all those who took the trouble to write. Some stories were fascinating, some tragic, but all added to my understanding of the dream, and helped shape this book.

Robin Royston

I would like to thank Wesley and Hazel Humphries, sadly no longer with us, for not insisting that I go outside and play games instead of keeping my nose stuck in a book; and for providing many of the books, too (as well as a love of Gilbert and Sullivan). Thanks also to Alison Humphries for encouragement and comic songs.

I benefited from the expertise of the Hales – Ian, Alan, Alice and Keith – on subjects ranging from movies and quantum non-locality to the American dream and how to deal with recalcitrant computers.

Thanks go to Andrew Whiteley and Gordon Rycroft, fellow members of the Phoenix quiz team, for their comments on superheroes.

Along with Robin, I acknowledge the tremendous support of Rebecca Winfield and Brenda Kimber, whose perpetual enthusiasm and conviction of the need for this book kept us on track.

Annie Humphries
September 2005

INTRODUCTION

'I've dreamt in my life dreams that have stayed with me
ever after, and changed my ideas; they've gone through
and through me, like wine through water, and altered the
colour of my mind.'

(Emily Brontë, *Wuthering Heights*)

Have you ever woken from a vivid dream and known,
instinctively, that this dream was very different from other
dreams you have had? Did it have an urgency, or a sense
of significance that isn't present in most of your dreams?
Its memory may have stayed with you for days – or for
years. You may have felt the need to record the dream at
once, because of your conviction of its importance. Often
it seems that such a dream contains knowledge or information that we simply could not have had during our
waking hours. If so, where did that knowledge come
from?

CAN OUR BRAIN HAVE TWO MINDS?

In this book, we will see that our dreams may contain the key to our future happiness. Some may even be capable of saving lives. The value of dreams has been recognized since ancient times, and they have been studied by medics, scientists, mathematicians, artists, writers and, of course, psychologists and psychiatrists puzzled by dreams and determined to unravel their meaning.

But if dreams have caught the imagination since the beginning of time, the significance of dreaming remains one of the great unknowns in the twenty-first century. Despite major scientific advances since Sigmund Freud published *The Interpretation of Dreams* in 1900, we still have not disentangled the relationship between the brain and the mind, the conscious and the unconscious. And although we know that dreaming is a biological imperative, we still lack a theory that fully explains why we sleep and what function dreaming plays.

Just as all of us are different, we all dream differently. And we *do* all dream, whether we realize it or not. The reason for this is hard to establish, but it is likely to be related to our personality: later we will look at Ernest Hartmann's theory of 'thick' and 'thin' boundaries in our minds, which may shed some light on this. Don't worry if you can't recall your dreams: if an important message is to be communicated, it usually gets through, even to people who supposedly never dream. John, in Chapter 8, is a good illustration of this.

SIGNIFICANT DREAMS

'We will speak to the people,' said God. 'We will ask them a few simple questions. Then you shall hear. In their sleep they will say what they truly know. That is another odd thing about mankind. When they are awake, they are deepest asleep. When they are asleep they are widest awake. Strange creatures!'

(Ted Hughes, *What Is the Truth?*)

The molecular biologist and Nobel Prize winner Francis Crick saw dreams as no more than a means of disposing of the vast amount of information we take in each day. Many dreams do, indeed, seem simply to reflect or play back our experiences, often in odd and unpredictable ways. People and places are transformed into surreal scenarios. However, not all dreams are like this.

Most of us experience at least one significant dream in our lifetime. For some, that dream may contain a creative idea or concept; or the dreamer may suddenly realize the solution to a complex intellectual problem. Sometimes the dream may act to persuade us that all is well. It is not uncommon for people who have suffered pain or loss to derive great comfort and reassurance from a dream. Dreams can also be predictive – and some contain vital clues that, if they are decoded accurately, may radically change our lives.

The Hidden Power of Dreams examines how dreams can function in this way. This is not a book about psychic predictions, nor is it a scientific treatise on the relationship between sleep, dreaming and brain function. Instead, by showing us how to understand and interpret the images conjured up in our night-time life, this book will help us to rediscover a source of wisdom and inspiration that has existed – within every one of us – since ancient times.

We will see how dreaming connects us to a reality hidden during our waking hours – and one that has a spiritual context that some may find surprising.

THE DREAMERS

In January 1994 I began a research study that attracted the attention of the national media in Britain. In articles published in the *Sunday Telegraph* and *The Times*, I asked people to write to me if they had experienced a dream that they felt was related to the subsequent diagnosis of illness. Over 400 people responded. Every one of them had an intriguing story to tell. Many said that their lives had been fundamentally changed as a result of a dream. Others had experienced dreams that told of events the dreamer couldn't possibly have anticipated in waking life. These case studies have led to the present book.

From the many responses I received, I have selected just eleven; each, in its own way, will tell us something different about how dreams can act as warnings or herald future events. But before we go further, there are two points we must bear in mind. The first is that the dream cannot be separated from the dreamer. We have come a long way since the *Victorian Book of Dreams*, whose author has no hesitation in asserting that dreams have universal meanings:

BAGPIPES – To dream of this musical instrument is always unfortunate; it denotes extreme poverty, and you will have to labour hard all your life. It also denotes that the marriage state will be unhappy, as your wife will be proud, pious and poor, and not very industrious.

It is not quite as simple as that. The meaning ascribed to a dream is relevant only to the individual dreamer and his or her milieu. We cannot assume that a similar dream would mean the same thing to another person, whose life may be very different.

The second key point is that dreams cannot be used as a straightforward diagnostic aid. Powerful, disturbing dreams are more likely to have a psychological cause than a physical one, however strongly they may seem to point to illness, as many dreams in the following pages do. All of the dreamer's circumstances must be taken into account. It is most likely that a dream predicting illness will only be understood after the event, so cannot be used to diagnose illness before the dreamer becomes sick.

PRODROMAL DREAMS

A prodromal – or diagnostic – dream is one that heralds the onset of an illness, and in this way it functions like physical symptoms. For example, when an infant becomes feverish we may suspect this is a sign of the onset of teething or an ear infection – though we may also be on the lookout for a more serious illness such as meningitis.

In the prodromal phase, the illness has not become obvious but it is nevertheless present.

Often our body is aware of illness before we feel any symptoms. Our immune system picks up the start of many diseases and can identify the source, even when medical tests fail to make the right diagnosis. Recently, psycho-neuroimmunology has explored the relationship between the mind and the immune system, the links between mind and body we look at in this book. Dreams that occur before there are any clearly distinguishable signs of illness often disappear once the dreamer has properly interpreted and acted on the message in the dream. It may be that the more serious the illness, the more urgent or acute the dream. Perhaps the dream itself senses the need to disturb the sleeper. It is as if in waking life we seek to take control of nature, but in our dreams nature forces *us* to listen. These dreams, it can be argued, have a basis in medical science.

PRECOGNITIVE DREAMS

If a prodromal dream is one that warns of an existing condition, a precognitive dream is simply one that fore-tells the future. Obviously there are times when the precognitive and prodromal overlap. 'Telepathic' dreams appear to transmit an idea from one person or entity to another. Occasionally, this can happen while we are awake – when a thought, such as knowing someone is in danger, strikes us like a flash of lightning.

JENNY'S DREAM

Let me describe the dream of one of the people I worked with, whom I shall call Jenny. A qualified paediatrician, Jenny has had a great deal of experience caring for sick children. One night she had a puzzling dream. She was sitting at a bus stop when ten people approached her – eight women and two men. They wanted directions to the 'Maison Dieu' (House of God), an historic house on the corner of Water Lane. She then heard that a pregnant woman had died from a pulmonary haemorrhage. That was the entire dream; yet she knew it had a meaning.

Three days later, Jenny and I met again. She had finally made sense of it, she told me. Two days *after* the dream, a coach had crashed on the M2, very close to where Jenny had seen herself sitting. The only way the emergency services could get to the victims was via Water Lane in Ospringe. The Maison Dieu was originally a monastic hospital and hostel for travellers. Ten people had died, some from pulmonary haemorrhage, a rare occurrence in adults except in the case of crash victims who have sustained chest injury. Of the victims, eight were women. Most importantly, perhaps, Jenny said that she had known all along that the dream was not about her.

Some dreams are so powerful that we are sure they are predictive. The images and the force with which they take hold may make our sleep highly unsettled; or the dream jolts us into consciousness, its haunting images demanding our attention. Finding a rational explanation for such dreams is frequently a long and complicated task, for their predictions function at a spiritual or metaphysical level.

If we accept that Jenny's dream was not a coincidence –

and many will not – might the ten people have been the souls of the crash victims? Did Jenny witness the future? Perhaps she was tuning in to events already known, even though they had not yet happened in the time scheme that we understand. So how could they have arisen in her mind?

CALL IN THE EXPERTS: FREUD AND JUNG

Can't you see I'm dreaming?
In a dream you are never eighty.
(Anne Sexton, 'Old')

As we all know, Freud understood dream images as having deeply embedded sexual meaning: they stood for repressed and unacceptable wishes. Dreams, according to Freud, were a form of wish-fulfilment, and he distinguished between the 'manifest dream' (the dream itself) and the 'latent dream', which contained our repressed desires. Though much of Freud's work has been criticized – not least for its views of women as representing the threat of castration and otherness to the male, and for the theory of penis envy – his theories were the first full formulation of unconscious functions, and he remains influential today.

So are dreams simply a reflection of our repressed anxieties and desires? In my view, they are a great deal more than that. To understand how they can help us to move beyond the limits of our individual mind in order to gain a sense of harmony and connection with others, we need to look at another leading figure: Carl Gustav

Jung, who had equally strong opinions on what goes on in the dreaming mind.

Where Freud looked at dreams from the point of view of Captain Smith on the bridge of the *Titanic*, Jung took the point of view of the iceberg. In Jung's model, our daytime consciousness is surrounded by the personal unconscious. Here we find events and knowledge from our own individual lives. We can recall some of this immediately, but many details may be impossible to remember, even some things that once really mattered to us. The personal unconscious does not exist in isolation: beyond it is a deeper layer of the mind, which contains all the knowledge acquired during the evolutionary history of humanity. When we encounter unfamiliar symbols and images in our dreams, we need to consider whether these would have made perfect sense to our ancestors. Next time you realize that you know something – but have no idea *how* you know it – remember that your mind may be acting as a receiver of information. This rich source of human knowledge is the collective unconscious.

THE ARCHAIC MIND

Do we know our own mind? Can we always control what we think? The human brain and its connected nervous system form an intricate structure that has developed over millions of years. As the nervous system slowly increased in complexity, at some point along the line consciousness developed.

Just as the nervous system is built up of multiple levels, it is reasonable to assume that the human mind too has many layers underlying consciousness. In our brain, a vast amount of activity goes on below the surface: we can become aware of some of it if we pay attention to our thoughts as we let our minds wander and see ideas floating in and out.

Dreaming is the most obvious example of a kind of thinking over which we have no control but which happens nonetheless. We could simplify this by saying there is a primitive mind within all of us, a mind that thinks less in words and more in images and feelings. The consciousness we know is supported by this archaic consciousness.

THE INTERNET

the single worldwide computer network that interconnects other computer networks ... enabling data and other information to be exchanged.

(*Collins English Dictionary*, 4th edition)

Jung's concept of the collective unconscious is remarkably like the Internet. Think of your mind as a PC (or an Apple Mac) with a hard drive that contains programs you only gradually become aware of. Some you may never locate or find a use for. This is the personal unconscious. But the PC is linked to a much wider network, stretching far into time and space and connecting with the lives of all of humanity – vast numbers of unknown people, many of whom will undoubtedly seem alien and even bizarre. The Internet: a world beyond the confines of the individual, and one that has much to teach us.

If our unconscious mind, in dreams, connects with the

minds and lives of others, this may help to shed light on Jenny's puzzling experience. Even if she thought she didn't, her mind knew of the accident that was about to happen – though why it told her is a mystery that is hard to unravel. It seems that the dream can know more than the dreamer. If so, instead of asking, 'What do we want from our dreams?' we need to ask, 'What do our dreams want of *us*?'

SHAMANISM: HARMONY WITH THE WORLD

> All nature is but art unknown to thee;
> All chance, direction which thou canst not see;
> All discord, harmony not understood;
> All partial evil, universal good . . .
>
> (Alexander Pope, *An Essay on Man*)

Shamanism originated in northern Asia and spread throughout many areas of the world. Nowadays we probably associate it mainly with the medicine men of the tribes of North and South America. It is based on the belief in the eternal battle between good and evil spirits, and only the shaman can control these: his skill and power determine the future of the community. The shaman may inherit his role, or he may be 'chosen', sometimes through falling ill. Often his sacred vocation is revealed to him in a dream. The shaman (there are also female shamans) is a master of the sacred – not a businessman looking for a knighthood. At the centre of this world is not ambition, but harmony, something that

so many in the stressful western world are searching for.
It is not easy to achieve:

> The grant of shamanic powers occurs after a deliberate
> quest ... candidates withdraw to mountain caves or
> solitary places and seek, by intense concentration, to
> obtain the visions that alone can determine a shamanic
> career.

As Igjugarjuk, a Caribou Eskimo shaman, explains: 'The
only true wisdom lives far from mankind, out in the great
loneliness, and it can be reached only through suffering.
Privation and suffering alone can open the mind of a man
to all that is hidden to others.'

The shaman has to be at one with his world – and with
his own unconscious mind – if he is to carry out his
function. Controlling his psychic flight, he acts and
dreams on behalf of the group, whose future is in his
hands. In primitive societies, these dreams reflected both
the individual shaman's history and that of the tribe.

Not many of us live out in the great loneliness.
Withdrawing to mountain caves is not always an option,
however much we want to save the planet. All of this may
seem far away in the dim, distant past and of little
relevance to us as we struggle to cope with the conflicts
and demands of life at the start of the twenty-first century,
when we hardly have time even to *read* about spiritual
harmony. But we can learn a lot from the shaman and his
world; and this knowledge will benefit us, and the earth
as a whole. Primitive societies, both past and present, do
not pollute and destroy the world they live in.

SO WHAT WENT WRONG?

> We [the British] are the first race in the world, and
> the more of the world we inhabit, the better it is for the
> human race.
>
> (Cecil Rhodes, quoted in Niall Ferguson, *Empire*)

Over the centuries, as traders in search of wealth and
explorers in search of glory brought 'civilized' customs to
dark continents, the old nature spirits and gods faded
away, unable to withstand the power of an enlightened
era. It is hard to see how they could have survived.
According to Niall Ferguson in *Empire*, his account of
'How Britain made the modern world', in just twenty
empire-building years, from 1880 to 1900, around 10,000
African tribal kingdoms were transformed into forty
states. Thirty-six of them were under direct European
control.

As tribes became the enemy for settlers to conquer and
attempt to eradicate, then exotic objects for anthro-
pologists to study, the harmony of humanity and the
natural world came under threat. Not everyone thought
this new civilization an improvement. In the fifteenth century Leonardo da Vinci saw 'God's handwriting' in the
natural world and his scientific work as a quest for
spiritual understanding, but 300 years later the Romantic
poets were damning science and its microscopic analysis.

> Our meddling intellect
> Misshapes the beauteous forms of things –
> We murder to dissect

Wordsworth fumed in 1798, while Keats reclaimed the rainbow from 'the dull catalogue of common things' and placed it back in the sky, where it belonged. Art and science, man and nature, were farther apart than ever.

I

THE RIDDLE

What shall I say they are but they are just my Brownies,
God bless them! who do one-half my work for me while I
am fast asleep, and in all human likelihood do the rest for
me as well, when I am wide awake and fondly suppose I
do it for myself. That part which is done while I am sleeping is the Brownies' part beyond contention; but that
which is done when I am up and about is by no means
necessarily mine, since all goes to show the Brownies have
a hand in it even then.

(Robert Louis Stevenson, *Across the Plains*)

Dreams are notorious for their ability to find creative
solutions to problems. We wake in the morning and all at
once we know the answer that the night before we'd
found it impossible to work out. In our sleep, our mind
discovered that elusive bit of information. Once it was
thought that as the sun goes down, the mind takes a rest.
Now we know that the sleeping brain is nearly as active

as the waking brain. And some of that activity is quite unusual.

First of all, let's look at what psychiatrist Dr Morton Schatzman found, in his research on dreams and problem-solving. He placed some puzzles in the *Sunday Times* and asked readers to think about them when they went to bed, and to contact him if a dream provided any solutions. This may seem optimistic, especially since the puzzles weren't exactly easy. Here is just one of them:

First, What is curious about this sentence: show this bold Prussian that praises slaughter, slaughter brings rout?

Second, Which of the following verbs does not belong in this group: bring, catch, draw, fight, seek, teach and think?

One reader's dreaming mind was remarkably ingenious:

On Tuesday night (two days after the article appeared), before going to sleep, I memorized the problems, without much expectation of success. Between 3.00 and 3.30 a.m., I woke up aware of terrible indigestion and of having had a rather weird dream. In my dream I'm watching Michael Caine in one of his spy roles, possibly *The Ipcress File* . . .

He walks up to a door marked Computer Room and opens it; behind the door is a heavy wire-mesh screen. He passes a folded copy of the *Sunday Times* to someone behind the screen.

From the Computer Room come sounds of whirring tapes, clickings and other computer-type noises. I see that through a slot in the grille is being pushed a coloured comic postcard with a caption at the bottom. Michael Caine takes it, looks at it, chuckles briefly and hands it to me.

The postcard comes to life and I'm sitting in an audience watching a stage show. On the stage, a comic Elizabethan figure in doublet and hose, wearing a hat with an enormous feather, is kneeling with his head in a guillotine. He looks apprehensively at the audience and rolls his eyes. The audience rocks with laughter, and the comic figure struggles to his feet, comes to the front of the stage and says, 'Sh-she-sh! Laughter is a capital offence!' More riotous laughter from the audience. The comic figure doffs his hat with a flourish and bows extravagantly.

For some reason I feel very grateful to Michael Caine, and turn to thank him. He says nothing, but points over his shoulder to indicate that he must 'dash', and with a friendly wave walks off.

I woke up, turned on the light and from my bedside table picked up the *Sunday Times*, which was open at the article on dreams . . .

Unaware, at first, that any of this story related to the puzzle, the dreamer now sees that if the first (capital) letter in each word is lopped off, the sentence reads: 'How his old Russian hat raises laughter, laughter rings out.' As if that wasn't complicated enough, there is more to come:

In my rather sleepy state I wondered what had happened to the answer to the other problem, which I felt I should know.

Before actually falling asleep again, I saw Michael Caine looking rather irritable and repeating the pointing gesture over his shoulder. I realized that he was performing a mime and that . . . pointing over his shoulder indicated past tense.

Again I switched on my bedside light and looked at the problems. I saw that the only one of the verbs whose past tense doesn't end in –ght was 'draw'.

UNRAVELLING THE PUZZLE

. . . a riddle wrapped in a mystery inside an enigma.

(Winston Churchill)

Here the dream has worked out the answer when the conscious mind did not know the solution. The idea of beheading is repeated – decapitation *and* doffing the hat with its enormous feather. There is an emphasis on 's' ('Sh-she-sh'), as *slaughter* becomes *laughter*. Laughter is a prominent feature of the dream. However, Michael Caine is forced to make another appearance, to point over his shoulder yet again: this time he is not friendly but irritable. Perhaps the dreaming mind is impatient, as it speeds about making connections for us.

What is fascinating is the complexity of the verbal puzzle that seems to be solved by a part of the brain that does not use language. How much easier it would be if the dreamer could just pick up a sheet of paper containing a written explanation. No need for Michael Caine and feathered hats at all. But dreams do not work like this, presumably because they cannot. Our conscious mind has to help. Alfred Alvarez, the writer and critic, quotes the French philosopher Lacan:

> Jacques Lacan once said that dreams are 'like a charade where the participants must guess an utterance known to them, or its variant, with the sole help of a mimed scene'. Lacan had a gift for going too far, but for once he seems not to have gone far enough. Dreams are not *like* charades, they *are* charades – inner dramas in which mental activity expresses itself physically in signs and gestures. They are ideas in dumb show, thinking in mime.

THE SEA AND THE SHORE

> I shall tell you how I did it – and it has nothing to do with rising with the larks. It was by sleeping! Yes, sleep! I would go to sleep with some half-formed idea in my head and the next thing – tap, tap – something would wake me up . . . I've no idea who or what it was . . . But there was the answer, the solution to the problem, I had found the mystery . . . All that was left for me to do was write it.
>
> (Gaston Leroux, author of *Phantom of the Opera*)

On the shore of conscious life, we are surrounded by a sea that we can explore but never conquer. Our daily life may be plagued by problems, but even if we cannot dispose of all of them, we usually know exactly what they are. Dreams are a less straightforward matter. We will see numerous examples of the convoluted language of dreams in the chapters that follow, and we will look at ways of unravelling them. For now, let us acknowledge that dreams are predominantly visual; they use image and metaphor in order to 'speak' to us.

Metaphor – one of the most widely used figures of speech – is crucial to the communication process. In the interpretation of dreams, it is also a key concept. In *Dreams and Nightmares* Ernest Hartmann describes metaphor as 'a basic foundation of our thought and mental functioning. Indeed, it may be older, broader, and deeper than speech itself.' Just before this he writes:

> Metaphor is learned and understood early in life. A number of studies have shown that children understand metaphor quite easily at the ages of four to seven, when they have not yet mastered the propositional logic that supposedly allows us to explain metaphor, and certainly long before they have any notion of a 'rhetorical device' . . . Metaphor is by no means a figure of speech, but rather a basic part of our being in the world.

Whether or not it predates speech, we know that metaphor is dealt with in a different part of the brain – something we will look at in more detail in Chapter 2. It arises in parts of the mind that are constantly at work behind the scenes, spinning images and making links, influencing us all the time. Language does crop up, but on the whole dream language simply enjoys playing with words – it is a *Times* crossword or a pun, not a speech. The dream does not lecture: it paints.

Yet, for Freud, the dream revolved around language. In modern thinking, his is a 'cognitive approach' to understanding dreams. Beginning with a word or a thought, the dream used images to elaborate on it. One classic example he cites is from Plutarch's *Parallel Lives*. In 32 BC Alexander the Great was laying siege to the Phoenician city of Tyre. After seven months, he was worried that it was taking such a long time. Then, in a dream, he saw a satyr, who mocked him at a distance and eluded his grasp until finally, after much coaxing, the satyr surrendered. Aristander, the seer, interpreted this as foretelling success: when the Greek word *satyros* is divided into *sa* and *Tyros* it means 'Troy is to be thine'.

We will not delve deeply into Freud's theories of dreams, but this example encapsulates the mixture of image and language that we will look at more closely in relation to Nancy's dream later in this chapter. Interestingly, it also strongly suggests that, at least at times, there can be a correct interpretation.

LIKE A BOLT FROM THE BLUE

The best songs are the ones that come to you in the middle of the night and you have to get up and write them down . . .

(John Lennon)

Dreams are riddles. They have to be sat with, thought about, allowed to develop. They often yield a meaning – maybe not *the* meaning – when given this freedom and attention. Like a bird incubating an egg, they may hatch spontaneously – or they may not.

Intuition, inspiration, a hunch ... So many of the world's leading thinkers rely on this. Albert Einstein was famous for his prolonged periods of intense thinking. First he had to have the glimmer of an idea – such as his visualization of a tram or sledge travelling faster and faster until it approached the speed of light. As this played around in his mind over time, he used the rational thinking characteristic of maths and physics to transform the basic image/idea into a workable theory. Words and numbers combined with imagery: the two modes of thought are equally vital to the work of creation. The mathematician Roger Penrose describes this cooperative process:

> Almost all my mathematical thinking is done visually ...
> Often the reason is that there are simply not the words available to express the concepts that are required ...
> When one 'sees' a mathematical truth, one's consciousness breaks through into this world of ideas, and makes direct contact with it ... this 'seeing' is the essence of mathematical understanding.

Dreams are one way of finding a way through what Francis Galton, the scientist and explorer, called the 'mathematical landscape'.

There was a time, not long ago, when engineers and scientists would have opposed anything so irrational as 'seeing' ideas; categorized as clairvoyance or mysticism, such an approach would have been laughed out of laboratories and rejected by serious research publishers. Today, science has a wider concept of creativity.

CREATURES FROM THE ABYSS

We may not all be budding Einsteins, but the inner life to which dreams give us access is the source of a rich variety of creative endeavour. The word itself has its own magic: 'Last night I dreamt I went to Manderley again . . .' The opening words of Daphne du Maurier's *Rebecca* have mesmerized millions of readers.

Earlier we met Robert Louis Stevenson's brownies. Clearly, they had a hand in writing *The Strange Case of Dr Jekyll and Mr Hyde*. As Stevenson explains:

> I had long been trying . . . to find a body, a vehicle, for that strong sense of man's double being which must at times come in upon and overwhelm the mind of every thinking creature . . . For two days I went about racking my brains for a plot of any sort; and on the second night I dreamed the scene at the window, and a scene afterwards split in two, in which Hyde, pursued for some crime, took the powder and underwent the change in the presence of his pursuers.

In the following three days, desperate to keep hold of the essence of his dream, Stevenson wrote incessantly. Admittedly, following criticism by his wife, who thought the tale not moral enough, Stevenson threw the manuscript on the fire. But although he abandoned his original draft, the dream kept its hold on him and he continued to write compulsively. 'Jekyll was conceived, written, re-written, re-rewritten and printed inside ten weeks,' he claimed.

While living at Bournemouth, Stevenson got to know

Sir Percy Shelley, only son of the poet. Along with the urn containing Shelley's heart, Sir Percy's wife Jane had preserved the papers of Mary Shelley. Seventy years before *Jekyll and Hyde*, Mary's imagination had created another immortal icon. She was eighteen years old when Frankenstein's monster came to her in a dream. Along with Byron, and her husband Percy, Mary had been reading ghost stories in the Villa Diodati on the shores of Lake Geneva. Byron challenged each of them to write a supernatural tale of their own. In her Introduction to the 1831 edition of *Frankenstein, or The Modern Prometheus* Mary tells what happened:

> Night waned upon this talk, and even the witching hour had gone by, before we retired to rest . . . My imagination, unbidden, possessed and guided me. I saw – with shut eyes, but acute mental vision – I saw the pale student of unhallowed arts kneeling beside the thing he had put together. I saw the hideous phantasm of a man stretched out, and then, on the working of some powerful engine, show signs of life, and stir with an uneasy, half vital motion . . .

Whether this was a dream or a hypnagogic hallucination – a vision that occurs as one passes into sleep – Mary's story was the only one to be completed. The Gothic tale that flowed from her dream has itself inspired an entire genre of film and literature.

CELTIC TWILIGHT

Not long after Mr Hyde was laying waste to London, a very different dream creature surfaced across the Irish Sea. William Butler Yeats, one of the era's foremost poets and dramatists, explained to his friend Lady Gregory the genesis of his character Cathleen ni Houlihan:

> One night I had a dream almost as distinct as a vision, of a cottage where there was well-being and firelight and talk of a marriage, and into the midst of that cottage there came an old woman in a long cloak. She was Ireland herself, that Cathleen ni Houlihan for whom so many songs have been sung and about whom so many stories have been told and for whose sake so many have gone to their death. I thought if I could write this out as a little play I could make others see my dream as I had seen it . . .

Dreams and visions were a central part of Yeats's creative experience; a member of the Hermetic Order of the Golden Dawn, he studied Tibetan spiritualism, alchemy, Buddhist thought, telepathy and clairvoyance. At the time of his dream, as he said, Cathleen ni Houlihan was already a familiar figure. Along with Roisin Dubh (Dark Rosaleen) she was a representation of the sovereignty of Ireland, and perhaps even the Virgin Mary, created by Irish Jacobite poets of the eighteenth century. One of them saw her as a lonely figure who kept watch by the shore for the arrival of her true lover, Charles Stuart. In his two plays about Cathleen, Yeats extended her influence; and she made such an impression on Irish nationalists that he later worried that she had inspired the leaders of the 1916 Easter Rising to go to their deaths. She remains an important symbol of Ireland today.

FIVE APPEAR IN A DREAM

'Make way, please,' said the policeman, politely. 'Everything is all right. These children were locked in the light-house and couldn't get out. Make way, please. There is no need for any excitement!'

'No – that's all over now – isn't it, Ju?' said Dick. 'Whew – it was just a bit *too* exciting at times!'

(Enid Blyton, *Five Go to Demon's Rocks*)

One of the most popular, prolific writers of the twentieth century (though reviled for her undemanding and repetitive plots), Enid Blyton knew all about the unconscious mind. She believed she had harnessed its power and had it well under control:

I shut my eyes for a few minutes, with my portable typewriter on my knee – I make my mind a blank and wait – and then, as clearly as I would see real children, my characters stand before me in my mind's eye. I see them in detail – hair, eyes, feet, clothes, expression . . .

The Famous Five, the Secret Seven, the Five Find-outers and Dog . . . the list is almost endless. Even Noddy lives on into the new century, if in a more politically correct form. Enid Blyton was extremely articulate, and quite specific, about how she wrote, and noted that ideas and characters often surfaced as she drifted into sleep. As she explained in correspondence about the creative process with psychologist Peter McKellar:

> . . . my conscious mind has nothing whatever to do with it except record what it sees . . . when you are at one and the same time, creator and interpreter, using your unconscious and your conscious intermingled for hours, it is sometimes very muddling! Which is really which?

Whether or not we enjoy the dozens of accounts of midnight feasts and catching smugglers, Enid Blyton shows that dreams can at least be a reliable source of income.

THE COMMITTEE OF SLEEP

> It is common practice that a problem difficult at night is resolved in the morning after the committee of sleep has worked on it.
>
> (John Steinbeck)

If scientists, novelists and poets draw constantly on their dream world for inspiration, so do artists, architects and musicians – as well as inventors, engineers, teachers and many who work in the world of business. Creativity is needed in every field. Igor Stravinsky dreamt of a sacrificial virgin who danced herself to death; then he composed *The Rite of Spring*. Beethoven is said to have been another persistent musical dreamer. Paul McCartney dreamed his greatest success, 'Yesterday'. As he later said, the music was so clear that at first he was convinced that it must be a well-known tune; he called it 'one of the most instinctive songs I've ever written'. Since then, there have been over 2,500 recorded versions, by artists ranging from Elvis Presley and Frank Sinatra to Placido Domingo and Tammy Wynette. A piece of music with truly universal appeal.

Frank Gehry, one of the world's leading architects, also finds inspiration in dreams. His most well-known creation is the Guggenheim Museum in Bilbao; another of his buildings is the quirky Maggie's Cancer Care Centre in Dundee, which won the 2004 Building of the Year award. He designed it free of charge in honour of his great friend Maggie Keswick Jencks, the Scottish artist, who died of breast cancer.

'She came to me in dreams,' said Gehry. Insisting he has no time for the supernatural, he went on: 'I didn't see Maggie, I heard her voice – she had a beautiful speaking voice – and she was saying to me, "Calm down, Frank. You're going over the top." And do you know something? I was. My design was good but not what Maggie would have liked.'

Working out his ideas was not an easy task. Gehry 'agonized over designs for the building' and ended up with a unique structure that, he said, 'looks like a lighthouse from one side and a rustic farmhouse from the other'. The unusual folded roof is based on the creases in a shawl worn by a woman in a Vermeer portrait he had seen with Maggie.

'IT FADED ON THE CROWING OF THE COCK . . .'

No bird soars too high, if he soars with his own wings.

(William Blake, *The Marriage of Heaven and Hell*)

Every one of us is creative. We all have something unique to say, and can find our own way of saying it. We have just seen how the unconscious mind can instigate or enhance creativity by communicating through dreams, and that it does so in many different ways – from Gehry's struggle to Stevenson's feverish rush to capture every idea before it vanishes; from Mary Shelley's dark, atmospheric vision to Enid Blyton's bright enthusiasm.

It seems that in dreams we are immersed in the free-wheeling world of the older, archaic mind, in tune with knowledge whose sources we may be unable to identify. It is a world that contains echoes and reflections of our own; but sometimes it seems so alien that we feel we have no contact with its wild nature. As we awaken, the gates of sensation are opened and the incoming life of the every-day takes over. We must turn our mind to the 'real' world, where we have to function in a predictable way, like everyone else. Just as the infuriating anonymous 'person from Porlock' arrived on business at Coleridge's Exmoor retreat, stayed for an hour and put an end to the poet's mystical vision of Xanadu, day-to-day life brings our imaginative efforts to an emergency halt.

When we think using logic in the daytime, we move from idea A to B to C to D; in dreams we 'move from logic to a floating sea of imagery revolving around an initial idea', according to Ernest Hartmann, in *Dreams and*

Nightmares. We need to venture out on that ocean. In our dreams we are already making connections not obvious in waking life. What successful creative thinkers have done is to gain access to this infinite sea. At the end of the book you will find practical guidance on how to work on this. For now, let me introduce you to Nancy.

Nancy

When Nancy responded to my newspaper article she was fifty-seven and had had a mastectomy after a diagnosis of cancer. She still clearly recalled two dreams she had had years before, while working on a psychology degree to add to her nursing qualification. She described these dreams as 'vivid, strong and clear'.

I was walking on the campus in a crowd of students. Suddenly I was pushed through my back and into my chest from behind, and thrown over a concrete barrier and into a garden below. I picked myself up and continued walking, only to be pushed powerfully from behind, once again, over the barrier and into the dirt of the garden.

I got up and thought, 'Who is pushing me? The next time I'll be prepared and I'll grab them.'

The push came again, but this time I was ready. I whirled round and grabbed a hooded figure behind me. I wrestled with the figure, knocking us both to the ground; then I sat on the figure and punched him or her repeatedly with my fist. The hood fell back from the figure's face, and I was astonished to see myself.

I kept on hitting the figure, shouting, 'BAD NANCY, BAD

NANCY!' as I pounded the face and chest. Then I woke up.

The dream was so powerful that I wrote it down immediately, trying to capture as much of the colour and imagery as possible, and the mood and atmosphere. I felt very depressed for a few days and remember bursting into tears. My reaction puzzled me. After all, it was just a dream — wasn't it?

Five months later, Nancy found a lump in her left breast. After examination by her doctor, she was booked into hospital for a biopsy. While waiting to go into hospital, Nancy was cleaning cupboards at home when she came across a cartoon she had had on her wall during her exams that spring. It featured a woman standing in a snowdrift with a shovel and declaring, 'I am invincible!' On the snowdrift, Nancy had written all the things she had to do that spring, such as exams, seminar presentations, papers and reports, all connected with her university work.

I grabbed a pen and thought, 'I have one more thing to conquer . . . CANCER!' I began to write the word on the cartoon and suddenly realized that I was not writing 'cancer' but had begun to write 'malignancy', beginning with MAL . . . (the French word for bad). Then I realized that the end of the word was NANCY, my own name. I had written 'malignancy', not 'cancer' – and the words were an echo from the dream. I rummaged through my papers to find my record of the dream and was astounded to see the imagery in the dream and think of its connection to my current reality.

Following the biopsy, Nancy eventually had a lumpectomy and a course of radiation. Six months later, she underwent the same course of treatment for her other breast. Her life moved on: she finished her degree and started to work as a puppetry and visual arts specialist in a rehabilitation hospital.

It was about four years later that she noticed a third lump, this one in her right breast. She was told by her oncologist and her surgeon that it was just a cyst; nothing to worry about. However, after a month or two Nancy felt it was enlarging, so she asked for another opinion. Again she was told to stop worrying. She had had so much radiation that, it was thought, she couldn't possibly have another tumour.

Another month passed. Then Nancy had such a powerful dream that she was wakened by it.

> I was in an open village square. A crowd was gathered round, listening to a hooded figure who was preaching on some subject which I didn't seem to understand. I pushed through the crowd to the front and began to argue with the figure, shouting that I didn't understand. He ignored me. I was so angry that with my boot I kicked the mound of white crusted snow that lay between us. I made a hole in the crust and out came a slurry of white and black rabbits in a greenish syrupy fluid. Everyone reacted with horror, but my attitude was: 'I told you so.'

Next day, Nancy talked to a friend. She then contacted her surgeon and insisted on a biopsy. The result showed a cyst filled with fluid and containing both live and dead cancer cells. Following this diagnosis, she elected to have a total mastectomy on both sides.

At the time when Nancy wrote to me she had been well for five years and was extremely active. She had had one more health scare: suffering acute abdominal pain, she had a scan and the doctor suspected that she had a tumour on her kidney.

> I had to wait several days for another test to confirm this. At first I panicked with fear, but then I realized that I had had no 'warning' dreams of any kind, so I felt very confident that it was just some error in the test. To my great joy, I was right!

INTERPRETATION

I find it quite intriguing that the key to the dream is contained in the words she used – BAD NANCY – and in particular by the curious way in which she was tricked into writing MALIGNANCY by the unconscious. She had *meant* to write CANCER. It is only at this moment, in the act of writing the word, that understanding dawns and the dream becomes sensible and understandable. Such moments of enlightenment, which are common to us all, are captured in James Joyce's influential concept of epiphany: a 'sudden spiritual manifestation' when the significance of an experience is made clear to us in what seems a trivial incident. These moments come into our minds from some other place fully formed; we are presented with the knowledge even though it is, quite reasonably, tempting to claim responsibility for them: 'It was my thought.' Or was it?

Earlier I said that the language of dreams can have an essentially playful, crossword nature (however serious its implications) and Nancy's dream is certainly a good illustration of this. Nancy is given a verbal as well as a visual clue – with 'malignancy' offering the type of multi-lingual pun that Joyce himself would have appreciated. But the play this time is aggressive and dark. The tone is consistent with the diagnosis: Nancy's two dreams appear genuinely to correlate with her physical state.

In Nancy's first dream, when she is forcefully pushed, I suspect this is a dramatic way of indicating that she is thrown off balance, bowled over by the serious diagnosis. It also serves to get her attention.

Once she knows she has cancer, she has to confront what has happened to her, and she has to own it. So many people with cancer use denial as a coping strategy. While they may consciously acknowledge the illness, in their actions and speech (or lack of it) they show that they do not really want to know what is happening. Many refuse to take the problem to a doctor until they are forced to do so; others comply in a passive way, but take no active part in their treatment. Nancy is quite different. She struggles with this unknown figure, and at last understands that it is herself: presumably she is struggling with the discovery that she has cancer. It is only after this great effort that she can see who or what she is fighting. It was always Nancy herself. She is the 'bad Nancy' – the malignant part of her own body.

THE RIDDLE

MYSTERIOUS FIGURES

In my dreams the hooded figure of Death rode over Barcelona, a ghostly apparition that hovered above the towers and roofs, trailing black ropes that held hundreds of small white coffins. The coffins left behind them their own trail of black flowers, on whose petals, written in blood, was the name Nuria Monfort.

(Carlos Ruiz Zafón, *The Shadow of the Wind*)

Hooded figures appear in both of Nancy's dreams. Perhaps what is hidden under the hood is the unknown, or what is about to become known, like a figure almost veiled in the shadows or a stranger lurking outside the door. Prodromal dreams, as we saw in the Introduction, concern illnesses that already exist but that lie beneath our conscious awareness. In Nancy's case, the cancer was upon her, but she did not know it. The dream was trying to force her to confront the problem and deal with it.

Many other people sent me dreams which featured hooded figures, sinister faceless figures that turned out to be related to death. It is an archetypal image: from the medieval conception of Death as the Grim Reaper, draped in a black hooded cassock and carrying a scythe, to more recent ominous manifestations – think of the last of the Christmas spirits to visit Ebenezer Scrooge in Dickens's *Christmas Carol*: 'a solemn phantom, draped and hooded, coming, like a mist along the ground, towards him'. Tolkien's imagination was populated with mystery hooded figures. Like the mask or the veil, the hood is an obvious means of disguise which alerts us to the fact that something is being concealed; the difficulty lies in establishing, for each individual, what that something may be. For Nancy, her struggle with the hooded figure may represent her struggle with death.

There are even more blatant images of death than hooded figures. Perhaps the grave is the most obvious: when the body is faced with a terminal illness, dreams may communicate with a directness that cannot be misunderstood. At the age of eighteen, Delta Goodrem was writing and recording songs as well as working long hours as an actress in *Neighbours*. When she noticed a hard lump in her neck she paid no attention to it, or to further signs; then one night she dreamed of 'a dark face and a grave'. She woke soaked in sweat, knowing it was a warning. As she explained in an interview for *Glamour* magazine: 'Your body tries to tell you things but if you ignore it, like I did, then I think your unconscious has to do the job instead. Physically, I wasn't listening to my body, and that was the only way it was going to get through to me.'

As her album reached number one in Australia and number two in the UK she was undergoing surgery for multiple tumours in her neck. Now recovered, she is going from strength to strength.

As for Nancy, she took on her battle with great courage. There was no flinching: just determination to find out who the hooded figure was. She showed – as one would expect, for dream life and conscious life are interwoven – the same bravery in her battle for health. She confronted the fact of her illness, acknowledged it and, at the moment of putting cancer on her list of tasks to deal with, understood the meaning of the dream.

Nancy found her dreams and the disentangling of their meaning illuminating. It was a positive experience for her at a distressing time. By working through the dreams, she said, she learned to trust what they were telling her and to be aware that powerful dreams are likely to have a message she should listen to. Hence her certainty that because she had *not* had a dream, the cancer could not have returned.

TO BE CONTINUED: SECOND DREAMS

And for that the dream was doubled unto Pharaoh twice; it is because the thing is established by God, and God will shortly bring it to pass.

(Genesis 41: 32)

A 6-year-old girl dreamed she was with her grandmother. In the dream she said, 'Grandma, I can make myself disappear.'

'Nonsense, child!' exclaimed the grandmother. 'Nobody can do that.'

At that point the child woke up, sat up in bed, looked around her darkened bedroom, then lay down and went back to sleep.

As sometimes happens, she re-entered the same dream, whereupon her dream grandmother looked at the girl and said, 'Lord, child, how did you do that?'

(Marie-Louise von Franz, *On Dreams and Death*)

The phenomenon of the repetition of an image has long been held to emphasize the importance of the image. In

Nancy's second dream the hooded figure returns, but now there is a change. At this stage she is challenging the doctors who refuse to acknowledge her intuition. She really is up against an outside force now. This time the rage is not directed at Nancy herself. It is the kind of rage any one of us would experience if threatened with serious illness in the midst of life – and confronted by the blindness of the medical profession. Perhaps that is the reason for the sense of satisfaction she feels on kicking the snow while everyone else is horrified. It is so interesting that the snow is taken from Nancy's earlier cartoon depicting the issues and problems she has to overcome. The white and black rabbits can be seen as representing the mixture of live and dead cancer cells – indeed that was Nancy's own interpretation; and the third lump that appears in Nancy's breast may have been foreshadowed by the third push she suffered in her earlier dream. The second dream acts as confirmation that she is right – she already knows the truth of the recurrence. Nancy has passed beyond the stage of fear and dread and now only has a need for diagnosis and treatment.

The choice of cartoon turns out to be wonderfully ironic. No sooner is the gauntlet thrown down – 'I'm invincible!' – than a problem that is not so easily brushed aside rears its head. It is almost as if Nancy knew what was ahead – *without* actually knowing it.

Not only do dreams cloak their meaning (sometimes it is literally in disguise), but they sometimes seem incapable of conveying all that they wish to say at once. It is almost as if they have second thoughts, or return to add a postscript. We saw this earlier in the chapter, when Michael

Caine reappeared to solve the second of Morton Schatzman's riddles. Dreams, creative in their very nature, may also take their time when it comes to literary work. W. B. Yeats explains how he came to write 'The Cap and Bells', a haunting poem about a jester and a young queen:

> I dreamed this story exactly as I have written it, and dreamed another long dream after it, trying to make out its meaning, and whether I was to write it in prose or verse. The first dream was more a vision than a dream, for it was beautiful and coherent, and gave me the sense of illumination and exaltation that one gets from visions, while the second dream was confused and meaningless. The poem has always meant a great deal to me, though, as is the way with symbolic poems, it has not always meant quite the same thing. Blake would have said, 'The authors are in eternity,' and I am quite sure they can only be questioned in dreams.

Dreams, then, can tell us more when they think we need to know. But they prefer lateral thinking to multiple-choice questionnaires. Usually, that is.

During my psychotherapy training, a senior analyst told me of a dream he had had many years ago. At the time he was studying with Jung, who allocated him a patient as part of his training. After the first meeting with this patient, he dreamed the word MADMAN. Very agitated, he went to Jung the next morning, complaining that he had been given a schizophrenic as a training patient. 'Yes, yes – it will be very good experience,' Jung replied.

The point is the extreme simplicity of this dream. The

word is presented directly to the trainee and the meaning is absolutely clear to him. So dreams *can* do this – there is no neurological reason why they cannot. Yet they – or our minds – seem to enjoy playing with words, concocting riddles. The need for clear, unambiguous answers is a modern, scientific concept, alien to our ancient mind.

THE DREAMING MIND

Was it a vision or a waking dream?
Fled is that music: – do I wake or sleep?
(John Keats, 'Ode to a Nightingale')

Where does our dream world end and waking reality begin? Can we be sure that we dream only when we're sleeping? What about the visions experienced by the shamans, or by mystics such as Bernadette, to whom the Virgin Mary appeared eighteen times at Lourdes? Or by the poet William Blake, who saw angels in a tree and communed with the biblical Prophets? The creative mind continues its activity on both conscious and unconscious levels – there is no sharp dividing line between the two. As Louis Jolyon West, a renowned psychiatrist and cult expert, notes, 'dreaming may occur all the time . . . (just as the stars are always in the heavens, but not visible during the day)'. Our instinctive understanding of this is embedded in our language in everyday phrases such as 'dream up an idea' or 'dream on'; or when we say the car 'went like a dream'. The 1940s 'dreamboat' turned into the less imaginative 'dream girl' or 'dream guy' ('in your dreams', that is). We're familiar with the 'American dream'. Most strikingly, Martin Luther King drew on the powerful nexus of dream associations in his commanding 'I have a dream' speech of August 1963. It is a phrase he used with stunning effect in many speeches that summer.

We have seen how writers and others make use of the older way of thinking to conjure up new ideas and tales, moving in and out of a seamless world of the imagination, just as the shaman has always done. Jung said it is likely that we continually dream, but that our consciousness creates so much noise that we don't hear what our dreams are saying. Now, more than ever, it is vital that we listen.

2

'THIS LIFE'S A FICTION'

Just like the digital codes of replicating life held within DNA, the brain's fundamental secret will be laid open one day. But even when it has, the wonder will remain, that mere wet stuff can make this bright inward cinema of thought, of sight and sound and touch bound into a vivid illusion of an instantaneous present, with a self, another brightly wrought illusion, hovering like a ghost at its centre. Could it ever be explained, how matter becomes conscious?

(Ian McEwan, *Saturday*)

The relationship between the mind and the brain continues to be controversial. There is no doubt the brain is the source of the mind: the experience of red, thinking of an old friend, laughing at a joke – all of these are the result of the actions of nerves. Just as the body performs many functions automatically, such as digestion, control of blood pressure and causing goosebumps, so the majority of brain actions occur below the level of consciousness. At the lower level, the mind is produced by the brain. But is there a higher level, where the mind has ascendancy and controls or affects the brain? And where is the mind? In the head? In the ether?

Scientific experimentation has not yet been able to pin down the precise location of the mind. Some would say that science has nothing to do with the issue; or that there never can be a final and irrefutable answer. At one end of the spectrum lie the materialists, who believe the brain and the mind are not only one and the same, but that the mind is merely an epiphenomenon (or by-product) of brain activity. At the other extreme is the biologist Rupert Sheldrake's theory that just as a magnet is surrounded by a field, the mind literally extends beyond the physical body to touch the minds of others. In Jung's concept of the collective unconscious, which earlier we visualized as the Internet, the individual mind merges on its deepest level with the wisdom of all humanity.

Of no fixed abode or trapped in the prison-house, wherever it resides, the brain/mind gives rise to dreams. The existence of a link between the mind and the brain is indisputable, and before we explore dreams any further it will help if we take a brief look at the functions of the parts of the brain that are involved. Note that although some scientists, as well as psychics, spiritualists and others, argue for the existence of a sixth – and even a seventh – sense, here I will be discussing only the universally accepted five senses, with which we are all familiar.

WHAT'S GOING ON IN YOUR HEAD

I am a Bear of Very Little Brain, and long words Bother me.

(A. A. Milne, *Winnie-the-Pooh*)

A few names of parts of the brain are unavoidable, but they are not too long or complicated. We don't need to go into much detail; we will simply look at how the brain works in order to gain a few insights before moving on to Geoffrey's unusual dream.

In normal waking, the brain receives information from outside itself: both from the body and from the external world. Our senses import sight, sound, touch, smell and taste to the 'I' that is locked away somewhere in the brain; and from these we discover what is happening 'out there'. Of course, all that we are consciously aware of is that we're part of the great experience of the world.

Our inner self is separated from the outside world by the relay station of the **thalamus**: a large structure deep inside the brain's core, which originated in the distant past of human evolution. Incoming information passes from surface receptors and is then carried in the form of electrical impulses to the thalamus. When we are awake the thalamus simply sends all of this along, distributing sensations to the relevant parts of the outer layer of the brain: the **cortex**. Here it is integrated with other related data and translated into, say, a bird, or a ball moving at speed, or pain in an infected ear.

At the back of the brain, the **occipital cortex** receives information from the eyes. The middle section, which consists of the **temporal and parietal cortices**, relates to the recognition of objects, movement and the other senses. At the forehead, the **frontal cortex** then decides which information we attend to, and is vital in enabling us to do this. All of this essential activity is carried out automatically. For example, you can drive for miles with little awareness of having done so until you come out of your reverie and realize you have not been concentrating – the brain has been on autopilot, dealing with everything without your conscious control, perfectly safely. Things are fine until you stop and think about what you are doing: then it all collapses. Any sports champion will tell you that games are won or lost not on the playing field or the golf course but in the mind. It's a phenomenon that is evidently well known. Variants of the following anonymous poem can be found in children's books and scattered across websites on subjects ranging from running, yoga, religion and business to sculpture, Canadian bartending and bondage:

> The centipede was happy quite,
>   Until the toad in fun
> Said, 'Pray, which leg goes after which?'
> Which worked his mind to such a pitch,
>   He lay distracted in a ditch,
>   Considering how to run.

As one website explains: 'We can become so caught up in trying to analyse *how* we should be running the race set before us as followers of Jesus that we fail to *just do it*.' This toad seems to be a close second to Coleridge's anonymous 'person from Porlock' in the unpopularity stakes.

MAKING SENSE

When in that House MPs divide,
If they've a brain and cerebellum too,
They have to leave that brain outside,
And vote just as their leaders tell 'em to.

(W. S. Gilbert, *Iolanthe*)

So a vast amount of activity in our brain is happening automatically. Now the information that has been gathered must be brought together into a coherent form, if we are to make sense of the world. It is in the cortex that the miracle happens and, for example, a flood of nerve impulses is converted into sight. We can see. All areas of the cortex are involved in this, and all are necessary: if the occipital cortex is destroyed, we are blind – even though the eyes work perfectly. To construct our vision of the world, the visual area works with the areas that recognize objects and patterns, found in the temporal and parietal cortices, areas that also integrate the other senses – touch, hearing, smell and taste. The help of memory is needed, so that we can compare the patterns we're receiving: 'That's a box.' 'It's Henry.' 'Ah, it's a waltz – the *Blue Danube*.' 'Sounds like Oasis, to me.' And at the head of all this activity is the conductor of the orchestra, the **frontal cortex** or lobes.

This is the most recently developed part of the brain in evolutionary terms. It is by far the largest in man compared even to the apes. It coordinates the other areas of the cortex as well as deciding exactly what information to concentrate on and what to ignore. It makes us human.

As well as keeping us on the road, the frontal lobes get

us out of bed, help us concentrate on a problem and overcome our frustration enough to stick with it; they stop us smacking someone even if they are *really* irritating. They make us civilized. Other parts of the brain are far more primitive in evolutionary terms and have a more basic attitude. Like Stevenson's Mr Hyde, they want to do their own thing – fight, have sex, eat, and so on. The frontal cortex has to restrain potential mutiny; like the British Prime Minister, it has no department of its own but must control and organize all the others.

WHAT'S GOING ON WHEN WE DREAM

I have come to the borders of sleep,
The unfathomable deep
Forest where all must lose
Their way, however straight,
Or winding, soon or late;
They cannot choose.

(Edward Thomas, 'Lights Out')

When we fall asleep the thalamus shuts its gate. No more information is admitted, even from the body. It's a lock-in. Of course a big stimulus *can* get in – but people have slept through hurricanes, and babies have been known to slumber unaware of the neighbour who is knocking down a wall in the next room. But despite this apparent shutdown, as we noted earlier, the brain is at times as active as ever. A part of it that generates images and metaphors and builds narratives comes to the fore; Jung called this its mythopoetic function, although the structures involved are not clear. Constantly intermingling thoughts and images behind the scenes, now that the brain is no longer turned outward it can revel in its own spontaneous show.

Wherever this drama comes from, it is back-projected on to the very same cortical areas that, a minute ago, were transforming all the incoming information for us, from light waves to nerve impulses to inner experience, in an effort to make us understand the outside world. Although the occipital cortex 'sees' just as clearly now, the vision is not 'out there' – it is hallucinated. We experience movement as we lie still in bed. The whole cortex is alive as it creates a drama just for us, a private screening in a cinema where we don't have to pay for a ticket. Enid Blyton again:

> My simile of a 'private cinema screen' is the best I can think of. But it's a 3-dimensional screen, complete with sound, smell and taste – and feeling! This is why I can describe things so realistically in my stories, 'as if I had been there'. I *have* been there – but only in my imagination . . . my conscious mind has nothing whatever to do with it except record what it sees.

This private, secret world, controlled by the thalamic gate, remains shut until we awaken, when it opens once more and 'reality' floods back in with the morning sun.

'PARADOXICAL SLEEP'

In the real dark night of the soul it is always three
o'clock in the morning.

(F. Scott Fitzgerald, *The Crack-Up*)

Strange things happen in sleep. In 1953 a postgraduate
student, Eugene Aserinsky, in Chicago, together with his
professor, Nathaniel Kleitman, noticed that bursts of
rapid eye movement (REM) occurred at regular intervals
during sleep. There are differing versions of this story.
According to one, Aserinsky was watching a baby,
possibly his own, as it fell asleep. Only for the first few
months of life do we go from being awake straight into
REM, so he was fortunate to see these strange eye movements as the child nodded off. In time, together with his
colleague William Dement, the team were able to show
that these REM periods appeared to correspond to
periods of vivid dreaming. Kleitman later worked with
Dement and they found that the REM periods were
repeated throughout the night, building to a crescendo
towards the time of waking. The rest of the sleep cycle
was termed non-REM (NREM), with the deepest sleep
during the early part of the night. The French physiologist
Michel Jouvet called REM 'paradoxical sleep' because of
the apparently wakeful brain activity that takes place
during these phases. We emerge from the depths of non-
REM early in the night to a state where we have every bit
as much energy on the EEG as when we are awake. The
deeper stages of non-REM sleep have also been termed
slow wave sleep (SWS).

At first it was thought that REM sleep was associated

with dreaming and that non-REM probably related to resting. But it did not take long to realize that some form of mental activity was taking place in non-REM sleep too. The jury is still out on whether or not non-REM dreaming – sometimes called 'mentation' sleep – is as vivid and bizarre as REM dreams. It is probably fair to say that REM dreaming is, in general, characterized by imagery, while non-REM is more like thinking.

There *are* very distinct differences between REM and non-REM physiologically. In the REM stages of sleep we are profoundly paralysed. Many of us will be familiar with dreams in which we cannot move, even though we're running flat out. There is a good reason for this mechanism: it protects us when we're asleep from acting out our dreams and seriously injuring ourselves. Apart from our eyes, the only parts of the body that can move to some extent are the small muscle groups, such as fingers and toes. In an experiment on cats, Jouvet showed that when paralysis in sleep is prevented, cats do in fact walk and appear to act out a dream in REM. Some people can wake from REM still paralysed, a condition called sleep paralysis, which can occur in those with irregular sleep patterns, such as shift workers or junior doctors. Often this is treated simply by providing conditions conducive to healthy sleep, but in more severe cases an antidepressant drug at night may help.

DREAMING BEFORE BIRTH

> Those who have likened our life to a dream were more
> right, by chance, than they realized. We are awake while
> sleeping, and waking sleep.
>
> (Michel de Montaigne, Essais, II, xii)

In the history of evolution, species slowly developed from
primitive organisms to reptiles and then mammals. We
know that non-REM is found in earlier species, so it is
probable that it is the old form of sleep, with REM, or
dreaming, the newcomer, found in almost every mammal.
However, there is some evidence that the sleep of reptiles
may be REM in form. If so, this would help explain why
we become cold-blooded in REM and possibly why REM
is the earliest type of sleep that the foetus experiences;
right at the start of our life we are in a reptilian stage of
existence. But, if that is the case, far from clarifying anything it only deepens the mystery. Why should reptiles
need to dream? What does the foetus dream of?

We are paralysed in REM but not in non-REM, so in
that stage of sleep we can move. It is in the very deepest
stages of non-REM that sleepwalking occurs, as do other
so-called sleep transition disorders, such as sleep-talking,
teeth-grinding (bruxism) and night terrors. None of these
conditions is associated with dreaming in the normal
course of events. Geoffrey's experience was rather different,
as we will see later in the chapter.

THE ABSURDITY OF DREAMS

When we dream, not only are our muscles paralysed, but the frontal cortex is down too. This means that, with our 'organ of civilization' off-line, we have no conscience, no morality, no ability to distinguish the absurd from the rational. We experience flights of fancy and we take the most ridiculous events in our stride; know that the man who looks nothing like Winston Churchill *is* him. On waking, when the frontal cortex is back on line, we may smile indulgently and dismiss the outlandish events of the night. No one has captured the essential oddity of the dream better than W. S. Gilbert, in the Lord Chancellor's song from *Iolanthe*:

> For you dream you are crossing the Channel, and tossing
>   about in a steamer from Harwich –
> Which is something between a large bathing machine
>   and a very small second-class carriage –
> And you're giving a treat (penny ice and cold meat) to a
>   party of friends and relations –
> They're a ravenous horde – and they all came on board
>   at Sloane Square and South Kensington Stations.
> And bound on that journey you find your attorney (who
>   started that morning from Devon);
> He's a bit undersized, and you don't feel surprised when
>   he tells you he's only eleven . . .

So far we have a part of the brain that creates images and metaphors, active all the time and projecting back on to the cortex during sleep so that we can experience these pictures as real. As a vital part of this, we need access to

memory, which provides the material for our dreams. A great deal of this comes from the recent past, especially the last week (Freud called this the 'day residue', thinking it was specifically from the previous day).

Finally, we need the involvement of the emotional brain, or **limbic system** – an old primitive part of our brain that gives rise to all our passions and causes so much trouble in the world, as well as positive emotions such as love. This adds the tone – how we feel in the dream. Indeed the memory and emotional circuits are probably closely interlinked. Emotion gives the dream its peculiar power, or lack of it.

IN TWO MINDS

'Now, what I want is, Facts . . . Facts alone are wanted in life.'

(Mr Gradgrind, in Charles Dickens, *Hard Times*)

Imagination is more important than knowledge. For knowledge is limited, whereas imagination embraces the entire world.

(Albert Einstein, 'What Life Means to Einstein')

As well as the cortices, located from the front to the back of the brain, there is a difference between sides. Like a walnut in its shell, the brain seen from above is divided into two: these **cerebral hemispheres** are joined at the bottom of the crevasse by a broad band of fibres, the **corpus callosum**.

In mammals, all the way up to chimps, there is very

little difference in function between the two sides of the brain. The left half controls the right side of the body and receives sensation from it, and vice versa. As far as we humans are concerned, it was not until Cro-Magnon man came on the scene – from around 100,000 years ago, probably in Africa – that brain development suddenly took off, with the development of art followed by, almost certainly, speech (though this did not really happen until 50,000 or so years ago). The two sides of the brain became specialized, with the crowning glory – speech and language – located in the left brain. Mathematical ability, reading, writing and logic are also associated with the left brain. The right brain deals with more artistic abilities: visual and spatial, musical and the recognition of emotional values. So, while the left brain can recognize a nose, eyes and mouth, the right brain can tell not only that it is a face but also whose face it is – and whether the expression is an angry, sad or baffled one. One poor farmer who had damage to his right brain could no longer tell his cows apart.

It is the right brain that fills in the blanks, reads between the lines. Socially, the left (logical) brain is relatively incompetent. Autism resembles pure left brain. The right brain makes sense of a situation, giving it context and emotional significance: it is skilled in reading others' intentions, the nuances of negotiation and intuition: 'The left brain may see 132 trees, while the right sees a forest.'

ONLY (DIS)CONNECT

Do what you will, this Life's a Fiction
And is made up of Contradiction.
(William Blake, *The Everlasting Gospel*)

Although the exact areas of the brain that give rise to dreams are unknown, the following discussion may help us to visualize some of the processes underlying the activity of our minds during sleep.

For the first time, in the 1940s, a major operation was performed to limit severe cases of epilepsy. To prevent the seizure from spreading throughout the brain, the corpus callosum was cut, severing communication between the right and the left hemispheres of the brain. When a fit started in one side of the brain, it was then unable to cross to the other half and affect the whole brain. When the hemispheres were divided it was observed that this, perhaps not surprisingly, allowed the two sides, or 'personalities', to come into open conflict. If the patient chooses cornflakes with his right hand, the left hand puts the packet back and picks up the Shredded Wheat. The right hand starts to button up his shirt; the left hand tries to undo the buttons and take it off. Here the left hand clearly *does* know what the right hand is doing – but it wants to do something else. The 2000 film, *Me, Myself & Irene* is a perfect fantasy depiction of the condition and, interestingly, makes the right brain feminine.

In 1981, Professor of Psychobiology Roger W. Sperry won a Nobel Prize after working for twenty years with patients who had had this operation. He saw them as having two separate spheres of consciousness, each with its own experience, knowledge and memory. These people had enormous difficulties in negotiating daily life: one man took socks from a drawer with his right hand, only to have it painfully slammed shut in the drawer by the left. One woman overslept, but was woken when her left hand slapped her. While walking into town, a man found that his left leg refused to go, and tried to head off in another direction. Later he realized that if he'd followed it he would have ended up at his ex-wife's house. Some left hands have unexpectedly slapped relatives, or even attempted to throttle the hand's owner – a condition brilliantly illustrated by Peter Sellers in Stanley Kubrick's classic 1963 film, *Dr Strangelove*. Often this is referred to as 'anarchic hand' or 'alien hand syndrome'.

ATOMS ON THE RED SEA SHORE

The Atoms of Democritus
And Newton's Particles of light
Are sands upon the Red sea shore,
Where Israel's tents do shine so bright.

(William Blake, 'Poems and Fragments from the Note-Book')

In Chapter 1 we saw that metaphorical thinking is probably older than conscious reasoning and our examination of the brain underlines this. Scientific thinking can be conceptualized as left brain – systematic, pursuing a clear train of reasoning. The right brain, artistic and emotional, associates outwards: the mind drifts, allowing images to surface, making connections, expressing feelings. This innate way of thinking seems to be hardwired into the brain; and on it we have superimposed the hard work of logic. Inevitably, this is a somewhat simplistic summary of complex processes. In normal life, the two sides cooperate like the two hands of a pianist. The differing contributions come together seamlessly, producing harmony from the dialogue. That does not mean they do the same things.

I have described the sorts of serious problem that arise when the right and left brain are totally separated. These cases are relatively uncommon. But if the left brain deals with language and the right brain with imagery, there are certainly opportunities for confusion to arise. In Chapter 1 we explored the dreaming brain's creative use of language in the solution of Morton Schatzman's obscure word puzzles and in the surprising pun that surfaced in Nancy's dream. Our next dreamer's experience, while in some ways similar, does have significant differences, and from these we will learn more about how we relate to our dreams.

Geoffrey

Geoffrey had just retired from the Church, where he was a canon. His background, however, was not ecclesiastical: his father had been a postman. After leaving grammar school, Geoffrey was conscripted for two years in the RAF. It was the time of the Korean War. 'If you were standing up and breathing they strapped the aeroplane to you,' he told me. 'They were desperate.' Partly due to the influence of a fellow pilot, Geoffrey became a committed Christian; later, while studying history at Cambridge

University, he changed course to study theology. In 1997 he wrote to me about his dream, and on a subsequent visit we discussed it further.

> About three years ago I dreamt that I was wading through a sub-terranean waterway. The bed of the stream in this tunnel scenario comprised pebbles and smooth boulders. Then – suddenly and horrifically – one of the boulders turned out to be the shell of a huge, spider-like crab ... collapse of stout party, long time getting back to sleep, work next day, near to the frazzle level.

Geoffrey would thrash about, fighting off the spider-crab in his sleep. Even though the nightmare had occurred so long ago, it was still vivid in his mind: 'There were huge pebbles and huge creatures. I used to kick my wife and lash out, trying to fight them off. It was as fierce and terrible as that. That's all there was to it.' The dream kept on for some time – for almost six months, on average about once a fortnight – and his wife would regularly find herself on the floor.

After five months, it was discovered that Geoffrey had cancer of the colon. Following treatment, he was given a colostomy. As soon as the diagnosis was made, the nightmares stopped.

INTERPRETATION

The interpretation, then, seems very simple and clear. As in a virtual reality experience, Geoffrey was walking along his own colon in the dream and witnessed the events that had been occurring inside him.

The large boulders seem to be an image of the lining cells of the large bowel and it is usually one of these cells that turns malignant. As cancers take a few years to develop from the time when the first cell undergoes the change from normal to malignant, the dream appears to be showing something that happened to Geoffrey a few years previously. He did not experience the dream when the cancer first began to grow, but at a stage when it was about to become a problem clinically and have a strong impact on his life. The seriousness of the illness is translated into the terror Geoffrey feels.

The resemblance to Morton Schatzman's example is striking: the dream has an important message, but presents it as a puzzle that must be solved. However, where Jacques Lacan said that 'the dream *is* a charade', this goes one step further. Geoffrey is not just watching a charade: he is an acting and suffering subject in the theatre of his own colon. He witnesses the moment of birth of his tumour as he stands on the lining cells nearby, a real part of the drama. He is not a member of the audience, surrounded by others, watching actors move around among props on the stage. He is thrown into the middle of the action and as terrified as he would be if a sci-fi spider-crab materialized before him as he walked down the road.

ACTIVE IMAGINATION

The Imagination may be compared to Adam's dream – he awoke and found it truth.

(John Keats, letter of 22 November 1817)

In the late 1970s Robert Bosnak, a Jungian analyst, pioneered a new form of dream therapy inspired by Jung's work on alchemy and by his technique of active imagination. According to this, the dreaming mind sees dreams as real events in real surroundings; as Picasso is reported to have said, 'Everything you can imagine is real.' Bosnak's method is based on inducing a hypnagogic state, between wakefulness and sleep (we will look at this further in Chapter 8), to enable people to get back into their dreams and play an active part in re-experiencing them. The dreamer 'becomes' each of the elements, staying with a figure or object until, quite suddenly, they *are* that person or thing. Geoffrey, for example, could have become the boulder. Perhaps then he could have sensed the nature of the boulder and viewed things from its perspective.

SHOUTING IN PICTURES

... the time will come when you will hear me.

(Benjamin Disraeli)

This is as clear an example of a prodromal dream as one could wish for: a dream that heralds the onset of an illness, while the illness exists in the body but has not yet become manifest. One can almost sense the urgency of the dream, its intensity reflecting the frustration of the unconscious mind as it fails to communicate with the dreamer. It could not have sent a more powerful message and it could not, in its own terms, have been clearer. But Geoffrey cannot hear it; he does not understand this language. The unconscious might as well be using Greek semaphore, for all the good it is doing.

As we know, the right side of our brain deals with imagery, is possibly where the menacing spider-crabs are created, and shouts its message – but has absolutely no access to our language. Or at least not in a straight-forward way. Nancy did manage to decipher the 'malignancy' clue that her dream offered. Here, while Geoffrey's mind does not state CANCER, it does make use of the simplest symbol to hand: the crab, the astro-logical sign for Cancer. It may have been combined with the spider because Geoffrey is arachnophobic. A neat piece of fusion.

Yet Geoffrey acted out his terrifying struggle with the spider-crab, fighting with his wife and kicking her out of bed. If he was able to do this, his dream must have occurred in non-REM sleep, despite its alarming REM-style images. Although there is a condition called REM sleep behaviour disorder (RBD), in which a small area of damage in the brain prevents paralysis, just as in Jouvet's cats, Geoffrey's violent night-time activity ended when his dream disappeared. Interestingly, if he had had the dream during an REM stage of sleep – if he had been paralysed and not attacked his wife – some of the urgency might have vanished from the situation.

The dream does not give up – and it does not change tack. It keeps on driving the same message home, again and again, like a boxer with a good left hook or a child who knows the answer, waving her hand in the air, desperate to attract the teacher's attention. Undoubtedly it succeeds, but all that happens is that Geoffrey grows more anxious. He becomes increasingly disturbed, not least by the effect the restless nights are having on his marriage. He knows he needs help and considers going for counselling; it is only with the onset of minor symptoms that he decides to seek medical advice.

POST-TRAUMATIC STRESS DISORDER

He often went out alone, and when he came back you were never absolutely certain whether he had had an adventure or not. He might have forgotten it so completely that he said nothing about it; and then when you went out you found the body; and, on the other hand, he might say a great deal about it, and yet you could not find the body.

(J. M. Barrie, *Peter Pan*)

There is evidence that the nightmares of post-traumatic stress disorder (PTSD) occur in non-REM sleep and are not strictly dreams but intrusions, just like flashbacks in waking consciousness. Before the age of ten, the corpus callosum has not completely matured; even then the connection between the two sides of the brain is not entirely perfect. Negative emotional experience is more likely to be processed by the right (intuitive) side of the brain, and possibly stored there. It is thought that an overwhelmingly powerful experience – especially one that is sudden and unexpected, and particularly if it occurs during childhood – may remain stuck in the right side of the brain: it is 'too big' to cross the gap all at once, so cannot be processed by the conscious side and placed in the normal boxes in which we file experience. So it stays alive, crashing into our awareness in the form of startling flashbacks and nightmares. The life-threatening nature of Geoffrey's condition makes his dream behave in exactly this way.

It is interesting to note that Geoffrey rarely dreamed. He had no interest in dreams. Yet all of a sudden an overpowering and disturbing nightmare actually broke through the normal protective mechanisms of sleep and forced itself into his waking mind. There was a clarity about this that was striking, and that characterizes lucid dreams, which we will look at in the next chapter. His dream, at least from a subjective point of view, has similarities with the nightmares of PTSD. It is repetitive, terrifying, causing him to thrash about violently; it is also predominantly visual. The difference is that whilst Geoffrey's trauma lies in the future, the PTSD victims of war, terrorism or abuse are reliving their harrowing experiences.

Earlier we noted Professor Sperry's conclusion that two separate spheres of consciousness may exist in the brain, and on a clinical level his findings seem very helpful. Studies of normal dreaming are complex and do not show a clear right-sided predominance, yet the dream does behave *as if* it is pure right brain. And it appears to know something that the dreamer does not – again just like the people whose two sides were in dramatic conflict.

We all have two sides to our brain, but the degree to which they cooperate varies from one individual to another. From trauma victims we can learn more of how the brain works, even if we may not yet know the exact nature of the underlying mechanisms. Could the nightmares of PTSD help us to account for the presence of convincingly real people and events in our dreams? Are they simply expressions of powerful emotional experiences stuck in one side of our brain, or could there be other explanations?

3

MIND INVADERS

Where do people go to when they die?
Somewhere down below or in the sky?
'I can't be sure,' said Grandad, 'but it seems
They simply set up home inside our dreams.'
(Jeanne Willis, 'Inside Our Dreams')

In the REM stages of sleep we dream: we cannot avoid it. Yet we all know people who claim they never have dreams; or who think they do, but can't remember them. Ernest Hartmann has devised a theory of the relationship between different parts of the mind which has relevance to our understanding of what goes on when we dream. Just as some of us appear to have better or worse access to our memory banks or our emotions, he proposes, there are people who have high dream recall and very vivid and lengthy dreams. Night after night they immerse themselves in them. At the other end of the spectrum are those who have no memory of their dreams, and no interest in dreams.

77

Just as different mental abilities exist, the brain contains many different structures that do different things. Some are concerned with balance, some with memory, and so on. Although they are separate, they have to relate to each other so that we can coordinate incredibly different activities into a seamless whole. In Hartmann's view, access to images and dreams varies depending on the boundary between certain parts of the brain. If the boundary is 'thick', access is difficult and fantasy will be low, while if the boundary is 'thin', dreams will not only be rich and detailed, they will also be easily remembered.

Imagination is one aspect of this idea. We have already seen that creative people have easy access to the source of their material: in Hartmann's terms, they have 'thin boundaries'. This means that the walls within the brain have more gaps – possibly between the left and right brain – so more conversation goes on. Extending this, we can visualize the corpus callosum as more open in thin-boundaried people; less so in those with thick boundaries. Think of it as the difference between 2Mb Broadband and Dial-up Internet. This is, of course, theoretical: there is no hard and fast evidence that the right brain is the dreamer and the left the thinker; but it is a useful metaphor to bear in mind. Hartmann's idea is a general assessment; even those who say they never dream may have a single startling experience, as we will see later.

When Hartmann devised a research questionnaire and analysed the responses of 800 people he found that there was a high correlation between dream recall and what he termed 'thinness' of boundaries. The dreams of those with very thin boundaries were independently rated as significantly more vivid and emotional and showed more interaction of the characters within them. Further, he found that thinness was highly correlated to a personality measure called 'openness to experience'. People who suffered from lifelong nightmares also had thin boundaries.

In the last chapter we highlighted the difference between normal and PTSD dreams. Interestingly, Hartmann's study showed that those with nightmares of PTSD had normal, not thin, boundaries. If Geoffrey had completed the questionnaire he would, I am sure, have been categorized as 'thick-boundaried', for he had no interest in fantasy or the imagination and was a very practical, down-to-earth man, not a dreamer. We will return to the boundary issue in Chapter 8, when we meet John, the most thick-boundaried dreamer of them all.

LUCID DREAMING

If a man could pass thro' Paradise in a Dream, & have a flower presented to him as a pledge that his Soul had really been there, & found that flower in his hand when he awoke
– Aye! And what then?

(Samuel Taylor Coleridge, Notebook entry, 1815–16)

The term 'lucid dreaming' was coined in 1913 by Frederik van Eeden in 'A Study of Dreams', but the concept was not taken seriously until scientific research during the 1980s started to find evidence to validate it. Lucid dreams are those in which we consciously realize we are dreaming. We feel we can direct the course of the dream; we have the ability to alter the content of the story and control our actions. While experiencing an apparently real dreamscape, we can simultaneously recall events of our waking life. In his experiments with lucidity, van Eeden had the following dream:

> I dreamt that I was lying in the garden before the windows of my study, and saw the eyes of my dog through the glass pane. I was lying on my chest and observing the dog very keenly. At the same time, however, I knew with perfect certainty that I was dreaming and lying on my back in my bed. And then I resolved to wake up slowly and carefully and observe how my sensation of lying on my chest would change into the sensation of lying on my back. And so I did, slowly and deliberately, and the transition – which I have since undergone many times – is most wonderful. It is like the feeling of slipping from one body into another, and there is distinctly a double recollection of the two bodies. I remembered what I felt in my dream, lying on my chest; but returning into the day-life, I remembered also that my physical body had been quietly lying on its back all the while. This observation of a double memory I have had many times since. It is so indubitable that it leads almost unavoidably to the conception of a dream-body.

The lucid dream may feel 'hyperreal' – as if it is an enhanced and powerful version of daily life. Thin-boundaried people are often lucid dreamers, or 'oneironauts'. Some people take this type of dreaming for granted and are surprised to discover that it doesn't happen to everyone. We cannot consciously decide to become thin-boundaried, but we may be able to create the conditions in which we become susceptible to lucid dreams. This is one way of helping nightmare sufferers control their problem.

The key point is that the existence of lucid dreaming shows that our conscious awareness can persist while we are dreaming. In these dreams we can make decisions and take charge of events. If we want to fly to Saturn, we do it. If the dream takes a frightening turn, we can always make a hasty exit. In early hunter-gatherer societies lucid dreaming formed the basis of religious practices, and indeed this type of dreaming was the origin of a belief in gods and the soul. According to A. J. J. Radcliffe, 'Man's earliest conception of dreams is just this literal belief; what appears before him in dreams is as real as what appears before him awake, and the people of his dreams stand veritably before him.' The possibility of employing lucid dreaming for healing both oneself and others has been explored but it is not known whether suggestions and actions made during the lucid state can bring about effective improvements to physical conditions or illnesses.

OVERLAP STATES

Up by 4 a-clock and walked to Greenwich, where called at Captain Cockes and to his chamber, he being in bed – where something put my last night's dream into my head, which I think is the best that ever was dreamed – which was, that I had my Lady Castlemayne in my armes and was admitted to use all the dalliance I desired with her, and then dreamed that this could not be awake but that it was only a dream. But that since it was a dream and that I took so much real pleasure in it, what a happy thing it would be, if when we are in our graves (as Shakespeere resembles it), we could dream, and dream but such dreams as this – that then we should not need to be so fearful of death as we are this plague-time.

(Samuel Pepys, *Diary*)

Before moving on to primitive ideas, it is worth making a diversion to look at conscious states related to lucidity.

The search for consciousness is the modern Holy Grail of science. How can a mass of protein, fat and chemicals give rise to seeing red or to thinking about our place in the universe? There are many theories, but as yet no clues. It is known that a small stimulus, for example stroking the skin very lightly, can be detected in the nerves of the cortex but fail to become conscious. If the stimulus is increased a bit more then it may suddenly be strong enough to enter awareness. So consciousness lies on the top of a very complex process.

On its own, this is a big enough problem to figure out. But now we have to add dreaming awareness: not just REM but NREM, which, as we have seen, are fundamentally different physiological states. Add to that the awareness of dreaming; that is, wakeful consciousness against the background of REM dream experience.

There are some unfortunate individuals who, due to damage especially of the frontal lobes, lose the brain's normal 'reality monitoring' – the ability to tell reality from dream. It is not that they have more dreams, but that they cannot determine what is a dream and what is a perception. According to Mark Solms, one person 'woke from dreams and believed that they were real events. On one occasion, after dreaming that he had been bitten by a poisonous snake, the patient's wife had to seek the help of neighbours to calm the patient. He was convinced that this had actually occurred and was demanding to be taken to hospital.'

'False awakening' is similar, but with a different emphasis. First described by van Eeden – who called such experiences 'wrong waking up' dreams – these create a normal world, into which the dreamer wakes, but finds that something is odd. On full awakening the illusory nature of the transitional state becomes obvious. The most striking examples I have seen occur when the dreamer gets into a loop: dreaming of a horror then waking with relief, only to gradually realize that the thing has not gone and the horror is repeated, only to awake with relief, slowly to realize that it is still with them – on and on. A good illustration of this is Linda Caine's false awakening in *Out of the Dark*, the story of her terrifying fight for self-discovery.

Linda had what could be described as 'traumatic' false awakenings. In the most vivid, she awoke from a nightmare and was terrified. Roger, the senior nurse on night duty, came into the room at that moment and sat on the bed reassuring her that she was safe in her room in Ticehurst House Hospital, a private psychiatric hospital in south-east England, and that she was not back in her childhood nightmare.

His hand was resting on her leg as reassurance and

Linda began to feel less terrified. Then she noticed his hand moving up her leg and 'his touch changed' so that it now felt sexual, not reassuring. At that moment of terror and helplessness, she suddenly woke up. As she did so Roger entered the room and sat on the bed, reassuring her. She felt immense relief and began to calm down. He placed his hand on her leg to reassure her but she suddenly noticed his touch change and his hand move up her leg. Terrified and unable to move she felt powerless but then suddenly woke up. As she did so Roger entered the room . . .

Narcolepsy provides a slightly different angle. This is a syndrome characterized by daytime sleepiness that often leads to sudden entry into a REM phase of sleep, with muscle paralysis (cataplexy), sleep paralysis and hypnagogic hallucinations. In this condition, REM is too easily accessed in waking life. The trigger is often laughing: the typical sufferer abruptly loses muscle tone and becomes floppy. They may suddenly fall asleep at the table as they are eating.

Finally, there is sleep paralysis. Normally, as we emerge from sleep, muscle tone is restored and up we get. But occasionally the paralysis persists into waking life for a short while; it can last as long as a minute or two. As if this were not frightening enough, dream images may also continue, giving rise to waking (or 'hypnopompic') hallucinations. Only when these fade − or if we have experienced them before − do we recognize them for what they are. We will see some examples in Chapter 8.

So the boundaries of reality are somewhat blurred. The brain has to sort incoming sensation from internal information and, even at the best of times, is making up some of what it perceives. Consciousness would seem to be a relatively 'simple' issue if it were not for dreaming. We still have no idea why nature had to include a paralysed state in the dark where a form of madness is allowed to break out, and it is difficult to assume that natural selection is the prime cause. Dreaming must be essential, but perhaps a simple biological answer is inadequate. Does the dream have more than a biological function?

THE SHAMAN'S WORLD

You are not a human being in search of a spiritual experience. You are a spiritual being immersed in a human experience.

(Teilhard de Chardin)

Primitive man lived in a world peopled by forces outside himself. The whole of nature was suffused with life and spirits: in rocks, trees, birds, water . . . It was vital that he remain connected to these unseen forces and that he entrust his being to some special part of nature with which he had a profound relationship.

In early societies, the dream world constantly mingled with the daytime world. As A. J. J. Radcliffe noted in *A History of Dreams*, 'It is at this stage that man realizes, as much from . . . dream experiences as from any other observation, that he is not just a body, but first a spiritual being; he has a soul.' For primitive cultures this experience of the world was real: the forces had to be obeyed or propitiated. If a dead relative appeared in a dream it was their spirit, and what this spirit had to say was of great significance. The view of nature as allegorical is a much later abstraction, unknown to early man. According to Jung:

> We can understand why higher and even divine knowledge was formerly attributed to the soul if we remember that in ancient cultures, beginning with primitive times, man always resorted to dreams and visions as a source of information.

For millennia, dreams were meetings of spirits with the dreamer: his soul could leave his body and wander far and wide, scouting, hunting or even travelling to the farthest points of the heavens. There were dangers in this: the soul might not return safely, so often there was a taboo on waking a sleeper. Radcliffe reported that 'The Indians of Guiana ... say a man sleeps and wakes according to whether his soul is abroad or in the body; waking is the sign of the soul's return.'

Central to many cultures was the shaman, a dream visionary. As noted in the Introduction, shamanic initiation can partly be hereditary; but it may also involve important encounters in dreams. In their early life, future shamans have often been different from their peers – isolated, perhaps suffering from epileptic fits or other problems. They may have grown into inadequate adults. After often harsh initiation rituals, they would undergo instruction from shaman elders. In a view quite alien to our modern attitude, sickness itself may be seen as an initiation, transforming the ordinary person into a 'technician of the sacred'.

Joseph Campbell, in the first volume of his comprehensive survey of mythology, *The Masks of God*, describes Igjugarjuk, a Caribou Eskimo shaman. As a young man he had constant dreams that he did not understand. They were extremely clear and vivid, and contained strange, unknown beings. Once his destiny was realized, he spent over a month fasting in the cold wilderness, during which time he 'sometimes died a little' but thought only of the Great Spirit and tried to keep his mind clear of everyday things. 'Toward the end of the thirty days there came to him a helping spirit in the shape of a woman. She came to him while he was asleep and seemed to hover in the air above him. After that he dreamed no more of her, but she became his helping spirit.' In Chapter 10 we will meet Vicky, whose dream bears a remarkable resemblance to this experience.

According to Eliade, the renowned historian of religions:

A shaman's instruction often takes place in dreams. It is in dreams that the pure sacred life is entered and direct relations with the gods, spirits, and assorted souls are re-established. It is always in dreams that historical time is abolished and the mythical time regained – which allows the future shaman to witness the beginnings of the world and hence to become contemporary not only with the cosmogony but also with the primordial mythical revelations.

Eliade comments that the dreams are 'stereotyped', rather than unique. 'The available documents on shamanic dreams clearly show that they involve an initiation whose structure is well known in the history of religions.'

So, not just anyone could go to the tribal elders saying they had had a dream and wanted to be a trainee shaman. The dream itself had to conform to a pattern recognized not only by each tribe as part of the shamanic profession but also found throughout the history of religions. It could not be faked. Shamans seem to have understood these dreams in a way unknown to our modern, scientific outlook.

What has been described here is a process referred to as dream incubation, which is important in dream work in all ancient civilizations. It was an essential aspect of the use of dreams in primitive cultures, for example in the treatment of illness, and laid the foundations for more developed cultures.

JOURNEYING

If the Sun & Moon should doubt,
They'd immediately Go out.
(William Blake, 'Auguries of Innocence')

In shamanism, the oldest healing tradition known on earth, the journey is central. In 'journeying' the shaman moves into an altered state of consciousness in order to send his dream body to the various realms of the upper and lower spirit worlds. Here he will communicate with a range of helpers; often these take the form of animal guides, elemental spirits or ancestral ghosts, who can reveal to him wisdom and healing. Strength and subtlety are required in this bargaining, for supernatural spirits, it is believed, at times cause sickness, or even death. They may even be hostile to any living beings they find among them. At times the shaman intervenes simply because energies are out of balance. The energetic imprint of a traumatic event continues to exert its damaging power until it is overcome by the shaman's skill in the techniques of soul retrieval.

Shamanic cultures believe that there is a spirit aspect that can leave the physical body during sleep and wander abroad, for example exploring the tracks for the next day's hunting. If the soul gets lost, the individual suffers, possibly becoming depressed, and must be made whole again. In Chapter 10 we will see how a tribe took extreme action to retrieve one man's soul. The Andaman Islanders (Ongees) believe that when the 'body double' steps out of the sleeping 'body physical' it retraces the steps of the outer body from the previous day's wanderings and collects 'the smells scattered by the individual'; it can 'smell things that Ongees did not notice the first time around'. As they retrieve the smells, so they strengthen the spider's web which, they believe, links us all.

The shaman is the prototype of the lucid dreamer. He undertakes his journey with a specific purpose, acting for the benefit of the individual or the tribe. Paradoxically, strict discipline and the observance of ritual enable the freedom of his flight. Intention is the key: positive energy is conjured up by the intensity and control of his thought. If he is assailed by doubt or a lack of focus, the journey fails.

FLIGHTS OF IMAGINATION

Open wide the mind's cage-door.
She'll dart out and cloudward soar.

(John Keats, 'Fancy')

Protons, neutrons and electrons
are the human body, the planet and the stars.
From the unconscious consciousness came
so in us the planet loves and dreams.
It is the Earth singing this *Cosmic Canticle* in me.
    The music of the spheres . . .
'If our eyes were more perfect
we would see the atoms singing.'
    They say the proton sounds like a Bach fugue.

(Ernesto Cardenal, 'The Music of the Spheres')

The sense of spiritual interconnection which lies at the heart of animistic beliefs was shared by the Romantic poets at the end of the eighteenth century. Contemplating the divine presence in the natural world, they saw imagination as the vital force: it is through imagination that we raise our human consciousness to become one with the world's creator. Coleridge elevated Imagination far above the mechanical 'Fancy' of humdrum and prosaic writers, which 'merely toys with the wooden jigsaw pieces supplied by memory and association'. Literally 'inspired' poets, by drawing in the breath of the divine, identify with the creative mind of God and through active imagination can then express in their work the spiritual meaning that pervades the world. Incidentally, it was Coleridge who coined the term 'psychosomatic', combining mind

90

and body in a single word (Greek *psyche* and *soma*).

The Romantic movement has often been seen, above all, as glorifying the individual at the expense of society. Yet, as in shamanism, the emphasis on escape from physical and temporal limitations is equally important: we must cast off social restrictions and our own 'mind-forg'd manacles' if we are to become part of the eternal spiritual world. Blake – a visionary and undeniably a lucid dreamer – believed that it is only our bodily limitations that prevent us from seeing that all of creation is one:

How do you know but ev'ry Bird that cuts the airy way,
Is an immense world of delight, clos'd by your senses
five?

he wrote in his 'Memorable Fancy'. In his dreams he debated with biblical prophets and Isaiah clarified the issue: 'I saw no God, nor heard any, in a finite organical perception; but my senses discover'd the infinite in every thing.' Much earlier than Blake, Sir Thomas Browne wrote of his ability to control his dreams; in 1642 he claimed, 'in one dream I can compose a whole Comedy, behold the action, apprehend the jests and laugh my self awake at the conceits thereof.'

From another century, and a very different context, comes the following remarkable tale. In 1891 Ambrose Bierce published 'An Occurrence at Owl Creek Bridge', a story of the American Civil War. It tells of Peyton Farquhar, a supporter of the Confederate cause, who is captured and hanged from a bridge. Losing consciousness, 'as one already dead', he drops down into the river. He awakens in the cold and dark, hears a terrible roaring and realizes that the rope has broken. His neck aching horribly, he forces his way to the surface, now fully alert. After eluding the Unionist gunfire he makes his way home at last:

> All is as he left it, and all bright and beautiful in the morning sunshine. He must have traveled the entire night. As he pushes open the gate and passes up the wide white walk, he sees a flutter of female garments; his wife, looking fresh and cool and sweet, steps down from the veranda to meet him . . . She stands waiting, with a smile of ineffable joy, an attitude of matchless grace and dignity. Ah, how beautiful she is! He springs forward with extended arms. As he is about to clasp her he feels a stunning blow upon the back of the neck; a blinding white light blazes all about him with a sound like the shock of a cannon – then all is darkness and silence!
>
> Peyton Farquhar was dead; his body, with a broken neck, swung gently from side to side beneath the timbers of the Owl Creek bridge.

What is unusual about this lucid dream is, of course, that the fictional dreamer is dead. From the earliest shamans to Aldous Huxley and Carlos Castaneda the spiritual flight or dream journey from everyday life to another reality has been a magnetic theme for thinkers and writers – including songwriters: 'Green, Green Grass of Home', a hit for Tom Jones and Elvis Presley, is a lucid dream. Lucid dreaming shapes the plots of the films *Nightmare on Elm Street*, *Vanilla Sky*, *Waking Life* and, most notably, the

Matrix trilogy. Which is the true reality? To characters in Audrey Niffenegger's intricate 2004 novel *The Time Traveler's Wife* it remains a puzzle:

'You still haven't proved you're real,' Clare says.

'Neither have you.'

'Do you ever wonder if I'm real?' she asks me, surprised.

'Maybe I'm dreaming you. Maybe you're dreaming me; maybe we only exist in each other's dreams and every morning when we wake up we forget all about each other.' . . .

'How do you know? I mean, if I was making you up, and I didn't want you to know you were made up, I just wouldn't tell you, right?'

I wiggle my eyebrows at her. 'Maybe God just made us up and He's not telling us.'

Jane

I now turn to the strange tale of Jane, who had a very striking dream experience. Towards the end of her years at school she had become aware of a slow build-up of psychological problems, and when she left to begin her nursing studies she had a serious mental breakdown. It is hard to understand the impact of such an event unless it has happened to you. Jane suffered a frightening loss of inner control, which she described as 'a sort of mental paralysis'. She found it difficult to study, with the result that her career 'got derailed'. Despite this, she later managed to return to college and was in the middle of a degree course in history when I met her. To me, her symptoms suggested depression.

Unlike Geoffrey, Jane had been interested in dreams since childhood and was a clear case of a 'thin-boundaried' person, to use Ernest Hartmann's term. Lucid dreams were familiar to her: 'For some years I kept a dream diary but gave it up because eventually it was taking too much time. I found I could change things in the dream if I concentrated on them. Flying, for instance. I was curious to see what I could do ... After the exams, I was flying but I began to sense I must not go too far or I might not be able to get back.'

As a child, Jane had powerful dreams; often she would find herself flying around Greek temples. She would also hear dream voices. The vivid dreams never left her; indeed, they were one reason why she later chose to study Ancient Greek, as well as history. 'To me the dream world is a contact with the spiritual world,' she said.

Jane had contacted me following one particular series of dreams she experienced around the time when she had an infection. Although its nature was not serious, it manifested itself as a skin rash which was uncomfortably itchy and painful, and extremely persistent. Despite various forms of treatment it continued to return. Jane, of course, constantly dreamed. This time, however, she could tell that something odd was going on:

For some time before the onset of the illness I had the experience of seeing these very strange creatures appearing in my dreams. They were so peculiar-looking as to mark themselves out as quite different and something I had never dreamed of before – they seemed to me like visitors from somewhere else, because they didn't really do anything except appear and lurk. They were about six inches in height or so, they were definitely a white colour. It is very difficult to describe. They weren't human-looking, except that they did seem to have heads and bodies, but it's more that they had something rather grotesque and alien about them.

On the night before the start of the rash appearing I had a vivid dream of these creatures flying in a swarm – a huge swarm – out of the kitchen. They were all white, and similar to locusts. Over the next few months I kept seeing them in my dreams.

Remarkably, one night I had a dream that all the creatures were dead – their bodies were shrivelled and their wings all dried up. The last one just lay there completely dead. I woke up feeling quite relieved to realize that these creatures wouldn't trouble me any more.

INTERPRETATION

I do not know whether I was then a man dreaming I was a butterfly, or whether I am now a butterfly dreaming I am a man.

(Chuang Tzu, 4th century BC)

Jane was right: it was the last she saw of the illness. The

creatures who invaded her dreams evidently represent the fungal infection, with their numbers possibly paralleling the numbers of spores. Curiously, there does not appear to be the same intensity of feeling that we find in many of the other dreams in this book: perhaps because the illness is not life-threatening. Naturally, Jane did not know when the rash was about to start, or when it would finally vanish, but the dreams anticipated both, tracking its onset and returning to lurk as a reminder until the infection's departure. Unlike many repetitive dreams, this example seems to have a dynamic relationship with the illness. The creatures grow in number rather than repeating a single image. Then, as the illness reaches its conclusion, the active dream equivalents die. The pattern here is marked, and quite unlike the progression evident in Nancy's two dreams of the hooded figures.

In our discussion, Jane told me that at first just one of these peculiar beings had appeared in her dream. She had found it disturbing and felt that something odd was happening. The creature kept returning, always alone, for a couple of months. All of a sudden there was a multitude and, unlike the solitary creature, these ones had wings: 'like locusts or some kind of strange butterfly'.

Jane's dream raises the problem of whether all the elements in our dreams belong to us or whether some are part of a much bigger whole.

Marie-Louise von Franz, a leading authority on myths, fairy tales and dreams, in an interview described a powerful dream of Jung's. He entered a small chapel and was surprised to find no statue of the Virgin on the altar, and no crucifix:

... but only a beautiful flower arrangement. And then he saw on the floor in front of the altar a yogi sitting in the lotus posture, in deep meditation. Jung realized with a shock that this was the yogi who was imagining him, and that in his trance, a kind of active imagination, he was imagining the life of Jung, dreaming him. Jung knew that when the yogi woke up, he, Jung, would no longer exist. The ordinary Professor Jung was the dream of that great inner figure.

Questioner: And yet, at the same time, the yogi figure was a dream of Dr Jung's.

Referring to Chuang Tzu, von Franz said: 'A butterfly is a symbol of the Self. Are we the dream of the Self or is the Self our dream? We just don't know.'

I find it fascinating that Jane does not interact with the creatures – merely observes them. The overall feeling is of strangeness, of something alien encroaching on her dream world. The first being 'came into the dream and drew attention to itself', she explained. She was certain that the dream wasn't *about* the creature, that it had an independent existence: 'It was as if it had its own consciousness. It was like it could dream about you. I suppose you could say it had embryonic consciousness.'

The sudden swarm of insect-like creatures may sound like something from the Hitchcock film, *The Birds*, but Jane insisted that these weren't nightmares. On the contrary, she saw her experience in a positive light. Later she wrote to me: 'The conclusions I took from having the dream were optimistic, really, in that I believe there is some kind of association between one's dreaming mind and physical life, and I have the notion that if I were to become ill again, then I would have some sort of dream about it . . . having dreams about illness serves in a way to lessen my fear of illness. Broadly, I seem to have taken the attitude that although illness is not within my control, there is some component of it that is.'

Interestingly, these creatures were not in any way familiar to Jane. Remember, she is an experienced – one might say sophisticated – dreamer. While not claiming absolute control over all elements of her dreams, she did feel they were part of her. However, again and again, she described these creatures as alien to herself, as 'intruding' on her dream world, as if they were separate from it. She was sure the creatures had 'their own thinking'.

Is the fungus appearing in her dream, or is she dreaming about the fungus?

DREAMS AND DEATH

About ten days or so
After we saw you dead
You came back in a dream.
I'm all right now you said.

And it was you, although
You were fleshed out again:
You hugged us all round then,
And gave your welcoming beam.

How like you to be kind,
Seeking to reassure.
And, yes, how like my mind
To make itself secure.

(Thom Gunn, 'The Reassurance')

It seems natural that we should dream of dead family members or friends, and many of us do. After all, they have played such important roles in our life that it would be surprising if we did not. Consciously, and perhaps subconsciously, we do not want to forget. Other dead people appear in our dreams too, and here the connection is more uncertain. Why should we dream about Liberace or Vivien Leigh? Or that man who used to have a fish stall in the market? And why now? We may not have given them a thought for years (if ever), yet there they are, doing often quite extraordinary things (or indeed ordinary things). No dream dictionaries can give a convincing reason, though they do seem to agree that to dream of any kind of death denotes a marriage; as night opposes day, in these books everything seems to represent its opposite. In the Introduction, we saw that the interpretation of figures that appear in dreams depends on individual circumstances. Liberace may not mean the same to you as he does to the legendary man on the Clapham omnibus. Trying to establish the nature of these figures leads us up some intriguing paths.

As can be seen, there are many possible ways of interpreting a dream figure. To the shaman it is *really* that person; to a modern therapist it is an aspect of their client's personality, and some characteristic of the dream figure is a part of the dreamer they probably are uncomfortable with. It is easier to see the problem (that is, to project it) in someone else first. However, not all figures should be seen as personal; especially when the dreams are of people who have died, the situation becomes more complex.

On Dreams and Death, published in 1984, is the final book of Marie-Louise von Franz, who was a leading disciple of Carl Jung. During the forty or so years that von Franz worked with Jung, she also became an expert on alchemy and in the interpretation of dreams. In her illuminating study of the rituals and beliefs of many cultures, von Franz gives us many insights into the relationship between dreaming and the dead.

One reason why a greatly missed relation appears in a dream is, of course, because we want to know they still exist somewhere; if they can't be with us in waking life, they are at least present in our dreams. To reassure us that they are still alive on another plane, our memory bank retrieves stored images for us. We are consoled by the feeling that those we love live on.

In Jung's terminology, this type of dream is subjective, and he interpreted most images in this way – seeing them as symbols of ideas and images already present in the mind of the dreamer. In other words, it is all in the mind. There is another way of approaching the interpretation of figures that appear in our dreams and that is to view them objectively: it is *not* all in the mind of the individual dreamer. The dream figures really do have their own independent existence. In this wider perspective, we take into consideration the continuing, post-mortal life of the dead person, not just the life of whoever is encountering this figure in their dream.

Von Franz gives an account of one such case:

I . . . was once asked by a young woman analyst to study the dreams of a patient of hers, a young girl who had lost her fiancé, a pilot, in an airplane accident. She dreamed of the pilot almost every night, and the analyst and I at first interpreted the dream figure as the image of her own animus, which she projected onto the fiancé. The unconscious seemed to be suggesting that ... she detach herself from her tie with the dead. But there were six dreams which somehow I could not interpret in this manner. Therefore I told the analyst that in those dreams the appearance of the pilot was probably the dead man himself. The somewhat rationally inclined colleague was indignant, asked for a consultation with Jung and presented the whole dream series to him. Without hesitation, Jung (who knew nothing about my choice) picked out the same six dreams and interpreted them on the objective level.

Understandably, the younger analyst is taken aback by von Franz's view that the pilot had entered her dream from his continuing existence after death. Presumably she felt she had to accept the interpretation when Jung endorsed it. Von Franz herself admits that it is hard to establish 'universally valid criteria' to demarcate subjective from objective experiences of dead people who appear in dreams. To her, both exist: the 'real' dead person and the dead person as 'a symbol for some inner reality' of the dreamer's mind. So she suggests that analysts proceed as far as they can with interpretation of the dream on a subjective basis; if that leads nowhere, the objective approach should be considered, as in the above example.

If, of course, the dead person is alive in a world other than the daily one we recognize, the objective approach to dream interpretation might seem less strange. If, as the Japanese novelist Haruki Murakami writes, 'Death exists not as the opposite but as a part of life.'

4

THE PANTHER'S PARTING GLANCE

IDIOT – To dream of an idiot is a good dream, showing that you are about to derive some great benefit from a stranger. It also denotes great success in trade, and prosperous times. If a maiden dreams that her lover is an idiot, it implies that they will soon be married, and that he will receive a legacy through the death of a distant relation that he has never heard of before, and who has recently returned from abroad to his native town.

(The Victorian Book of Dreams)

Every dream is embedded in the life of the dreamer, the inner event shaped by and informing the outer drama, just as each jewel has a value in itself and is also enhanced by its setting. The more I learned about the dreamers, the more complex the whole picture became and what had at first appeared simple began to merge into the life of which it was a part. As the background – initially largely unknown and hazy – becomes sharper it crowds in on the originally clear event of the dream.

Many dreams are so full of intricate detail that it is hard to know which parts are important. Our task is to draw out the special qualities of the individual dream without losing sight of its context and history. Here we will spend more time on background than we have done so far, to illustrate the vital connection of dreamer and dream.

The dream we will examine in this chapter is a dramatic one, and one that raises questions that are not easy to answer. In 1996 I presented it to the Association for the Study of Dreams, in San Francisco, and it then appeared in various publications on the subject.

David

Over the years, I had spoken to David on the phone and we had corresponded. When at last we met, I was able to fill in more detail about the life from which his dream had emerged. Born and raised in Old Trafford as one of a family of seven, David left school at the age of sixteen and in the same year became a professional singer with a band. They toured Germany, Belgium and all over Britain and for a while were quite successful: they had a record in the charts and appeared on *Top of the Pops*. Then, says David, 'We were ripped off blind like you are by managers and agents and after about four years we were broke. We had a lot of fun but we were absolutely broke. We were playing in terrible places.' Unlike the Beatles, David's band played Hamburg's Star Club on their way down, not up.

David abandoned the singing career. He married, took

exams and made it to university, where he studied English literature and did an MA. 'I said, "The one thing I'm never going to do is teach," and of course that's what I ended up doing. I went through the mill doing that for twenty years.'

David liked some aspects of his teaching: 'especially the A-level work and the intense discussions we used to have and the improvisations you get involved with. It's like playing jazz with a group. You've got a basic theme and you start to improvise with ideas and bounce them off other people and they come in with ideas. I'm always very open about my life and they respond very well to that. And I've had a fairly chequered and interesting career.'

As the years passed, he moved up through the ranks until he became vice-principal of a college. Now he was in management, his life was becoming bureaucratized and the work more demanding: 'I found I was trying to teach A levels to groups of thirty, half of whom didn't really want to be there. It all started very rapidly turning into a sort of factory system.' The pressure increased; the amount he had to do was crazy. Then he became ill:

My stress symptoms show themselves in the body. The real reason I gave up teaching was the shaking – it wasn't too bad at first, but then it became worse and eventually in all sorts of situations I'd just shake uncontrollably. It frustrated the hell out of me, as mentally I'd be perfectly confident about what I was doing. I used to get very angry about my body for letting me down and yet I had to turn that round somehow and say: 'Well, trust your body, it's trying to tell you don't do this.'

So David listened and took a year off, during which time he did some writing. But for financial reasons he had to return, and ended up teaching for three and a half days a week. He found he still enjoyed the work. But after about eight months or so his body again rebelled, and he suffered symptoms of anxiety and depression. Realistically, he knew he couldn't just keep taking a few months off. 'Would it be such a bad idea if you never went back?' his doctor said. For David, it was a revelation: 'Absolutely! That's the answer I'm looking for. Just get out of the whole damn thing.'

When David first wrote to me he had been experiencing stress symptoms for some time and, on his GP's recommendation, was going weekly for counselling. One day he told his counsellor he wished to describe a dream he'd had the previous night, because of its unusual vividness:

In the dream I was riding along on horseback with my wife and three children ahead of me, also on horseback. (I have not been on a horse in thirty years.) At first we were going slowly, then I spotted, lurking in the bushes on my right-hand side, two black panthers, crouched and watching us. Seeing the danger I urged my wife and family to gallop away, which they did, on down this dusty road, with me bringing up the rear, keeping between them and the panthers.

The panthers now began to chase me and I felt growing terror as they gained on me. At the climactic moment one leapt up behind me, trying to grapple me off the horse with its forepaws. I felt a sharp pain as the claw of its front paw dug into my back between my shoulder blades and just to the left of my spine.

I shook it off and galloped on, still pursued. Ahead, my family had arrived at the safety of a little town where several men in white coats saw me coming and waved me to turn to the right, while by waving things at the panthers they diverted them to the left. I felt I was saved, but looking back over my shoulder I saw the last panther turn its head and stare at me menacingly. At this point I woke up.

David and his counsellor could make little of all this, beyond seeing it as an expression of his general anxiety.

A month or two later, while he was shaving, David's wife noticed a new and unusual mole on his back, between his shoulder blades and just to the left of his spine. She persuaded David that he should go to his GP. The mole was removed and sent for histology. A week later David was informed that it was a malignant melanoma. With little delay, he was admitted to hospital to have it removed, along with a large area of skin around the melanoma in case any cancer cells had spread from the original tumour. A skin graft from his thigh was used to repair his back. The operation appeared to have been successful: 'Since then I have been in generally good health, though given the highly metastatic nature of melanomas, I sometimes think of the panther's parting glance.'

INTERPRETATION

As is generally known, we cannot manipulate dreams; they are, as it were, the voice of nature within us.

(Marie-Louise von Franz, *On Dreams and Death*)

107

The imagery is dramatic, powerful and precise. As readers, we feel caught up in a tremendous drama. It is typical of the dream world to thrust us suddenly into the animal kingdom and make us fight for our lives.

At first, the panthers are lurking. Perhaps they are slowly enlarging to the point where their growth is becoming an immediate problem for the dreamer – a more elaborate formulation than is conveyed in Geoffrey's dream of sinister crabs. The illness is now upon David and will start attacking his body in a very real way. From their still place, crouching stealthily behind the bushes, the panthers move into open assault. It is such a powerful way of expressing the biological nightmare that is about to overtake the dreamer, of which, at the time of the dream, he had not the slightest idea.

After the opening scene he goes to the doctors, the men in white coats. This represents the surgery that, it later turns out, David required. When we discussed his dream, he said he was extremely aware of the need to protect his family, which is another strong theme to emerge.

Like the disease, the panthers are black, menacing, very rapidly moving, stealthy and powerful. Indeed, 'melanoma' derives from the Greek word, *melas*, meaning black. The first panther – the one that leapt on the horse – is shaken off and disappears down the left path. There is the overwhelming relief of having been saved. It is only in the final moment of the dream that the significance of the second panther becomes clear as it turns and stares at David, although he has no understanding of this during the dream. All he is aware of is the enormous anxiety he feels at this 'parting glance'.

The major problem with malignant melanoma – and one that David had no idea about prior to his illness – is that the cancer can recur many years later, after the patient has apparently been cured of it. It may crop up at the original site, in David's case around the wound on his back, or in another part of his body to which it has spread and where it has remained dormant for reasons that are not known.

The threat of the second panther seems quite clear – 'I'll be back!' Like so many dark figures in books and films, it never really dies. It is possible that the second panther is a warning of what could happen. It may return; only time will tell. The dreamer is aware of this, and must live with the knowledge for the rest of his life. That on its own is enough to cause the abrupt, frightening ending to the dream. Alternatively, the second panther could represent a few cells that have escaped the surgery and are lying dormant, in wait, at some site in David's body and may come back to life in the future.

It is very significant that David had no warning of his physical problem at the time of the dream. He did not experience pain or bleeding, itching or, as far as he can remember, any change in sensation around the tumour. The dream certainly did not make him think of his back at all; I suspect this would have happened if he genuinely had had any change in feeling.

POWER ANIMALS

Each outcry of the hunted Hare
A fibre from the Brain does tear.
A Skylark wounded in the wing,
A Cherubim does cease to sing . . .

Kill not the Moth nor Butterfly,
For the Last Judgment draweth nigh.

(William Blake, 'Auguries of Innocence')

For David, the panther had at least two potential meanings. On the one hand it was a clear representation of the skin cancer. On the other, it was to do with the anxiety he felt in the face of what was for him a significant life change. Under pressure in his job, he no longer enjoyed it and needed to move on. Like so many of us, he was being prevented from doing so by his responsibilities: family, mortgage, bills, and so on. As a former musician, David felt hemmed in, the need for security creating considerable tension with the more adventurous side of his nature. So the panther may have had a third meaning, perhaps relating to his thwarted creativity.

The panther, like many animals, is surrounded by a web of meaning. For example, in Christian iconography it is a positive symbol, acting to protect the individual from the dragon, or the Evil One. In heraldry, it usually signifies fierceness, fury, impetuousness and remorselessness.

There is yet another way of interpreting the panthers, and it may be equally valid. In shamanism, it is believed that spirit beings often take the form of power or 'totem' animals whose function is to protect us:

The Buryat (Siberians) say that in the beginning there were only the gods and the evil spirits. Humankind was created by the gods, but cursed with illness and death by the evil spirits. Therefore, the gods sent the eagle to act as a shaman for suffering humanity. The humans, in their ignorance, did not understand the eagle; nor were they able to accept a mere bird as their saviour, so the eagle was given the power to grant shamanic abilities to the first person he encountered. This proved to be a young woman sleeping beneath a tree. The eagle mated with her and she gave birth to the first shaman – which, symbolically, tells us that shamanism is 'born' from the union of the enlightened consciousness which dwells at the top of our own internal World Tree with the feminine potency that sleeps at its base.

From the moment of our birth, each of us has at least one power animal, and we have an instinctive affinity with this animal throughout our life. If we lose this, we experience a loss of power, and often this means we become ill.

Journeying in the spirit world, the shaman encounters different animals, each with its own nature and way of helping. If he meets the same one three or more times, he knows it has chosen to be his helper. A multitude of power animals exist – from the crow and the rabbit to the buffalo and the deer – and all are part of the energy of the universe. We cannot choose our power animals: they choose us.

The Siberian story above reveals the primacy of the eagle, which is the totem of shamans in general. It perches at the top of the central pole of the Sun Dance Lodge of the Shoshoni, and eagle feathers are used in the healing ceremonies of many tribes. The ancient Celtic world also recognized individual animal allies and clan animals. If the adder, for example – with its qualities of wisdom and reincarnation – was encountered in the spirit world, it might be seen as indicating that one's way of thinking should be abandoned for a new path.

CULTURES IN COLLISION

After my presentation of David's dream in San Francisco I was attacked by three people in the audience. All of them were shamanic dream interpreters – modern shamans – and each just happened to have a panther as their totem animal. In modern shamanism, the power animal may be considered as a representation of our empowered self, rather than as a separate spiritual creature. These dream interpreters insisted that David's animal was important and that he should talk to it to find out why it was attacking him like this. Here we had a meeting of the ancient world with modern science; of old ideas of the natural world and research on cellular behaviour. David would have some sympathy with the shamans' position, but I feel that caution is needed. Pursuing this line of argument – that the panther has an important message but he is not listening – we would reach the inevitable conclusion that in some way David was responsible for his cancer. Perhaps he was. Should you talk to your tumour?

BODY AWARENESS

Man has no Body distinct from his Soul; for that call'd
Body is a portion of Soul discern'd by the five Senses, the
chief inlets of Soul in this age.

(William Blake, *The Marriage of Heaven and Hell*)

When he experienced this dream, David had no inkling of
the cancer in his body. It is helpful that he had talked to
his counsellor about it, so she was in a position to
corroborate the question of timing and provide solid factual
evidence. But if his conscious mind was unaware of the
melanoma, something deeper inside him evidently did have
knowledge of it and was actively trying to remove it.

Physiologically, our main line of defence is the immune
system, which contains an enormous amount of information about disease processes that affect the body. It
knows of the existence and site of the cancer and would
also have knowledge of any other sites to which it might
have spread. It seems to me quite feasible, indeed quite
likely, that such knowledge may well be able to be trans-
ferred to other parts of the nervous system.

Although they are very closely interrelated, each system
also has a certain autonomy. The immune system behaves
like a beehive or an ant colony: each cell responds to its
immediate conditions and affects its immediate neighbours, with the eventual result a coordinated response by
the system as a whole. It is a 'bottom up' system rather
than one with a central leader. When the system as a
whole has learned of an attack (in this case by a cancer),
although in one sense the immune system 'knows' about the
threat, can it pass this knowledge on to other systems such

113

as the nervous system? Once it is stored in the brain, perhaps the subsystem responsible for coordinating immune behaviour is able to pass the information to another subsystem capable of transforming this knowledge into imagery.

Such knowledge does not enter consciousness directly as an idea or thought. The nervous system is a network of slave functions all operating in an independent but coordinated way below conscious awareness. All we perceive is the tip of the iceberg. When people seem to sense a problem, or 'have an intuition', the information may be being passed more directly to waking consciousness rather than via a dream, but still the information cannot be made absolutely clear. Many brain functions operating outside conscious awareness may give rise to a vague feeling or hunch but the information has been integrated and the result deduced below awareness. The end result may be the body's attempt to communicate such information by means of dreams, using imagery rather than language. The parallel with Geoffrey's dream of crabs is clear. Another similarity is the huge emotional reaction within the dream. Given that both images were conveying a life-threatening illness, this should not be a surprise.

A LEAP OF INSIGHT

Strange how things in the offing, once they're sensed,
Convert to things foreknown;
And how what's come upon is manifest

Only in light of what has been gone through.
Seventh heaven may be
The whole truth of a sixth sense come to pass.

At any rate, when light breaks over me
The way it did on the road beyond Coleraine
Where wind got saltier, the sky more hurried

And silver lamé shivered on the Bann
Out in mid-channel between the painted poles,
That day I'll be in step with what escaped me.

(Seamus Heaney, 'Squarings')

David spent a lot of time thinking about his dream, trying to work out not so much what it meant as what the point of it was. In many of my other cases, the pattern was clear: the unconscious mind communicated with the dreamer, who could then decode the warning message in time to act on it. In comparison, David's case was puzzling. He could see that such advance warning was a valuable aid to early diagnosis. However:

In my case, the facts appear paradoxical. Looked at now, each element in the dream is clearly linked to subsequent events, but at the time it would have taken a fairly impossible leap of insight to infer a physical problem, let alone melanoma, particularly in the absence of physical symptoms.

Precise prediction, only visible in retrospect, is not particularly useful. So, if we assume that the unconscious does not put on displays like this simply for entertainment, and if we leave aside mystic speculations about outside spiritual agencies, I think it is legitimate to ask questions about purpose, or to be slightly more scientific, about function.

David approached the issue with an enquiring mind; neither a believer nor a sceptic, he wanted to discover the reason for such dreams. After all, as he later said, 'if you can't interpret them so as to arm yourself against this physical threat, what is the point of having them?' Is it merely that we impose symbolic meaning on our dreams in retrospect because we know what happened later? Eventually David saw his dream as the point when his anxiety about his career jumped from his mind to his body, taking a form he could no longer ignore. He concluded that for him it did play a vital role, but its purpose was existential rather than medical: as a result of the warning, he decided to take early retirement. Eighteen months later he left his career in education, at the age of forty-four.

When I discussed David's case with colleagues I found that medical opinion appeared to be somewhat divided. There are those who regard dreams and illness as a legitimate area of study and see David's dream as containing information which goes beyond the conscious position. On the other hand there are those who view the dream as simply stating the obvious.

I presented this particular dream, along with others, to a group of doctors at a local hospital. One specialist strongly stated his opinion that, due to publicity that summer, David would obviously have been acutely aware of the link between sunshine and malignant melanoma; someone on the beach probably pointed out his mole to him. In the specialist's opinion, David had forgotten about this and the information then surfaced in his dream. There was general consensus that he would have been aware of some symptoms from the melanoma at the time of the dream.

What this explanation seems to overlook is the fact that the dream did not prompt the dreamer to do anything. Medically, as David said, it was not much use. At the time, it simply made him worried. It was not until later that he became aware that significant bodily changes below the level of consciousness had intruded into his dreams, communicating metaphorically in a way that did – after quite some time – result in a major improvement in his life.

David dreamed a lot, often in cinematic detail, yet he had never bothered to write any of the dreams down. He told me of just one other dream that had made an impression on him, and perhaps the doctors might have been slightly less critical, had they known that David had experienced other dreams. This time, his dream was about someone else:

Last August – we'd been to Malta for a holiday – I got back on the Sunday night and I told my wife Joan on the Monday morning, 'I've had a really weird dream.'

It was about a sort of family do. I'm one of five kids and we were all there. We were searching for where this do was actually happening and we couldn't find it. What was strange was that Matt, my oldest brother, wasn't there. And I had my arm round Amanda, Matt's wife, who I've never been particularly close to. I had no idea why, I had my arm round her waist and I was just being nice to her.

At lunchtime on the Monday I phoned my mum to find out how things were as we'd been away for a fortnight. She's the news-keeper of the family, and she said, 'Well, I've got very bad news about Matt. He's got lung cancer, it's been diagnosed as inoperable and he's going to go for radiotherapy. But they're not very optimistic about it.'

So that was August, and in November we actually had a family do. Matt couldn't make it because he'd been ill the night before. Amanda was there and after a few drinks, later on in the evening, I found myself with my arm around her, sort of comforting her.

I'd forgotten all about the dream and we were driving home when Joan said, 'It was just like in that dream, wasn't it?'

Like his dream of the black panthers, this dream stayed with David. Where the first dream had been startlingly powerful, this one struck him as strange because it was so ordinary; there were no surreal elements at all. It came as a shock, following his conversation with his mother, when its meaning was confirmed almost immediately.

As mentioned, David left education and returned to the real love of his life: music. Perhaps surprisingly, at times when he had felt angry with his body for manifesting obvious and embarrassing signs of stress, he found that he had no problem with singing. He was quite happy to get up on a stage in front of an audience of 1,000. Performing in a concert was fine – but not in a classroom. Stress is not always found where you expect it. The sense of control is a key aspect. After leaving his job he started to sing with an eight-piece soul band of 'ageing musos' and felt he had come full circle.

Rediscovering his particular form of self-expression had meant a drastic re-evaluation of his life, but he felt it had been necessary, and worth it. Without the dream, who knows if his life would have changed direction. David cannot tell what the effects on his health might have been had he remained in teaching; he was just happy to slow his life down and enjoy the music.

NEGATIVE CAPABILITY

Several things dovetailed in my mind, and at once it struck me what quality went to form a Man of Achievement, especially in Literature, and which Shakespeare possessed so enormously – I mean *Negative Capability*, that is, when man is capable of being in uncertainties, mysteries, doubts, without any irritable reaching after fact and reason . . .

(John Keats, Letter of December 1817)

Like Jane's dream of alien creatures, David's panther dream is dynamic in the way that it tracks his disease from inception to location and then to treatment, even including a comment on prognosis. It also has similarities with Geoffrey's dream of crabs. But why should David have only one dream, while Geoffrey's was repeated? And why should neither dreamer have any idea of the meaning of their dream?

Research on our inner world continues. It is now known that the frontal lobes exert powerful inhibitory actions on other parts of the brain. This obviously happens automatically, below the level of conscious awareness. However, there are enormous variations between individuals and this has been found to support the idea of 'negative capability'. It was David who introduced me to Keats's idea.

THE TWO TYPES OF THINKING

In an experiment by Colin Martindale two groups were selected: those who scored high on general creativity and those who scored poorly. In the test they were asked to come up with a bedtime story for a child. After a few minutes they were asked to refine and improve the story. The two groups were called Creative and Uncreative while the tasks were the Inspiration phase and the Elaboration phase.

It will be noticed that this test looks at two types of thinking we have already discussed: Inspiration compares to non-linear or metaphorical thinking, with the Elaboration phase being the use of logical and focused linear thought.

First let your mind wander widely, making links between many thoughts as they bubble up from the depths. Your brain is in the Inspiration phase and the frontal lobes are having a rest. An idea may float in as the images come together before drifting apart again. Once the inspiration arrives, you have to start thinking: the frontal lobes wake, switch on the inhibition and turn the new idea into a properly reasoned concept. The first (Inspiration) phase is the equivalent of Hartmann's thin boundaries: areas of the brain that are more loosely structured are allowing greater connectivity with surrounding areas so that the associative mode can encourage metaphor. It shows on the EEG as 'beta waves', a state quite different from concentrated thinking, known as 'alpha waves'.

In the Elaboration phase a different brain mode is needed. Once Einstein intuited Relativity he still had to prove it mathematically using directed, purposeful thinking. The frontal lobes now suppress associative ideas and keep thinking on track. Jung wrote about this exact subject in *Symbols of Transformation* as long ago as 1911.

Although Martindale found that both groups showed increased beta activity in the Elaboration phase when increased frontal inhibition was controlling their thinking, there was a difference in the Inspiration phase. Here the Uncreative group still showed increased beta activity, but in the Creative group there was a dramatic change to alpha:

> Their frontal lobes were exerting much less inhibitory control, so that the process of reverie could take its course, and come up with some novel connections. They weren't 'figuring', they were daydreaming. And they knew, intuitively, when to dream, and when to stop dreaming and when to shape up.

Ending on a positive note, Claxton explains that this pattern of inhibition is for many people easy to break.

Just as no one knows precisely why we dream, there is

no one theory that can explain what dreams mean. Although we are gaining more understanding, the links between body and mind may always remain mysterious. As we explore 'that untravelled world', we need to welcome the discoveries that come to us while accepting that we can never know all the answers. As the poet Kathleen Raine says:

> The materialist ideologies of the West . . . expect us to know things by observation of an external object and they try to measure dreams by putting electrodes on the head of the dreamer. But that does not tell one the dream. That may measure something else, but it is the dream itself that is the sacred experience.

'THAT FINAL STARE'

David rang the week after the manuscript had finally been handed to the publisher: 'I have a final coda to add and I hope it is not too late for the book. I had two epileptic fits a few weeks ago and have just been told I have several secondaries in my brain. They are certain it is from the melanoma.'

We discussed the original dream that had occurred fourteen years ago, and I said I had always felt that it reflected the inevitability of a recurrence. David agreed. 'It was that final stare; it turned and looked me right in the eyes.'

It was a beautiful sunny summer's day. 'I am going back to the garden now to have a glass of champagne and enjoy whatever is left of my life,' he said.

How could the dream have anticipated all this? Only if there were malignant cells, like a terrorist cell, already settled at a distant site, awaiting a signal to move into action. Is the panther simply an anthropomorphized version of these cells, or does it ultimately have some other reality, related but separate?

David died a few weeks later.

5

THE ENERGY WITHIN

. . . angels in some brighter dreams
Call to the soul, when man doth sleep.
(Henry Vaughan, 'Beyond the Veil')

Dreams, like life, are about mystery and uncertainty: we need to listen to the world, both inner and outer, to try to find our path. Listen to the inner voice, literally, to find our vocation. David's dream of panthers, while in some ways a model of clarity, raised the baffling question of why the mind should have sent this message when it made sense only in retrospect. In this chapter we will see that dreams can perform a more obviously useful function. Just as an engine needs steam or petrol, so all of us need the drive of unconscious energies to push us on, even though we may remain unaware of them.

THE TALE OF ASCLEPIUS

Yes, sir, we practise Necromancy in all its branches. We've a choice assortment of wishing-caps, divining-rods, amulets, charms, and counter-charms. We can cast you a nativity at a low figure, and we have a horoscope at three-and-six that we can guarantee. Our Abudah chests, each containing a patent Hag who comes out and prophesies disasters, with a spring complete, are strongly recommended.

(W. S. Gilbert, *The Sorcerer*)

Dreams play a prominent role in both healing and creativity. They are not just ways of exploring our personalities, but the source of invaluable information on health and well-being. By studying dreams we may discover our deepest wishes and gain an understanding of how to heal both mind and body.

Our fascination with the dream world stretches back for centuries and links many traditions. It has inspired myths, poetry and strange tales, many of which have become part of our cultural heritage, enriching our imaginative life. Before we meet Rachel, whose dreams are at the centre of her creativity, we will look at some of the key legends that underlie our present knowledge of dreaming.

Long ago in ancient Greece, dreams were interpreted not only in order to diagnose illness but to suggest treatment. At the centre of this was the cult of the god Asclepius (known to the Romans as Aesculapius), son of Apollo and the mortal woman Coronis. Asclepius had a dramatic start to life. Angered by the discovery of Coronis's infidelity, Apollo sent his sister Artemis to kill her. Then, abruptly regretting his haste, Apollo snatched his unborn son from his mother's corpse as it burned on the funeral pyre.

After this unconventional birth, Asclepius was educated by the centaur Chiron, who taught him healing; he also learned surgery and the use of drugs, love potions and chanting. Athena, goddess of wisdom, is even said to have given him a magic potion made from the Gorgon's blood. But when Asclepius used his skill in medicine to raise the dead, Zeus killed him with a thunderbolt for daring to trespass on the territory of the immortals. Still, Zeus did honour Asclepius by making him a god and transforming him into the constellation Ophiuchus.

THE SNAKES OF EPIDAURUS

Be silent.
Be still.
Wait before your God.
Say nothing.
Ask nothing.
Be still.
Let your God look upon you.

(Edwina Gateley, 'Let Your God Love You')

Throughout the Greek world Asclepius, the foremost god of healing, was worshipped from around 300 BC to perhaps as late as the sixth century AD. People travelled for long distances in search of cures, especially to the main

Temple of Asclepius at Epidaurus. Here they made sacrifices and offered gifts through the priests who were keepers of the god's sacred secrets.

At night, patients slept in dormitory cells close to the temple, to undergo a healing process after a period of struggle and concentration called 'incubation'. Dream incubation, like the dream quest the shaman often undertakes, is an active process involving the journey, drugs, deprivation, the place itself, withdrawal and prayer and not just the fact of a dream. As they slept, hoping for a visit by the god in their dreams, the sacred dogs and (harmless) snakes of Asclepius moved among them. To dream of being licked by one of these creatures was a good omen, or the god himself might appear as a snake in their dreams. Priest-interpreters gave advice and would prescribe treatment.

In Third Dynasty Egypt, over 4,700 years ago, lived Imhotep, or 'He who comes in peace'. Poet, philosopher and astronomer, Imhotep is now known mainly as the architect of the Step Pyramid at Saqqara. Like Asclepius, he was a physician-priest who was later deified, and he was probably assimilated by the Greek god's cult. At the first Temple of Imhotep – believed to be the world's earliest hospital – pilgrims prayed to the god for healing, 2,000 years before Hippocrates. Imhotep's tomb in Egypt was a powerful site for dream incubation. Joseph, whose story is told in Genesis and who is one of the most famous dream interpreters, was imprisoned there, along with Pharaoh's butler and baker.

DREAM INCUBATION

We have moved away from the ancient practice of observation: looking at people with our eyes and listening with a compassionate heart to the sound of their voices telling us of their complaints. (The tone of the voice is the surest of diagnostic tools.) We need not only scientific precision, but also spiritual depth to resonate with the being of the person needing help. With this we can diagnose, make prognoses and heal.

(Oonagh Shanley-Toffolo, *The Voice of Silence*)

To us, the word 'incubation' is unlikely to conjure up images of sleeping in snake-infested temples. What it means is the application of heat to something and allowing it to develop in its natural way. By going to sleep thinking on a problem, we are doing just this.

Precisely the same process is found in shamanism. As we saw earlier, the shaman who has learned to be a lucid dreamer must activate the unconscious, in order to 'get its attention'. Altering his state of consciousness requires ritual, often involving danger and fear. For the shaman, these produce the tension that a great performer experiences in front of their most important audience. The dream plays a part in this, and may answer in dramatic form.

GENIUS LOCI

Put off thy shoes from off thy feet, for the place whereon thou standest is holy ground.

(Exodus 3: 5)

In dream incubation, a direct question is asked of the gods, spirits or, in modern terms, the unconscious. Associated with this is the *genius loci*, or spirit of the place. In itself, this was a potent element in the stimulation of dreams, not only in the Greek world but in ancient Israel and in Judaism. The Old Testament tells of how the prophet Samuel heard the Lord's voice calling him after he lay down to sleep before the lamp of God went out 'in the temple of the Lord, where the ark of God was'. Shamanic initiation takes place in dedicated holy sites, and the ancient Greeks saw certain conditions as likely to favour the creation of dreams: 'lonely caverns . . . regions of gaseous escape and ghastly cliffs and gorges' were best.

Holy places, like the chancel in modern churches, were fenced in by rules. According to Anthony Shafton, in *Dream Reader*, 'To enter the precinct to incubate, it was necessary first to be invited by the god in a dream.'

Very often the supplicant would fast, undertake a difficult or dangerous journey, sacrifice an animal and possibly sleep in its skin, pray to the god, and sometimes take drugs. All of these induce a powerful conscious state in readiness for the oncoming nights. Patience was usually essential. The dream might come either to the supplicant or to a priestess, for example, who lived in the temple. Interpretation might be immediate, by the dreamer; sometimes, however, only a priest or other expert could interpret dreams.

The dreams we have discussed so far in this book have been the result of pressure in the unconscious mind – a pressure of which the dreamer was unaware. It should be noted that the dreamers did not incubate them, nor did they set out in search of a solution. This is an important point, as it stresses the independence of the dream from the dreaming mind. Nancy, David, Geoffrey, Jane. None incubated a dream.

MAGIC RODS AND SERPENTS

Moses and Aaron went in unto Pharaoh, and they did so as the Lord had commanded: and Aaron cast down his rod before Pharaoh, and before his servants, and it became a serpent.

Then Pharaoh also called the wise men and the sorcerers: now the magicians of Egypt, they also did in like manner with their enchantments.

For they cast down every man his rod, and they became serpents: but Aaron's rod swallowed up their rods.

(Exodus 7: 8–12)

The symbol of Asclepius – a physician's staff entwined with a snake, or with twin snakes – is very ancient, and the Egyptian moon deity Thoth carries a similar magic rod. It is thought to represent the renewal of youth, because the serpent casts off its dead skin, so the staff of Asclepius makes an appropriate symbol for the medical profession. A similar staff is the caduceus of Hermes (the Roman Mercury), messenger of the gods, conductor of the dead and patron of merchants and thieves. In the early twentieth century the US Army Medical Department adopted this winged staff as its emblem, helping to spread confusion of the two staffs.

In ancient Egypt too it was assumed that illness could be cured by the interpretation of dreams. Like the Greeks, Egyptian patients slept in temples, where, after cleansing and purging rituals, prayers were offered to Serapis, the god of dreams. The pictogram for 'dream' uses the symbol of an open eye, implying that it is in dreams that we truly see. 'Open your eyes' – the first words we hear in the film *Vanilla Sky* – thus expresses a very old idea. (Incidentally, a copy of Jung's *Memories, Dreams, Reflections* can be seen on the table in one scene of the film.)

Rachel

The whole of dream life is childlike, playful, imaginative – like fairy stories. Almost as if the core of it is like a big child. Ordinary life, when we get up and during the day, is very boring in comparison to dream life. Dream life is so exciting!

Rachel's words at once tell us that dreams are important to her. After reading the letter in which she recounted her dream I visited her at her home in north London. It was a pleasant detached house but as we talked I gathered that she had been used to living in bigger houses and had once been financially well off. I found her an attractive woman, with a sharp mind and great enthusiasm for life. She had always been interested in psychological ideas but was not a fan of either Freud or Jung. Her interests were diverse and based on what intuitively seemed right to her. Rachel was a designer of both dresses and gardens. Lately, life had not been kind to her.

In her letter, Rachel explained that she had suffered gynaecological problems following the difficult birth of her son. For many years she had dreadful pain and discomfort. After numerous forms of treatment, including three operations, there was no improvement. Eventually, Rachel asked her specialist to book her in for a hysterectomy. At the time, her son was ten years old.

The gynaecologist was far from sympathetic. 'Don't be ridiculous,' he said. 'You don't look ill. You're young.' A short while later Rachel had a dream.

> In my house – which was beautiful – was a lovely modern kitchen. But in the middle of the kitchen was a huge old-fashioned boiler with rusty pipes running around the room.

Short and – well, peculiar. Or that is how Rachel described her dream, at any rate. At first she looked at it very literally and then it made no sense at all. She had a completely modern kitchen. The boiler was housed outdoors. 'I'd always had beautiful kitchens. A boiler in the kitchen has got to be the last thing ever! It was an ugly boiler and all the pipes were visible.'

THAT EUREKA! MOMENT

And immediately there fell from his eyes as it had been scales: and he received sight forthwith . . .

(Acts 9: 18)

The next day, as Rachel vacuumed the carpet, she pondered on what the dream could mean. Thinking: 'boiler, pipes . . . boiler, pipes', something clicked in her mind. 'I just knew at that point – "That's it! Boiler needs to come out of the kitchen. Pipes . . . it's my tubes. Whole lot's got to come out." '

Rachel described it to me as a blinding flash of insight, yet it turned out that the dream had been returning to her for the past two years. Different houses, different kitchens, different shapes of boiler and pipes – but always ugly. Some of us with less exacting standards of kitchen design may find Rachel's response an over-reaction. But, as she put it, 'I'm an artist, I'm a dress designer. I can't stand that hideous boiler!' She knew she couldn't get rid of the disreputable thing, however strongly she felt about it.

The latest dream, she explained, was much more vivid. With new determination, she returned to her specialist and demanded that he carry out the hysterectomy. 'I practically had to twist his arm,' Rachel said. Very reluctantly, he agreed. After the operation he confessed to her that the symptoms had given him no indication of the extent of her internal damage: she had been suffering from severe endometriosis. Rachel had desperately needed the operation.

INTERPRETATION

A general anarchy prevails in my kitchen.
(Samuel Johnson, September 1778)

For ten years Rachel had been trying for a baby; she was acutely aware of the workings of the body. To insist on a hysterectomy meant giving up, after all that time. It was a big decision. Her dreaming mind had been prompting her with the same image, over and over again for over two years. Now it had come to a head. Rachel agreed that the dream was the one thing that made her finally decide to have the operation: 'There was no indication from the surgeon's point of view. The dream was absolutely right.'

It is an intriguing illustration of the personal nature of dreams. I would have thought an oven, perhaps an old Aga or Rayburn, a better analogy than a central heating boiler, but Rachel's mind evidently runs along different lines: 'The boiler is like the hub, it's conventionally thought of as the central part of the kitchen.' The point is that it worked for her.

Rachel's dream seemed to display many of the features of others I had encountered. The key meaning took a long time to filter through. There was a moment of enlightenment after two years, no doubt due to the deterioration of her condition, with her symptoms wearing her down to the point where she knew she had to fight against the resistance of her medical advisers. Again it seems that the body, or some part of the mind, knew; yet she had no conscious awareness that she needed the hysterectomy, and it went directly against the recommendation of the specialist.

In contrast to the terror of the nightmare situations in which Geoffrey and David found themselves, Rachel's dream throws up a playful image. This is consistent with the diagnoses: they were suffering from cancer, while Rachel and Jane's conditions, although extremely unpleasant, were not life-threatening. The image was related to Rachel's creativity, the source of her ideas. The boiler clearly referred to her interest in interior design and made a big statement in that form, one that repeatedly puzzled her.

Like so many of the dreamers in this book, Rachel was struck by the obscurity of the message. If the brain can produce pictures of a whole catalogue of boilers, why not show an exact image of her internal plumbing system? Perhaps in the same way, many of us who have laboured over newspaper crosswords will find that sometimes the answer comes after much thought, sometimes never. When we do find the solution, however, it usually seems obvious. But unlike crossword puzzles, these dreams are involved in the serious struggle for survival. As David said, the dream seems to fail on that level: it does not make its point straight away. We simply do not know all the answers.

The important issue for Rachel is that, once she recognizes that the boiler represents her womb, she makes the vital link. Her dream gives her the assurance that she knows the way forward. It energizes her to fight the uncertainty and take control of her life, something often seen when an unconscious idea becomes conscious. This is not to say that people driven by an unconscious idea are *always* right; frequently they are mistaken. The point is the extreme conviction created by the energy coming from within ourselves. We can easily see how similar this is to being in love – it is exhilarating, but the outcome can be disastrous or ideal. Usually it falls somewhere in between.

SHADOW OF A GUNMAN

In Dublin, at lunchtime on 26 June 1996, the *Sunday Independent*'s crime reporter, Veronica Guerin, was murdered – shot by a motorcycle pillion passenger as she was waiting in her car at traffic lights.

Guerin had lived a dangerous life. As if on a personal crusade, she tenaciously pursued drug barons, bypassing the Gardai (police) and making direct approaches to the criminals themselves, among them some of the most notorious men in Ireland. Despite her high profile, she refused to give in to intimidation: 'I would, and do, take risks,' she said. 'I would meet anyone, go anywhere for a story.'

Her colleagues at the paper admired her, but were worried by the reckless life she led and the warnings she ignored. Immediately after her murder, John Waters, who also worked for the *Independent*, felt ambivalent about writing about her in his column. He had known her well, felt shocked and saddened by her death, but, he said, 'I couldn't think of anything . . . other than clichés. I couldn't think of a single word to write about her at that point, so I decided to just leave it.'

The following dream changed his mind:

. . . a strange thing happened to me. I went to bed on Saturday night, probably about ten days after she was killed, and at about five o'clock in the morning I woke up with a start . . . in a nightmare. And in the nightmare, a man had a gun pointed at my forehead and I was experiencing this sudden access to something which you can't imagine in real life. Now I understood exactly the fear she must have felt at the moment she was killed and it was absolutely terrifying.

I've never known terror and I was shaking. I got up and I wrote this article about her and about how great she must have been.

There was no mistaking the message in this dream. Waters, like Rachel, was inspired by an overpowering conviction, that he *had* to write about Guerin. The importance of the journalist herself and the work she did transcended whatever doubts he had.

NO REGRETS

Returning to Rachel, we can see how, having understood her dream, she acted decisively; but of course this meant abandoning her hope for a second child, something she had been unwilling to do for a long time. Now, she found, her need actually faded. She had expected to feel a sense of loss. The reality surprised her:

Wanting another child is 80 per cent biological and only 20 per cent what you really want. And after I could no longer have one, I really didn't want one at all. After the hormones or whatever goes along with it were taken away, I no longer had the desire. I had no regret and I haven't felt regret from that day to this. Now I have the most wonderful granddaughter who has made up for it.

THE BEAUTY OF SPEED

We affirm that the world's magnificence has been enriched by a new beauty: the beauty of speed. A racing car whose hood is adorned with great pipes, like serpents of explosive breath – a roaring car . . .

We want to hymn the man at the wheel, who hurls the lance of his spirit across the Earth, along the circle of its orbit.

(Filippo Marinetti, 'Founding Manifesto of Futurism')

Rachel told me about many of her dreams, describing some of them as 'real epic, fantastic adventures'. She welcomed them rather than feeling apprehensive. Occasionally a pattern would emerge:

I now know my body appears in dreams as a car. Whenever I have a car dream it's my body telling me about *me*. I might have a dream of climbing up a steep hill and my brakes fail and I'm going down. If I have that sort of dream, I know that however hard I've been pushing myself – whatever deadlines I've got – I've got to listen. And I do. I always have those dreams when I'm pushing myself. I'm used to deadlines all the time, but then I'll have a car dream. Why me? I'm not remotely interested in cars.

The car symbol seemed a good one to me, and many other people experience just this imagery. Cars could represent the energy that Rachel flows with in her work; if she over-does it she is in danger of burnout – crashing or running out of petrol. Given the unremitting pressure of her work, it was a practical image for Rachel.

DO AS YOU WOULD BE DONE BY

And now some one here may say, 'Sir, I can not love my neighbour, you may love yours perhaps, because they may be better than mine, but mine are such an odd set of neighbours, and I try to love them, and for all I do they do but return insult.' So much the more room for heroism. Wouldst thou be some feather-bed warrior, instead of bearing the rough fight of love?

It would be a good thing if some ladies loved their neighbours as much as they loved their lap-dogs.

(A Sermon Delivered on Sabbath Morning, August 9th, 1857, by the Revd C. H. Spurgeon)

Despite the artistic fields in which she worked, Rachel definitely had a practical streak. The next dream she told me about brought in money; sadly, she hadn't yet managed to dream the winning lottery numbers. At the time of this dream, Rachel's grandfather had been dead for fifteen years.

In this dream there was my grandfather. He was lovely, he was gorgeous — a very chatty, friendly man with a good sense of humour. He was just standing there. Next to him was a repulsive creature. I don't know what it was — a troll, or a slug, I don't know. It was something really horrible. Like a ghastly elemental creature.

I'm looking at this thing and then I look at my grandfather and pull a face. My grandfather smiles at me and says, 'Don't you be horrible — you be nice to this creature because it's very good to your grandmother.'

Rachel woke up and thought, 'I don't know any slugs or toads, let alone ones that are good to my grandmother.' Then she completely forgot about it until the next time she went round to the house and found that her grandmother's friend was visiting her. Rachel had never liked the woman:

> She was revolting. I don't mean she was a revolting person, but she looked ghastly. She was fat and horrible and she ate like a pig. She would shovel in food . . . She was a very generous woman, actually, quite a wealthy woman and she was always taking my grandmother here and there but I barely gave her the time of day – I would always beat a hasty retreat.

Now she realized: 'That's her, that's the toad-cum-slug thing!' The ghastly woman was in fact trying to persuade Rachel's grandmother to let her take her on a cruise. Rachel didn't know this but, impressed by the stern instructions her grandfather had given her in the dream, she made a big effort to be pleasant to the slug-woman. From then on, if she ever failed to behave well towards her, she could hear her normally easygoing grandfather warning: 'Don't you dare.'

After about a month, Rachel received a cheque for £500 in the post, with no letter or note. It turned out to be from her grandmother's friend. Rachel had seen the dream as having just one, unmistakable message: behave! This windfall was a bonus.

We went on to talk about Rachel's grandfather as he appeared in her dream. She was absolutely definite on one point: 'It was undoubtedly him, it was not *me*. It was nothing to do with me. He was cross and it was him' – her words echo the certainty Jane felt about the alien nature of her lurking figures.

THE LOST BROTHER

On Christmas Day 1911 I had the following dream. It began with flying and floating ... I saw immense and beautiful prospects – first a town, then country landscapes, fantastic and brightly colored. Then I saw my brother sitting – the same who died in 1906 – and I went up to him saying, 'Now we are dreaming, both of us.' He answered: 'No, I am not!' And then I remembered that he was dead. We had a long conversation about the conditions of existence after death, and I inquired especially after the awareness, the clear, bright insight. But that he could not answer; he seemed to lack it.

(Frederik van Eeden, 'A Study of Dreams')

Rachel wasn't surprised to meet her grandfather in her dreams; what she found hard to understand was the absence of her lost five-year-old brother, who had been killed on the road when Rachel was fifteen. For the family, it was an appalling tragedy. As Rachel explained: 'My mother had had twins. He was the survivor, because the other twin was strangled during the birth. So she lost two children. I am Jewish, and there is a Jewish saying that one twin calls the other. They were identical twins. The year before, he nearly drowned – he'd been having close calls a few times. Nobody knows to this day why he ran into the road.'

I pointed out to Rachel a pattern that she hadn't detected: the ten-year gap between her birth and that of her brothers, and the ten years that separated her own son's birth and her final decision to stop trying for another child. Rachel had just one dream about her brother, very soon after his death, then no more; she felt that her subconscious wouldn't allow her to dream about him – that it was protecting her from something potentially too painful. The death, she said, 'permeates every part of my life; it makes you terribly aware of your mortality'. Despite this, she now has a balanced view: 'Everyone has something in their lives that they have to deal with. But something like that . . . it leaves you open to believing that anything can happen. But also, thank God, it left me open to believing that good things can happen as well.'

I find patterns very interesting. Talking to patients I often begin to see a pattern forming around them. For example, Rachel told me that her father was a professional musician and that her son became a composer; at one time he was the top-selling New Age musician in the UK and the market for his music ranged from Tibetan monasteries to people with cancer. Rachel herself clearly followed her mother's path in life. The pattern makes the person and the person is also part of the pattern. Had Rachel's brother not died, her life would have been very different. I have found that the shock caused by an early tragedy may actually make people tune in more to the spiritual and imaginative side of life.

DREAM DESIGNS

Presently Ethel came back in her best hat and a lovly velvit coat of royal blue. Do I look nice in my get up she asked.

Mr Salteena survayed her. You look rarther rash my dear your colors don't quite match your face but never mind I am just going up to say goodbye to Rosalind the housemaid.

(Daisy Ashford, *The Young Visiters*)

Dreams were closely interwoven with Rachel's working life. As a designer, she welcomed the ideas they brought to her, which enhanced her daytime creativity. She described it as seeing 'the magic in all things'.

Arty people have their heads in the clouds, and if they're like me they have to work very hard, so their feet are on the ground. If you *haven't* got your head in the clouds then all you've got is what comes out of the ground. You've got to be prepared to accept a lot of things, be very open.

At school, Rachel's English teacher told her she should go to university and write, as her essays were so good. Then her brother was killed, and she couldn't function at all. So her mother intervened; deciding she'd have to make up her mind what would be best for Rachel, she removed her from school and sent her to the London College of Fashion.

Rachel went to work in her mother's clothes business at an inspirational time in the fashion industry. The shop in South Molton Street was right at the centre of the swinging Sixties:

It was fabulous, fabulous. My mother says she started South Molton Street. Well, she did in a way. She was a brilliant designer. It was that really exciting time, when Mary Quant started – exactly the same time. I was designing for this one shop. A lot of the stars came in there, all sorts of aristocracy.

As the new girl, Rachel was learning very fast. Experimenting with strange combinations of colour, she would make a dress and put it in the shop window. Soon she sold dozens of her weird new creations. She loved the work, but was under pressure to produce a complete collection – and soon. Added to this, the staff thought she'd got her job because she was the boss's daughter. Again, Rachel's creativity dried up and she found herself staring at the walls, getting nowhere.

Then, one night when I really needed it, I had this dream. In it there must have been seven dresses, multicoloured, down to the last detail. The minute I got up, I wrote them all down.

Now, in any dreams where you think you've discovered something, you think: 'That's brilliant!' Then you get up in the morning and it doesn't work and you think: 'How could I have been so excited about it? It's ridiculous.'

We lived in Marble Arch at the time, and I used to walk to South Molton Street, and in that time I went over these dresses, thinking, 'That would work, that's going to work' – but still thinking it would dissipate. It didn't. The whole lot worked and they were all winners.

Overnight, the dream solved both of Rachel's problems: she had an instant collection and the respect of the rest of the staff (although she didn't tell them the origin of her brilliant ideas). Her work now ranges from wedding dresses, embroidery design and beading to garden design.

THE CREATIVE ELVES

O body swayed to music, O brightening glance,
How can we know the dancer from the dance?
(W. B. Yeats, 'Among School Children')

That wonderful creative dream of the seven dresses came at a difficult time in Rachel's career. It seems to show that the unconscious enjoys the challenge of struggling with a problem and looking for a creative solution.

This is, perhaps, the real meaning of the story of 'The Elves and the Shoemaker'. In this fairy tale the old cobbler is down to his last piece of leather. The situation is serious and he can see no solution. Out of the crisis, an unexpected source comes to his aid: the elves or, as Robert Louis Stevenson called them, the brownies. The elves of the unconscious are aroused by the urgency of his problem. Although the man is himself a cobbler, something is not working and he is sliding into poverty. A creative solution is presented to him as he wakes and he never looks back. Is the driving force behind Rachel's life her creative unconscious, or is her own imagination the reason her unconscious has become involved with her conscious struggles?

AXIS MUNDI AND THE AEOLIAN HARP

> ... the initiation dreams, the general schema of the
> shamanic flight, and the figures and adventures they
> encounter, are not a shaman monopoly: they are, in fact,
> the basic experience of the poetic temperament we call
> 'romantic'.
>
> (Ted Hughes, *Winter Pollen*)

Rachel had thought a lot about creativity; after all, it was
essential to her business. 'I don't believe artistic inspiration comes from yourself at all,' she said. 'I think there is
a whole pool. Everything comes out of it. It's almost the
allowing of yourself to be an empty vessel.'

Poets of the Romantic era used the Aeolian harp to
express the same idea. Named after Aeolus, Greek god of
the winds, this instrument was first constructed as a
stringed wooden box by Jesuit Athanasius Kircher and
later adapted by the Scottish violin player, James Oswald.
To expose it to the winds, the Aeolian harp was placed in
a window, or even perched in the branches of a tree, so
that nature itself could play on it without human intervention. Aeolian music, since it was played by the gods or
other eternal forces, was free of human impurity. Edgar
Allan Poe found it a source of celestial beauty and for
Ralph Waldo Emerson and the American transcendent-
alist philosophers it directly expressed nature's true spirit.

Just as Romantic poets breathe in – or 'in-spire' – the
divine music, and then transmit it to lower mortals,
primitive cosmologies held that the 'Great Wind' blows in
through the crack between earth and sky. As Mircea
Eliade explains, the *axis mundi* (Axis of the World)

passes through an 'opening', a 'hole'; it is through this hole that the gods descend to earth and the dead to the subterranean regions; it is through the same hole that the soul of the shaman in ecstasy can fly up or down in the course of his celestial or infernal journeys.

THE GODDESS NAMAJIRI

All things began in order, so shall they end, and so shall they begin again; according to the ordainer of order and mystical mathematics of the city of heaven.

(Sir Thomas Browne, *The Garden of Cyrus*)

Rachel, with her dream of dresses, shows how the spontaneous bubbling up of creative ideas works along with the conscious striving of the dreamer. Before we move on from this, let us make a brief detour to India where, in 1887, Srinivasa Ramanujan was born in his grandmother's house in a small village south-west of Madras. His father worked as a clerk in a cloth merchant's shop, and the family was not well off. After surviving smallpox, the young Ramanujan attended Kumbakonam Town High School, where he did well in all subjects. At the age of thirteen he began to work on his own in the bewildering world of pure mathematics.

Ramanujan never went to university, so lacked a solid grounding in mathematical theory. Like Einstein, he appears to have had extraordinary powers of concentration, endlessly writing, rubbing out and rewriting as he developed his theories. With little to write on, he used the same slate to work on, over and over. Ideas on pure mathematics flowed from him. When Ramanujan finally came to the attention of the Cambridge mathematician G. H. Hardy, serious doubts were entertained about his ability because his formal mathematical education was so poor. Attempts to train Ramanujan in the rigorous discipline of mathematics at Cambridge University proved difficult, often resulting only in the outpouring of yet more ideas.

One of India's greatest mathematical geniuses, Ramanujan made substantial contributions to the analytical theory of numbers and worked on elliptic functions, continued fractions, and infinite series. How he achieved this baffled many academics, but was no mystery to Ramanujan himself. According to him, the complex equations were whispered to him in his dreams by the goddess Namajiri, his local deity. 'An equation for me has no meaning unless it expresses a thought of God,' he said.

To Ramanujan's maternal grandmother this did not come as a complete surprise:

> Before Ramanujan's birth, Namajiri revealed to her that the goddess would one day speak through her daughter's son. Ramanujan grew up hearing this story. And he, too, would utter Namajiri's name all his life, invoking her blessings, seeking her counsel. It was goddess Namajiri, he would tell friends, to whom he owed his mathematical gifts. Namajiri would write the equations on his tongue . . . In a dream he saw a hand write across a screen . . . tracing out elliptical integrals.

IN TWO MINDS

> But man, the two-fold creature, apprehends
> The two-fold manner, in and outwardly,
> And nothing in the world comes single to him . . .
> (Elizabeth Barrett Browning, *Aurora Leigh*)

The conscious mind can never separate itself from the unconscious: it depends on unconscious energy just as a car depends on petrol. Yet the unconscious cannot exist without consciousness. The two exist in a dynamic equilibrium, with communication constantly flowing between them. Right at the centre of this conversation is the symbol, or idea.

Around this, the archaic mind weaves images. Just as throwing bread into a duck pond causes a frantic thrashing of the water where before it was smooth and still, so an idea can arouse the interest of the unconscious. This activity can be negative or positive, but the role of the hidden part of our mind must not be underestimated:

For it is the function of consciousness not only to recognize and assimilate the external world through the gateway of the senses, but to translate into visible reality the world within us.

6

'THE WHITE FLAME OF LIFE'

Listen. Before I go I will tell you this. I am your soul and all your souls. When I am gone you are dead. Past humanity is not only implicit in each new man born but is contained in him. Humanity is an ever-widening spiral and life is the beam that plays briefly on each succeeding ring. All humanity from its beginning to its end is already present but the beam has not yet played beyond you. Your earthly successors await dumbly and trust to your guidance and mine and all my people inside me to preserve them and lead the light further. You are not now the top of your people's line any more than your mother was when she had you inside her.

(Flann O'Brien, *The Third Policeman*)

Wherever a dream comes from, it seems to have its own laws. When we most expect or want some other voice to give its opinion, the dream is often silent. Then it suddenly comes to life, breaking through the oblivion that lies beyond its far shore and accompanying us on our return to the land of the everyday. Crossing Lethe with us into the bedroom, it is sometimes a comforting friend; at other times a terrible figure we struggle to escape from.

The great transitions of life – birth, death, loss, new beginnings – are likely to excite the dream world's interest. If the whole organism is under threat it would be surprising if this was not reflected in some way. Earlier we saw that the unknown presence of cancer in the body evoked vivid and disturbing dreams for Nancy, Geoffrey and David, while the less serious illness of Jane resulted in a less menacing dream. The problem is that the force of a dream does not necessarily reflect its importance. Like the powerful emotions, love and hate, so too with dreams: in time they may turn out to have less meaning than at first we thought.

So far the focus has been on prodromal dreams, which warn us of the existence of a condition of which we had been unaware. We now move on to explore precognitive dreams: those that tell of events yet to come. In the Introduction I gave the example of Jenny's mystifying dream of a coach crash; as we saw, its meaning could not become clear to her until the crash actually occurred two days later.

COINCIDENCE OR FOREKNOWLEDGE?

In 1865 Abraham Lincoln experienced a strange prophetic dream. He gave the following account of it to his wife Mary, and to Ward Hill Lamon, a lawyer who was an old friend and colleague:

About ten days ago, I retired late. I soon began to dream. There seemed to be a death-like stillness about me. Then I heard subdued sobs, as if a number of people were weeping. I thought I left my bed and wandered downstairs. There the silence was broken by the same pitiful sobbing, but the mourners were invisible. I went from room to room; no living person was in sight, but the same mournful sounds of distress met me as I passed along.

It was light in all the rooms; every object was familiar to me, but where were all the people who were grieving as if their hearts would break? I was puzzled and alarmed . . . Determined to find the cause of a state of things so mysterious and so shocking, I kept on until I arrived at the East Room, which I entered. Before me was a catafalque, on which rested a corpse wrapped in funeral vestments. Around it were stationed soldiers who were acting as guards; and there was a throng of people, some gazing mournfully upon the corpse, whose face was covered, others weeping pitifully.

'Who is dead in the White House?' I demanded of one of the soldiers.

'The President,' was his answer. 'He was killed by an assassin.'

Then came a loud burst of grief from the crowd, which awoke me from my dream. I slept no more that night . . .

Lincoln goes on to record that he was 'strangely annoyed' by the dream, and could not shake off the impression it made. A few days later, at a performance of *Our American Cousin* at Ford's Theatre, he was killed by John

Wilkes Booth. The President's body lay in state in the East Room of the White House.

It is hard to imagine a more clear-cut precognitive dream. It is both well documented and unequivocal in its message. Lincoln undoubtedly took it seriously, and recalled it in detail. Of course, he was already predisposed to believe in communication from the spirit world, his belief strengthened by the death of his favourite son Willie in 1862. The cause of Willie's death is unknown, but it may have been typhoid or TB, exacerbated by the poor sanitation in Washington. Throughout the boy's illness, Lincoln never left his side, sleeping and eating in a chair by the bed. After Willie died, his father had the body embalmed and interred in the Carroll family tomb where he would be able to visit it. Twice he had the coffin opened so that he could gaze on his beloved son, whose loss was said to be the greatest blow of the President's life. Lincoln's interest in – some would say obsession with – 'invisible power' was well known. In Britain, sheet music for 'The Dark Séance Polka' was illustrated with a picture of the President holding a candle. Can this completely account for the dream of his death?

Just as Lincoln foresaw his own assassination, Jenny witnessed the coach crash shortly before it happened. Neither of them could have known that the event was about to happen. Where did the information come from?

Before we answer this we will need to spend some time with the pioneering Swiss psychiatrist, Carl Jung.

THE THREE GIANTS

No man is an Island, entire of it self; every man is a piece of the Continent, a part of the main; if a clod be washed away by the sea, Europe is the less, as well as if a promontory were, as well as if a manor of thy friends or of thine own were; any man's death diminishes me, because I am involved in Mankind; and therefore never send to know for whom the bell tolls; it tolls for thee.

(John Donne, Meditation XVII)

At the end of the nineteenth century, three giants came together to lay the foundations for a new model of the mind. The unconscious was the object of their study, but they had differing opinions as to what it contained. Sigmund Freud, a neurologist and the founder of psycho-analysis, decided it was full of sexual dark energy. Alfred Adler, an Austrian psychiatrist, focused on power as the motivating force. Here we have the two great destructive energies of modern times, culminating in AIDS and war.

Carl Jung, who worked in collaboration with Freud, generally agreed with both Adler and Freud when it came to the treatment of neuroses in younger people, but his views on the unconscious diverged sharply. His independent research led him to become critical of Freud's emphasis on the psychosexual. When publication of his study *The Psychology of the Unconscious* led to a break with Freud in 1913, Jung went on to develop his very different 'analytical psychology'.

For Jung, the unconscious was a lot more than a patho-logical basement underpinning our waking life. Freud and Adler's theories were 'valuable', he wrote, but he objected that they did not do justice to 'the profundity and richness of the human psyche'. Gradually Jung came to realize that the unconscious mind is a part of our inheritance, just as the physical body is inherited: eyes vary in colour, but their presence is universal.

The individual does not start out as a blank slate. When a child is born it sets out on the journey of life with a considerable legacy. What we inherit is a vast library of possibilities, of potential forms and images laid down since life began. Jung called these potential forms archetypes. We do not inherit English nor do we inherit specific images; by living and developing we bring these things to life, shaping them according to our experience:

> every man, in a sense, represents the whole of humanity and its history. What was possible in the history of mankind at large is also possible on a small scale in every individual.

'AN EVER-WIDENING SPIRAL'

> Time present and time past
> Are both perhaps present in time future
> And time future contained in time past.
> > (T. S. Eliot, 'Burnt Norton')

For Jung, dream analysis operates on different levels. First there is the personal unconscious – the world of sex and power and whatever else troubles us mortals. So when interpreting dreams, part of the task is to discover what associations the dreamer has with each image: often they arise from events of the day or days immediately prior to the dream. These are little, or ordinary, dreams.

Occasionally, dreams emerge from the deeper layers of the psyche and have greater power. Although they may contain an image that makes no real sense to the dreamer, quite often they circle round and round it. David's panther is just such an image. Of course he knew what it was, but he had no specific personal associations with it; despite being highly intelligent and sophisticated, he was completely at sea in his own dream. This is precisely the point: the panther was *not* personal; it did not come from his experience. It was not a zoo animal or something seen in a film or even encountered on safari. Rather it emerged from within his psyche, from the collective unconscious, that historical part of the psyche whose 'primordial images' lie outside simple personal experience. Just as a malignant melanoma is a universal problem experienced within the individual, so the panther is not really David's.

As a result, discussion with his counsellor led to a different conclusion – that the panther *was* in fact personal, in that it related to his stress and sense of threat. In this case it would be perceived as an anthropomorphized expression of being under attack. Interpretation rarely sticks to the rule-book. Often our conscious attempts to make sense of such images lead us astray. As we know, for David the true meaning emerged later. Of course it could – and no doubt will – be argued that the panther is an aspect of David's psyche, his unlived instinctual aggression perhaps appearing from outside himself as an external force. Once he had gained an understanding of the dream, David

realized the frustration of the problem of interpretation.
When asked why dreams are so obscure, von Franz
replied:

> That has puzzled me too. I have often asked reproachfully,
> 'Why does this damned unconscious talk such a Chinese
> difficult language? Why doesn't it tell us clearly what is
> the matter?' Now Jung's answer was that it obviously
> can't. It doesn't speak the language of the rational mind.
> Dreams are the voice of our instinctive animal nature or
> ultimately the voice of cosmic matter in us. This is a very
> daring hypothesis but I'll venture to say that the collective
> unconscious and organic atomic matter are probably two
> aspects of the same thing. So the dreams are ultimately the
> voice of cosmic matter.

BIG DREAMS

> When I go to bed, to sleep, I see the characters again in my
> dreams ... Sometimes a character makes a joke, a really
> funny one, that makes me laugh as I type it on my paper
> – and I think, 'Well, I couldn't have thought of that myself
> in a hundred years'! And then I think, 'Well, who *did*
> think of it then?'
>
> (Enid Blyton, letter of 15 February 1953)

As Jung struggled with his ideas and their increasing
divergence from the theories of Freud, as far back as
1909, he had a momentous dream.

Accompanied by Freud and the Hungarian psychiatrist
and psychoanalyst Sandor Ferenczi, Jung was crossing

the Atlantic returning to Bremen from Worcester, Massachusetts, where he had been invited to lecture. In those days the voyage took several weeks, so they must have been able to discuss their theories at leisure. The 'big dream' Jung then experienced formed the blueprint for his theory of the collective unconscious:

I was in a house I did not know, which had two storeys. It was 'my house'. I found myself in the upper storey, where there was a kind of salon furnished with fine old pieces in Rococo style. On the walls hung a number of precious old paintings. I wondered that this should be my house and thought, 'not bad'. But then it occurred to me that I did not know what the lower floor looked like. Descending the stairs, I reached the ground floor. There everything was much older, and I realized that this part of the house must date from about the 15th or 16th century. The furnishings were medieval; the floors were of red brick. Everywhere it was rather dark. I went from one room to another, thinking, 'Now I really must explore the whole house.' I came upon a heavy door, and opened it. Beyond it, I discovered a stone stairway that led down into the cellar. Descending again, I found myself in a beautifully vaulted room, which looked exceedingly ancient ... I knew that the walls dated from Roman times. My interest by now was intense. I looked more closely at the floor. It was of stone slabs and in one of these I discovered a ring. When I pulled it, the stone slab lifted, and again I saw a stairway of narrow stone steps leading down into the depths. These, too, I descended, and entered a low cave cut into a rock. Thick dust lay on the floor, and in the dust were scattered bones and broken pottery, like remains of a primitive culture. I discovered two human skulls, obviously very old and half-disintegrated. Then I awoke.

Jung interpreted this house as an image of his own psyche. His consciousness was represented by the salon, which 'had an inhabited atmosphere, in spite of its antiquated style'. It was not strictly modern, as might be expected from a representation of his conscious self. The much older ground floor was the first level of his unconscious mind: the 'personal unconscious'. This represents those aspects of Jung's unconscious that result from the experiences of his own life; things forgotten and things that were not acceptable. From there he moved down into the depths, to find out what lay beneath the house:

> The deeper I went, the more alien and darker the scene became. In the cave, I discovered remains of a primitive culture, that is, the world of the primitive man within myself – a world which can scarcely be reached or illuminated by consciousness. The primitive psyche of man borders on the life of the animal soul, just as the caves of prehistoric times were usually inhabited by animals before men laid claim to them.

Beneath the civilized house was the dark cellar.

For Jung, the dream became a 'guiding image'. As can be deduced, the concept of the psyche that Jung created from this dream was far from a restricted personal system. As extensive within us as the world is outside us, it held all of humanity's evolutionary history. This is why certain symbols and images that appear in our dreams are mysterious and hard to decipher. The psyche, like the body, Jung assumed had a biological basis that contained traces of its developmental past.

Interestingly, Jung had had a similar dream before this crucial one. It had occurred while he was still at school and had to decide which way to go in his career. In the dream, he was digging a burial mound and found the bones of prehistoric animals. At this moment he knew he must turn to science and learn to understand nature. Recall that every dream must be viewed in relation to the individual dreamer; someone other than Jung might have seen the dream as telling them they should become a sculptor.

'THE HOURS ARE SUNS'

He whose face gives no light, shall never become a star.
(William Blake, *The Marriage of Heaven and Hell*)

The task of therapy – and, more generally, of life – is to tune into the unconscious. But first life has to be lived. You cannot learn golf without swinging a club; you cannot learn pottery without shaping the clay. But once you have had a go, you can start to make adjustments, work on where things are going wrong. If you swing the golf club too far one way, the coach corrects this and tries to move you back to a balanced position. The pottery teacher helps you to spin the wheel at the right speed. In the same way, Jung saw dreams as having a 'compensatory' role to play in our conscious life.

Talking of treatment, Jung noted that 'Since the meaning of most dreams is *not* in accord with the tendencies of the conscious mind but shows peculiar deviations, we must assume that the unconscious, the matrix of dreams, has an independent function.' If the therapist is on the right path, it 'will be confirmed by dreams indicative of progress . . . The course of treatment is thus rather like a running conversation with the unconscious.' The patient should feel 'an uprush of life'. If the wrong path is followed there will be nothing but doubt, resistance and deadlock. As illustration, Jung takes the case of an intelligent woman with whom he worked.

At first the therapy went well, but gradually Jung felt his interpretations were missing the mark. A dullness developed, and he had 'a steadily mounting sense of excruciating futility'. Finally he decided to confront this. The night before he was due to see his patient, he had a dream:

I was walking along a country road through a valley lit by the evening sun. To my right, standing on a steep hill, was a castle, and on the topmost tower, on a kind of balustrade, sat a woman. In order to see her properly I had to bend my neck back so far that I got a crick in my neck. Even in my dream I recognized the woman as my patient.

From this I concluded that if I had to look up so much in the dream, I must have been looking down on my patient in reality.

Jung told the woman about the dream, and his interpretation. At once the therapy changed dramatically: 'the treatment shot ahead beyond all expectation'. In the way that it creates a picture from an abstract expression ('looking down' on someone) this dream reminds us of Chapter 1's elaborate charade or puzzle dreams.

Sally

'I do believe there is a great power behind all this. I don't believe that things just happen.' Sally's words stressed the positive message she took from her dream – an obscure dream that came to her at a difficult time in her life.

It was a week since the birth of her daughter. The baby was premature, and for the first forty-eight hours it was touch and go whether she would make it. The odds for survival were poor – but then things seemed to improve. Sally and her husband were told that if their daughter made it through the first four days, there was hope. So a week later they were feeling optimistic.

Sally was a heavy sleeper; she hardly ever woke during the night: only if 'there is a loud bang or somebody has crashed the car', she told me. Yet one January morning she surfaced from sleep in the early hours with a dream vividly in her mind:

I dreamed I was walking along a street and saw a rather scruffy, bearded man who was wearing a belted raincoat and an old trilby hat. He was giving away bibles to passers-by so I asked politely if I could have one. 'Of course,' he replied, and handed me one.

The cover was stained and when I opened it I found the inside was mildewed so that some words were illegible. I asked if he would exchange it for another one, but he sounded angry. 'How can you criticize the Book of the Lord?' he said.

Meanwhile, many other people passed by and he continued to hand out bibles – some people even asked for three or four and were given them. I felt this was most unfair and pointed out that in asking for a replacement I was not being greedy. 'I would be quite happy just to have one other,' I explained.

'Then you must be patient and wait until I offer you one,' I was told.

At this point Sally awoke. Pondering on the significance of the dream, she looked across at the bedside clock. It was 4.20 a.m.

Just as her husband was leaving for work a few hours later, a policeman knocked at the door. (They had no telephone.) He informed them that their daughter had died at four o'clock that morning. Both of them were shocked, and Sally was especially distraught. Immediately, she realized what her dream had been about.

INTERPRETATION

When Sally awoke, she found the odd dream going over and over in her mind. She said she knew it had to mean *something*, but it certainly had no obvious connection with her baby daughter. There was no reason why she should link the two; after all, Sally's anxieties about the baby had lessened. All appeared to be going well, which made the child's loss even more devastating.

At the time when she had the dream, Sally was feeling optimistic about her daughter. Yet despite this the dream seems aware that her daughter will die and it occurs around the time of the baby's death. The scruffy man clearly has this knowledge but gives the impression that he is unconcerned about it; that is simply what Sally has been given. He also knows that if she is to have another child – or, in terms of the dream, a bible in good condition – she will have to be patient.

As far as one can tell, it is no good appealing to him, or begging him, or paying him. It is as if he hands out the bibles either according to his own preconceived plan or following the instructions of some other, greater authority. Perhaps he just gives them out on a whim. However, given the sternness of his approach, that does not seem to be in tune with the dream.

'You must be patient and wait until I offer you one,' the man told Sally. Happily, he did just that and twenty months later a healthy little daughter was born. Sally told me she could still picture the bearded man; and by listening to her dream she gained a calmness that greatly helped her the second time:

The message in my dream – to be patient – kept my spirits up throughout my pregnancy. When I was expecting my next baby I told myself I would never, ever, ever doubt in my mind again that there was a God if my baby came safe and sound. There's got to be a message in the dream that things will work out.

THE BEARDED MAN

Merlin departed from his master and came to King Arthur, that was in the castle of Bedegraine . . . And Merlin was so disguised that King Arthur knew him not, for he was all befurred in black sheep-skins, and a great pair of boots, and a bow and arrows, in a russet gown, and brought wild geese in his hand, and it was on the morn after Candlemas day; but King Arthur knew him not. Sir, said Merlin unto the king, will ye give me a gift? Wherefore, said King Arthur, should I give thee a gift, churl? Sir, said Merlin, ye were better to give me a gift that is not in your hand than to lose great riches, for here in the same place where the great battle was, is great treasure hid in the earth. Who told thee so, churl? said Arthur. Merlin told me so, said he.

(Sir Thomas Malory, *Le Morte D'Arthur*)

Who is the bearded, scruffy man in Sally's dream? If he represents fate or chance, it is accurate to say that he cannot be influenced by our entreaties. It is not uncommon for figures of wisdom or authority to appear as shabby or downtrodden, or as beggars. However, this man is clearly an authority; he is very firm and unsympathetic. His word is law. There is something of the Old Testament about him.

The beard also suggests the Wise Old Man, a figure Jung described as emanating from the collective unconscious. In the *Star Wars* films, Yoda is just such a figure. In *The Lord of the Rings*, he is Gandalf. In the Arthurian legends, Merlin is the old sage. All these 'wise old men' are benign and reasonably friendly; certainly they can be stern when required, but in general they are positive. Yoda looks odd, but he is not negative.

Perhaps the key lies in the first news the bearded man brings to Sally. Here his role is that of Death: his news is that the baby will die, or indeed has died. He is, then, a prophet of doom: the Grim Reaper, the old god Saturn, the Death of the medieval mystery plays – even Darth Vader, or the character of Death that stalks Terry Pratchett's Discworld.

THE SELF

I have said that the soul is not more than the body,
And I have said that the body is not more than the soul,
And nothing, not God, is greater to one than one's self
  is . . .
In the faces of men and women I see God, and in my own
  face in the glass;
I find letters from God dropt in the street, and every one
  is sign'd by God's name . . .

(Walt Whitman, *Song of Myself*)

The dream image – a combination of Wise Old Man and Grim Reaper – is a part of what Jung termed the Self. This, he believed, was the central core of the collective unconscious, the organizing principle not just of a life but of all life that we know. It is from the Self that the compensatory function of the unconscious emanates and it is the task of the conscious mind to try to establish and understand the right direction for the individual. All of this is very moralistic, and counter to the modern psychological approach based on personal freedom, but it is a direct continuation from Jung's religious roots. As he explained:

> If ... I make use of a God-concept or an equally metaphysical concept of energy, I do so because they are images that have been found in the human psyche from the beginning. I find I must emphasize over and over again that neither the moral order, nor the idea of God, nor any religion has dropped into man's lap from outside straight down from heaven, as it were, but that he contains all this *in nuce* within himself, and for this reason can produce it all out of himself.

For Sally, there is no personal judgement. It is not her fault. The bible is mouldy but it is the one she is given. This is not a punishment for something she has done wrong; it just *is*. The man in the dream is there to show Sally the way and that, if she learns acceptance, all will be well. The path through the darkness leads to light.

HEAVENLY HARMONY

God's in his heaven,
All's right with the world!
(Robert Browning, *Pippa Passes*)

In medieval and Elizabethan times, people knew the Grim Reaper only too well. Although it was taken for granted that Death was not the end of life, they still needed a way of living in middle earth, 'passing through nature to eternity', as Hamlet put it. The 'Great Chain of Being' offered a picture of how the world worked.

Everything on earth and in the heavens – from the 'glorious planet Sol' right down through monarchs and bishops to poor people and even insects – was thought to have its divinely ordained and unchanging place in the great scheme of things. Plagues, portents, mutiny, raging of the sea, and every kind of chaos followed any disruption to the harmony of the natural order. 'Unnatural' acts such as the murder of a king have dramatic effects throughout Shakespeare's tragedies; and birds of night 'hooting and shrieking' at noon may warn of them.

Elizabethans would have had no problem in understanding the reason for tsunamis or a rise in the number of anti-social behaviour orders; they would have attributed them to an imbalance in the true order of things.

This hierarchical view of society remained popular in the eighteenth century. 'One truth is clear, "Whatever IS, is RIGHT,"' Alexander Pope wrote in 1733. The Victorian poet and writer of religious tracts Mrs Cecil Alexander had much the same picture of the world, over a century later:

> The rich man in his castle,
> The poor man at his gate,
> God made them, high or lowly,
> And ordered their estate.

The words may be unfamiliar, yet most of us know the hymn they were once part of. In the twentieth century this verse was quietly dropped from 'All Things Bright and Beautiful' in practically every church hymnbook. Without the commas, the third line tells us that God decided who was to have the castle and who wasn't – but no one can *hear* punctuation.

The Great Chain of Being is one way of visualizing the unity of all creation; with its assumption of a hierarchy, it has now died out, but it was a long-lived concept. In shamanism, the web is similarly seen as connecting the world. In 1983, Moroie, an Ongee spirit medium (or *torale* – 'those who have vision dreams'), explained how he dreamed:

> I am maker of a dream, like a very large spider's web from which nothing escapes. It is a web that is unlike other webs. It spreads across the horizon and thus the *torale* is able to see, smell, move, and say more.

The Ongees of the Andaman Islands regard dreaming as a process where the soul or spirit wanders while the dreamer's body sleeps. 'Each individual's dream is like a spider web, but in the process of collective interpretation small webs get interconnected to form a large spider web.' It is vital not to wake the dreamer before he is ready, for the dream, or the spider web, must be allowed 'to inter-connect with the other Ongees' dreams and spider webs'. Perhaps if we are to make the vital breakthrough to see-ing the oneness of all humanity, we need to break away from our linear chain and realize that we are all part of a universal web.

When Jung climbed down to the cellar and discovered that the life of primitive man still remains within our mind, he formulated a universal concept that reverberates in the work of creative writers. Since the collective un-conscious stretches through both time and space and, by definition, connects all of us, this should not be surprising. As a unifying metaphor for the entire human race it holds out hope for the future to those who once found themselves gazing up from the lowest link of a chain. Or, like Jung's female co-worker, to those who felt themselves less than worthy.

TRADITION AND THE QUARK

We think in eternity, but we move slowly through time.

(Oscar Wilde, *De Profundis*)

The poet and critic T. S. Eliot claimed that all writing of the past formed a 'tradition' that is the literary equivalent of the collective unconscious. Poetry, he wrote, is 'a living whole of all the poetry that has ever been written'. New writers and artists must place themselves 'among the dead' – their vigorous ancestors who are as alive now as they have ever been. Eliot's perspective in the 1920s was European, but his ideas have much wider relevance. The artist, he said, must be aware that the mind of Europe – the mind of his own country – a mind which he learns in time to be much more important than his own private mind – is a mind which changes, and that this change is a development which abandons nothing *en route*.

Every creative artist or writer adds to this tradition and by doing so modifies it. The evolving tradition is a living whole that exists within each poet's mind. If writers do not grasp this, their creations will not be immortal.

When *Finnegans Wake* was published in 1939, James Joyce had spent over sixteen years working on it. His aim, he said, was to convey what goes on in a dream. His modern Everyman, Humphrey Chimpden Earwicker (Here Comes Everybody, etc.), has an eccentric and over-crowded night-life. Joyce unravels this in a flamboyant riot of puns using more than sixty known languages as well as a few of his own. It is here that he invented the word 'quark'; and compressed Matthew, Mark, Luke and John into Mamalujo. In this comprehensive, if impenetrable, master-work, words, like the images in dreams, shift and slide: they have many meanings, or none at all. Time and space, post-Einstein, lose their daytime meaning. Like Picasso and Einstein, Joyce broke all the rules. Past and present are deliberately entangled in a never-ending series of dreams within dreams. As Dr Mary Aldridge writes:

Essentially *Finnegans Wake* is a tale of the subconscious, that nebulous place with taproots plunged into the collective unconsciousness of the human race. Here, time is collapsed and finally annihilated.

It certainly feels as if all of human life is here, going round in a circle – with the end of the book leading us right back to the beginning.

THE WHITE FLAME OF LIFE

The 1930s was a busy decade for J. B. Priestley. He published *English Journey*, a documentary account of his travels around the country; he was also working hard on his complex 'Time' plays. *Dangerous Corner* had been produced in 1932, and now two more were to follow, in 1937. He was about to go to America, and felt exhausted.

And at this time, Priestley wrote, he had a dream that 'said more to me about this life than any book I have ever read'. Here is his inspirational dream: it makes a fitting end to this chapter:

I dreamt I was standing at the top of a very high tower, alone, looking down upon myriads of birds all flying in one direction; every kind of bird was there, all the birds in the world. It was a noble sight, this vast aerial river of birds. But now in some mysterious fashion the gear was changed, and time speeded up, so that I saw generations of birds, watched them break their shells, flutter into life, mate, weaken, falter, and die. Wings grew only to crumble; bodies were sleek, and then, in a flash bled and shrivelled; and death struck everywhere at every second. What was the use of all this blind struggle towards life, this eager trying of wings, this hurried mating, this flight and surge, all this gigantic meaningless biological effort?

As I stared down, seeming to see every creature's

ignoble little history almost at a glance, I felt sick at heart. It would be better if not one of them, if not one of us all, had been born, if the struggle ceased for ever . . . But now the gear was changed again, and time went faster still, and it was rushing by at such a rate, that the birds could not show any movement, but were like an enormous plain sown with feathers. But along this plain, flickering through the bodies themselves, there now passed a sort of white flame, trembling, dancing, then hurrying on; and as soon as I saw it I knew that this white flame was life itself, the very quintessence of being; and then it came to me, in a rocket-burst of ecstasy, that nothing mattered, nothing could ever matter, because nothing else was real but this quivering and hurrying lambency of being. Birds, men, or creatures not yet shaped and coloured, all were of no account except so far as this flame of life travelled through them. It left nothing to mourn over behind it; what I had thought was tragedy was mere emptiness or a shadow show; for now all real feeling was caught and purified and danced on ecstatically with the white flame of life. I had never before felt such deep happiness as I knew at the end of my dream of the tower and the birds.

7

A MATTER OF LIFE
AND DEATH

For this dream of being awake suddenly was more urgent
than the condition of actually being awake. He felt like an
explorer who had at last walked into the true unknown
and found that the treasure of discovery was the realization that true awareness needs not only the fact, but also
the dream of the fact: these are the two vital ends to the
journey between.

(Laurens van der Post, *The Face beside the Fire*)

At high noon on 8 May 2004 a huge Medicine Wheel
ceremony took place. Many thousands of people gathered
at over twenty sacred sites in the western United States
and at similar locations throughout the world, from
Guatemala and Ecuador to Australia and the Middle East.
It was the realization of the vision of one man; a vision he
felt compelled to transform into reality.

In 1999, Bennie LeBeau of the Eastern Shoshone tribe

had started to experience a torrent of dreams. Their power and urgency impressed him: again and again, they told him he had to do something. He did not keep a record of the dreams, for to him the details didn't matter. The planet was calling out to him: he knew that action was needed.

Bennie LeBeau, living in the high mountains, had become disturbed by many changes in the land and the animals at Yellowstone National Park. Recently the signs had become more ominous. LeBeau had no doubt that the earth's energies were out of balance, and that the way to solve the problem was spiritual. At once he made plans and started to spread the word. The centre of the ceremony was to be in Wyoming: the Grand Tet peaks, or 'The Four Grandmothers Standing Tall'. Its perimeter would extend for about 600 miles in radius, encompassing the spine of the Rockies. The Medicine Wheel ceremony would take place right in the centre.

In the ancient Medicine Wheel rite, stones are used to mark the four main directions of the compass and other key points. With knowledge and respect, a sacred space is thus marked out; within it, people direct prayers, thoughts, feelings and actions towards a single idea.

'May 8th was a success, the energies connected and the pressures on Yellowstone were alleviated,' LeBeau later claimed. The purpose, he said, was to create stability – for the participants as well as the earth. By joining in such a massive event, people ground themselves and gain a clear sense of where they are, both spiritually and in relation to the earth itself.

IN THE CLEAR BLUE HEAVEN

The afternoon had been stormy but it cleared towards sunset. Gradually the heavy rain clouds rolled across the valley to the foot of the opposite mountains and began climbing up their sides wreathing in rolling masses of vapour ... I saw one very white brilliant cloud where the mountains ought to have been. This cloud grew more white and dazzling every moment, till a clearer burst of sunlight scattered the mists and revealed the truth. This brilliant white cloud that I had been looking and wondering at was the mountain in snow.

(Reverend Francis Kilvert, *Diary*)

Laurens van der Post, writer, conservationist and adventurer, understood the need to become attuned to the spirit of the land. In his writings, factual accounts of his travels merge with poetic and imaginary tales and speculation. Van der Post knew nothing about camels, yet in the Abyssinian campaign of 1940–41 he led a caravan of camels into the mountains, where he met Haile Selassie; in the 1950s he was sent by the Colonial Development Corporation to assess uninhabited plateaux in Nyasaland. In books such as *Venture to the Interior* he recorded his explorations and imaginings.

For van der Post, the mountains, like Africa itself, were both mystical and ominous – the visionary unconscious that conflicted with his conscious, European heritage. Inspired by the theories of Jung, he wrote: 'If we could but make friends with our inner selves, come to terms with our own darkness, then there would be no trouble from without. But before we can close our split natures we must forgive ourselves. We must, we must forgive our European selves for what we have done to the African within us.'

We have followed this path into the hills because that is where our next dreamer's story begins.

Mollie

Mollie was on holiday with her husband Paul, a Methodist minister. They were travelling in North America. After spending a day with a couple who lived in Montana they moved on to Yellowstone Park and started their tour. At first, Mollie said, they were having a wonderful time: 'You go through the tranquillity of the Teton mountains, Jenny Lake and the Chapel of the Transfiguration. It was beautiful and peaceful – crickets and birds and snow-capped mountains.'

They left the empty mountains, and abruptly the atmosphere changed:

We came to Jackson Hole in Wyoming, which is this cowboy town. It's hustle and bustle, wooden decks, noise, and everybody in almost a club atmosphere. Like one of the old westerns. A Doris Day kind of place. Denim and leather.

Mollie didn't like the motel they found; the doors leading on to the road made her feel uneasy. After checking in, Paul decided to go for a swim in the pool. Mollie was tired; it was about 9 p.m. and she wanted an early night. So she wrote a few postcards, had a bath, and went to bed.

I must have fallen asleep very quickly . . . I started to dream about taking our hire car to Jackson airport – not to Denver, Colorado, as planned. Somehow I was also over at the British embassy in Washington, DC, making arrangements for my husband's body to be flown home to England. He had died in Jackson.

Mollie woke in alarm. She turned over in bed, to touch her husband, but he wasn't there. Hastily, she pulled on a T-shirt and trousers and dashed round to the reception desk. She asked the receptionist to check the TV monitor to see if Paul was still swimming. No one was in the pool, the woman told her; anyhow, the area was locked at ten o'clock, and that was half an hour ago.

Trying not to panic, Mollie said that her husband was missing. The receptionist clearly thought her a crazy Englishwoman, to be worrying about him at such an early hour. The obvious place to find Paul, she said, was in the wine bar.

Brushing aside this attempt at reassurance, Mollie insisted that he would *not* be in the bar. At last the receptionist responded to Mollie's distress and reluctantly took her over to the pool complex. She unlocked the door and Mollie entered the men's locker room. On a bench she found Paul's unused swimming trunks and towel.

Repeatedly, Mollie called his name, searching the toilets and shower room until she found Paul. He was naked, unconscious, and bleeding from head injuries. Mollie shouted to the receptionist that it was an emergency, and told her to dial 911. Paul was taken by ambulance to hospital where, after tests, he was placed in intensive care. The medics said his injuries indicated that he had been mugged. Paul has no idea. He never recalled what happened to him that evening in Jackson Hole.

FOLLOW THE DREAM

I saw Eternity the other night,
Like a great ring of pure and endless light,
All calm, as it was bright.

(Henry Vaughan, 'The World')

I talked to Mollie about the evening when she had had her dream. Before that, of course, she had felt a strong aversion to the town; and events were to prove her intuition right. Distressed by the dream, she then had to overcome considerable resistance on the part of the receptionist, who treated Mollie as just some neurotic woman. 'But I follow my instincts,' Mollie told me.

After finding her husband, things got worse. As she knelt beside him in the locker room she was startled to find a gun next to her: it was in a policeman's holster. Unsympathetically, he asked: 'Has he been drinking? Has he got AIDS?'

It was touch and go whether Paul would survive until he reached the hospital. In the emergency room, a doctor told Mollie that Paul would have died had she not found him.

I am so thankful that I responded to my dream. It would have been very easy that evening to turn over and continue sleeping, for I was very tired. I don't have a lot of strong dreams, but if I do dream I always have to follow the dream. It's always right to respond to the dream.

INTERPRETATION

If a man will begin with certainties, he shall end in doubts; but if he will be content to begin with doubts, he shall end in certainties.

(Francis Bacon, *The Advancement of Learning*)

Paul searched his memory bank for any traces of the incident, and Mollie puzzled over the details of her dream. Washington, she thought, could have arisen from a previous visit: she had been there preparing to fly back to Britain when her father was terminally ill. There was no reason at all why she should have driven to Jackson, Wyoming, but, as we've already discovered, it is rarely possible to find a reason for *every* detail in a dream.

Mollie's mind predicted something that appears not to be predictable. Or perhaps it is predictable? The argument would probably run along the following lines: in her dream state she was aware that Paul was late in returning; knowing him well, she would know this was out of character. Now we probably need to invoke coincidence: all the worried dreamers who pick up some anomaly in their partners' behaviour will – by sheer chance, given the huge numbers involved – get it right once in many thousands of events. Mollie was the one who wrote to me; the thousands whose fears were *not* realized did not write. There would have been many others with similar dreams who woke and found all was fine; it was just a bad dream. However, I do not feel that any rational explanation is really good enough.

In his excellent book on the history of, and current research on, the unconscious, Guy Claxton gives an example of how a complex situation can easily give rise to a belief in the miraculous.

Juan Fangio, perhaps one of the finest of all racing drivers, was approaching a bend in the 1957 Monaco Grand Prix. Obviously, it was a corner he was familiar with, yet suddenly he found himself braking more than usual. Once round the bend he drove into a pile-up that had just occurred; but because he had slowed down he was able to manoeuvre round the debris and he went on to win the race.

He put this unusual series of actions down to divine intervention until, a few months later, on waking he relived the experience and became aware of the actions of the spectators. As Claxton explains:

> The great Fangio would normally (but unconsciously) have expected them all to be looking at him – but instead, as he saw in his waking reverie, they were all facing sideways, their attention drawn by the crash.

His awareness of this provided the true explanation – far more prosaic than the earlier divine one. Fangio's waking dream is an example of a hypnopompic hallucination, of the type that will be discussed in the next chapter. It is interesting that the dream didn't take place until several months after the race.

A SCIENTIFIC DETOUR

'We're looking at Andromeda's history. That's why they say looking out into space is like looking back into the past. The light, the information so to speak, we get in the future, even in ten years, is still Andromeda's ancient history.'

At this Rufus felt uneasy. He liked looking out into space. He didn't much go for looking back in time. He didn't think he was so different from everyone else, in that he looked up, hoping for things to come. The past he thought was safely behind him. He never expected it to be falling down on him from the stars.

(Carol Hill, *Amanda & the Eleven Million Mile High Dancer*)

The world was turned inside out at the start of the twentieth century. The laws of physics were sabotaged by Einstein; Picasso played havoc with the artistic status quo; Stravinsky redefined and reorganized music, just as Freud and Jung were revealing the inner mysteries of the human mind. We are not going to delve too far into quantum physics, but one aspect of it has an intriguing relevance to ideas on precognition.

Quantum theory tells us that when a quantum system such as an atom splits into parts, some of the particles generated may exist as linked or 'entangled' pairs. Each particle within an entangled pair is in an undecided quantum state until such time as the first of them interacts. The instant that one changes, the other one does too: it is not a question of mimicking – the change happens at exactly the same moment, however distant they are from each other: 'when a pair of photons are emitted from the same atom, their polarization is undetermined, although one is obliged to have a polarization opposite to the other. As soon as the polarization of one is measured, the other has the opposite polarization instantaneously.' This atomic behaviour is known as quantum non-locality.

David Deutsch, the quantum physicist, asks:

> What sort of reality is quantum mechanics telling us we live in? And of course it's hard not to wonder: 'well, if *something* gets there instantaneously, it is going faster than light. So in another reference frame it's travelling into the past. So it could create paradoxes; couldn't that solve the problem of consciousness, explain telepathy, summon up ghosts . . . ?'

Einstein, says Rupert Sheldrake, was unhappy about this, since it seems to imply a mysterious invisible influence that cannot be rationally explained. Deutsch aims to avoid the 'appalling mysticism' this line of thought might lead to, explaining that 'some information-carrying physical object' must be involved. At the same time, however, he endorses an idea that has been around since at least 1957 – that we live in a convoluted world:

> . . . The very structure of the [quantum] theory already forces upon us a view of physical reality as a *multiverse*. Whether you call this the multiverse or 'parallel universes' or 'parallel histories', or 'many histories', or 'many minds' . . . what the theory of quantum computation does is force us to revise our explanatory theories of the world, to recognize that it is a much bigger thing than it looks. I'm

trying to say this in a way that is independent of 'interpretation': it's a much bigger thing than it looks.

So will science provide explanations of phenomena such as telepathy and precognition? Only time will tell. Or perhaps it already has.

ATTACHMENT

When an individual (of any age) is feeling secure he is likely to explore away from his attachment figure. When alarmed, anxious, tired, or unwell he feels the urge towards proximity.

(John Bowlby, *A Secure Base*)

Returning to Mollie, she had had a terrible childhood, as I discovered when we talked. And she had told me she could rely on her instinct. This, linked with the story of her deeply troubled background, led me to consider that at the root of her dream was the issue of attachment.

In the 1930s and 1940s on both sides of the Atlantic observations were being made on children raised in institutions, and the problems they experienced. It was the beginning of a new way of looking at psychological problems and their origin; and it was in addition to – but also in opposition to – the views of Freud and his followers, who nevertheless held the centre ground for at least the next half-century.

Where Freud had worked with adults and looked back to imagined early difficulties, in London John Bowlby and his colleagues took actual known trauma and worked forwards, trying to establish how it had impacted on the development of the child. Unlike Freud's world of the individual's inner fantasy, Bowlby's theory was rooted in biology and outer reality.

After he trained first as a psychiatrist and then as a psychoanalyst, Bowlby's early work was on maternal deprivation and its consequences. He realized that the relationship between mother and child depended on many things, including the mother's own experiences of being cared for, and her support network. In other words, it was not all in the little person's head. This way of seeing child development moved towards freeing people from blame: it understood that the child would react in some ways that could strengthen the bond and in other ways could disrupt it. So if the mother herself is deprived, then she may find it hard to be a 'good enough mother', but just because a child has emotional problems it does not always mean it is the mother's fault. There may be a mismatch in the way they react to each other due to their innate natures.

SEPARATION RADAR

In the old days at home the Neverland had always begun to look a little dark and threatening by bedtime. Then unexplored patches arose in it and spread, black shadows moved about in them, the roar of the beasts of prey was quite different now, and above all, you lost the certainty that you would win . . .

Of course the Neverland had been make-believe in those days, but it was real now, and there were no night-lights, and it was getting darker every moment, and where was Nana?

(J. M. Barrie, *Peter Pan*)

Children who suffered early separation, it was found, had similar reactions to adults in mourning. They went through anger, searching behaviour, disbelief and grief. In 1971, Dr Mary Ainsworth, an American psychologist, identified patterns of attachment behaviour, which depended on the child's early experience. Once established, these patterns tended to remain constant throughout life.

She described three distinct patterns: secure, anxious resistant, and anxious avoidant. The anxious resistant tries to hold on, is clingy, and is also prone to aggression, while the anxious avoidant expects rejection and attempts not to get involved. The secure child will be distressed by separation but return to normal play when the parent returns, possibly after some comfort if needed.

It is easy to see how disrupted early relationships can leave someone 'anxiously attached'. All is well as an adult, until the threat of separation arises. Then the mind becomes hyper-alert and the individual may react in different ways, usually becoming distressed, mistrustful, anxious or angry. For our purposes here, we are concerned with the ability to intuit the separation. In those who have suffered this early wound, intuition is often developed to a high degree – at least with regard to 'separation radar'. In fact this appears to be a basic biological mechanism. Animals show a marked degree of intuition with the people to whom they are closely attached, as is shown in Sheldrake's work, *Dogs That Know When Their Owners Are Coming Home*.

Following her traumatic experiences in America, when I met Mollie, the most important person in her life, after her children, was her husband Paul, who had also been the first man she could really learn to trust. He protected her from the dark past by always being there for her, and in return Mollie gave him much strength and support. Their relationship was very close; coupled with the heightened intuition that resulted from the trauma of Mollie's early years, it may have been this bond that caused her to develop the instincts she knew she could always rely on; the finely sharpened intuition that had been expressed in her life-saving dream.

RADIOACTIVE TRAUMA

At all events the 'making of a medicine man' involves, in many parts of the world, so much agony of body and soul that permanent psychic injuries result. His 'approximation to the saviour' is an obvious consequence of this, in confirmation of the mythological truth that the wounded wounder is the agent of healing, and that the sufferer takes away the suffering.

(Carl Jung, *Four Archetypes*)

The theory that trauma gives rise to enhanced abilities such as intuition underlies the idea of the superhero. Set apart from ordinary people, superheroes possess heightened powers and senses, derived from a variety of sources: some are aliens (Superman), some are gods or their avatars (Thor and Wonder Woman), while others just have strange genes or unexplained magic.

Of greater interest to us are superpowers that compensate for injury. Here, it seems, nuclear science has a lot to answer for. One early radioactive hero – damaged by 'vita-rays' – is Captain America. The early 1960s saw a cosmic explosion of damaged superheroes. In 1961, the Fantastic Four suffered mutagenic changes when a solar flare increased the ionizing radiation of the Earth's Van Allen belt. Peter Parker, alias Spiderman, gained his arachnid superpower after being bitten by a spider that had been irradiated by a particle accelerator. Ironically, Parker was attending a demonstration on the safe handling of nuclear waste at the time.

From the Incredible Hulk (gamma radiation) to the X-Men (superhuman mutants known as 'children of the atom') and the Teenage Mutant Ninja Turtles (radioactive canister), a whole army of superheroes has been created from the byproducts of the nuclear industry. But while the mutagenic cause of superpowers may so often be predictable, the effects are not. Daredevil (radioactive waste), blinded in a freak accident, developed senses said to be heightened beyond even superhuman enhancement. He also gained a 'radar sense'. Spiderman, of course, became sticky. Yet the Fantastic Four, equally ionized, followed random trajectories, gaining qualities that varied from invisibility to superhuman strength.

Superheroes seem content to live with their unusual conditions; they have no choice in the matter. Real humans, on the other hand, may benefit from enhanced senses but that doesn't mean we have to give up trying to search out and heal the traumatic causes that lie beneath.

DREAMS AND THREAT REHEARSAL

... dream-analysis deserves very special attention. Sometimes, indeed, it is a matter of life and death.

(Carl Jung, 'The Practical Use of Dream Analysis')

In 1959, Rita Dwyer was employed by one of the pioneering companies in the aerospace industry. She was working in a research lab, dealing with high-energy propellants when the rocket fuel exploded. Luckily for her, her colleague Ed Butler was in the next-door lab. Hearing a muffled explosion and a scream, he rushed in to help her. The room was full of smoke but he managed to find Rita, drag her out and get her under a shower to put out the flames. Before the accident, Ed had experienced recurrent nightmares in which Rita was hurt in an explosion and he would then save her. Not wanting to frighten her, he did not tell her about the dreams. In fact, Rita wasn't even aware that Ed had saved her life until later, when she was recovering in hospital.

Like Mollie's dream, these nightmares saved a life. Yet Ed and Rita, who had been friends at college, were not romantically linked or unusually close. Their relationship wasn't remotely like that of Mollie and her husband, yet the result of the dreams was similar. So it seems that the existence of close bonds between two people is not essential: warning dreams may still occur. Ed interpreted the repeated dreams as a 'rehearsal' for the event. They enabled him to practise his response to an accident; by running through it again and again he was learning how to react more quickly. He felt he had done this so often that by the time the explosion happened in waking reality he was ready to deal with it. This supports Revonsuo's 'threat simulation theory': the view that dreams can perform a valuable biological function by simulating threatening situations. As illustrated by Ed's dream, they help us to perceive and avoid danger – a skill that would have been vital in our evolutionary past. This raises the possibility that dreams were originally a social phenomenon, part of the group matrix.

'LISTEN WITH A COMPASSIONATE HEART'

If a form should appear, and a voice tell me that a particular man had died at a particular place, and a particular hour, a fact which I had no apprehension of, nor any means of knowing, and this fact, with all its circumstances, should afterwards be unquestionably proved, I should, in that case, be persuaded that I had supernatural intelligence imparted to me.

(Samuel Johnson, as reported by James Boswell)

Oonagh Shanley-Toffolo, born to a poor family in Ireland, has had an unpredictable life as nurse, nun and counsellor. She has brought love and healing to the poorest of the world, as well as nursing the Duke of Windsor just before his death. Later she acted as spiritual guide and healer to Princess Diana. A woman of great independence and courage, she radiates serenity and continues to inspire others. Throughout her life, she has used dreams to guide her. This one came to her while she was working with the poor in Calcutta.

In August I received word that my father was very ill. On the night of the 26th, we prayed that he might be cured. I remember going to bed at 9 p.m. . . . It was very hot as I pulled the mosquito net around me and settled beneath the sheets.

At once I caught sight of a figure, parting the curtain which surrounded the bed and approaching. I thought I was seeing Christ – he was wearing a white robe with a sash. He put both his hands to my face and kissed me – exactly as my father used to do. I was spellbound. I could not speak . . . The apparition put his hands to my face again, kissed me and left . . . I got up, looked at the clock and found it was only 9.10 p.m. All this had happened in ten minutes. My soul was exalted. I did not return to bed but prayed and enjoyed the gift I had received. Next morning, I told my charges that maybe our prayers had been answered, that my father had been cured.

On my return from the local hospital late that morning, my Superior called me to her office. A telegram had come saying that my father had died at 3 p.m. with my name on his lips, thanking God that I was looking after God's poor in India: 3 p.m. in Ireland would have been 9 p.m. in India . . . My soul felt an incredible peace. The vision I had had of him the previous night stayed with me and consoles me even to the present day.

So it seems that whilst dreams may prevent death, they can also show us that this, the ultimate journey, should not necessarily be feared.

8

RITES OF PASSAGE

A death-blow is a life-blow to some
Who, till they died, did not alive become;
Who, had they lived, had died, but when
They died, vitality began.

(Emily Dickinson)

In this chapter we will meet John, whose puzzling dream
gives us food for thought. But before we leave the land of
experiences that may be explicable by rational means, let us
look at two short, simple, but immediate dreams. They
could be easily explained away; equally they may be in keeping with the world of the shaman.

THE HAND THAT ROCKS THE CRADLE

When Irene wrote to me after reading of my research, the
dream that concerned her was not her own, but her
mother's.

My mother, in her fifties and not suffering any obvious signs of illness, was deeply distressed by an urgent, insistent dream in which her own mother – who had been dead at this time for more than fifteen years – appeared in a long brown robe, pointing to her breast. No words were spoken but my mother woke up with a profound feeling of danger.

She was puzzled by the brown robe, as her mother loathed the colour and never wore it. Only later in the day did she remember that her mother had been buried in a Carmelite convent, and although my mother had not seen her prepared for burial she knew her own mother would have been dressed in the Carmelite habit.

She was so disturbed by the dream, she visited a doctor so that he might examine her breast. He said there was absolutely nothing wrong with her. Reluctant to tell him about the dream, she went to another doctor, who said that a small rash which had now appeared on her breast was eczema and that he would prescribe a lotion. My mother was sure that any doctor would simply dismiss or ridicule her story about the dream.

She went to a third doctor, who said she undoubtedly had a growth in her breast and arranged for her immediate admittance to hospital. The surgeon found a large malignant growth, and performed a mastectomy. The following day, as we waited to hear the results of this, the chemist's delivery boy arrived with the eczema lotion.

Although my mother eventually died of cancer, she had another twenty years of life which I am sure she would not have had if she had ignored her dream and accepted the first two doctors' diagnoses.

The striking feature in this dream is the clothing. It seems to be the key – the bait on the end of the dream's hook that catches the eye of the dreamer and draws her towards its purpose. Only on reflection does the meaning arrive; and it takes Irene's mother by surprise. It is by contemplating the dream as if looking at a familiar painting and noticing something curious for the first time that she begins to make sense of the brown robe – just as Fangio became aware of the unusual behaviour of the Grand Prix spectators.

If we are to believe the rationalists who explain the dream as 'simply' using a dramatic form to express the dreamer's already perceived problem – in other words, Irene's mother had already felt a breast lump – then why the need for funeral attire? Perhaps the Carmelite scapular serves to emphasize the figure's other-worldliness. Interestingly, according to the Order's website:

> the Brown Scapular of Our Lady of Mount Carmel . . . came to symbolize the special dedication of Carmelites to Mary, the Mother of God, and to express trust in her motherly protection.

LIFE BEFORE AND AFTER

> A bridge, now nearing, I shall walk alone –
> One pier on earth, the other in the unknown . . .
> (Walter de la Mare, 'The Bridge')

Another correspondent, Ethel, told me of a similar dream that returned often over a period of several weeks or months:

My dreaming, I believe, saved my life. I was having persistent dreams of two hands coming through the bedroom door and trying to put themselves round my throat – but I always managed to jump up when they were a couple of feet away. One night I wasn't quick enough and the hands just managed to touch my throat lightly. I recognized the hands, which were so close, as my deceased mother's.

Ethel could not believe her mother would wish her harm. Puzzled, she examined her throat in the mirror and found a small swelling. It wasn't causing her any pain, but she now noticed that it had a tendency to come and go. Eventually she wondered if she might have a thyroid problem. Like Irene's mother, she had difficulty in convincing her doctor and was reluctant to tell him about the warning hands in her dream. Yet, when she was referred to the hospital it was found that she required a thyroidectomy. 'I was in a bad way for several months,' Ethel wrote. 'The surgeon said I should have been seen much sooner.'

Because Ethel had no obvious symptoms, she might well have gone on for much longer unaware of her pressing need for treatment. Far from wishing her harm, the dead mother's hands seem to have been reaching out in a desperate attempt to help. In the early stages, this recurrent dream makes no sense to Ethel. The sudden realization that the hands belong to her mother comes at the critical point, when they are close to her throat, and only then does Ethel really question the dream and take it as a warning. Ethel must have had a positive relationship with her mother, so her dream may have been to do with her attachment to her mother. As we saw in relation to

Bowlby's theory in Chapter 7, this can have a strong formative influence.

As we might expect, the mothers who intervene in these dreams are protective, leading their daughters towards the healing they need. Mollie's dream alerted her to her husband's danger in the motel swimming pool; the closeness of family bonds may play some role in this type of warning dream.

John

Peace, peace! He is not dead, he doth not sleep –
He hath awakened from the dream of life –

(Percy Bysshe Shelley, *Adonais*)

In Chapter 3 we met Jane, who was bewildered by the odd alien beings that invaded her dreams then flew away. She was sure they weren't creations of her mind; but at least they did relate to her illness. Our next dreamer felt that his dream had nothing at all to do with him.

Earlier in the book we looked at Hartmann's theory that people can have 'thick' or 'thin' boundaries: some of us have better access to memories and images, and richer, more striking dreams than others (see pp. 77–9). John, whose dream we now turn to, is without doubt the individual with the thickest boundaries of all the people we meet in this book.

John was a cheerful, easy man to talk to and I'm sure would not be offended by the above comment. He was not a 'dreamer' in either the literal or the metaphorical sense. As an extrovert, his attention looked outwards to the world rather than moving from the world inwards. He had little interest in the inner realm; much more in his job as a metalwork teacher. A few years earlier, John had had cancer. He had no dreams at all regarding that. Now he wrote to me about a dream that had made a strong impression on him.

It was twenty years ago when I had this dream on a Sunday night.

I was sitting in the back row in a room where a lecture was taking place. The room was in darkness, lit from the front, and all I could see was the silhouettes of people. On my left was an aisle. Someone walked down the aisle to the back of the room and, in passing, placed a baby in my lap.

I became aware that the baby was wet so I picked it up, went out at the back, changed the baby and returned to the lecture room. I was confused on returning because no one accepted the baby. I asked whose it was and was told, 'Nobody's.' It was a boy.

Next morning, John told his wife he had had the most incredible dream. At work, he told other teaching staff at breaktime and talked about it quite often that Monday, for he found the dream quite amusing.

That evening, his brother-in-law rang to tell them that his wife Deborah had given birth to a stillborn baby on Sunday evening. It was a boy. It was then they both understood – in that strange way that some dreams lend us conviction – the real meaning of John's nocturnal experience.

WHY ME?

Angel: And thou art wrapped and swathed around in
dreams
Dreams that are true, yet enigmatical.

(J. H. Newman, *The Dream of Gerontius*)

To me, this was not only a strange and powerful dream; the oddest thing was that it should have been dreamed by John. The more we talked, the more the mystery deepened. John's wife Joan stressed that, although he loved his daughters, he wasn't a modern style of father:

> When I was pregnant, people would ask him, 'Are you going to have a son and heir or a bonny daughter to spoil?' And he said, 'I'd give anything to be having a big dog!'
>
> He came to see Ruth the day she was born. In those days, babies were kept in the ward's nursery. After visiting, I could never understand why my baby was always asleep when everyone else's was wide awake. I then discovered that it was because my husband walked straight out of the ward and out of the front door after visiting. All the other fathers went to see their babies!

At the time of his dream, John's children were very young. He didn't have a son and he'd never changed nappies, yet he did this in the dream. Nor was he very close to his sister-in-law; they had a polite, rather than warm relationship. If the baby was her son, why did he appear in John's dream?

INTERPRETATION

It was incredibly vivid. Even now I can sort of see everything. It's so literally black and white because it was so powerful.

The first thing to strike those who knew John was his amazement at the impact of the dream: he told everyone who would listen. As we know, this was completely out of character. At first he simply thought the dream amusing, and was struck by its significance only when he heard of the death. In the dream he had expected the child to be a girl, since he had daughters, and here events unfolded as they do in waking reality, when we think one thing only to be surprised when it turns out to be wrong. So the baby, he found, had nothing to do with his own children – it was not even a girl. Then, later, came the connection. When Joan's brother rang on the Monday evening and told her the baby was a boy, she instinctively answered, 'Yes, I know.' It took a while before he realized what she had said: how could she have known?

John's dream seems to suggest something akin to ancient ideas of the transition between life and death. Many cultures believe that the soul of an individual who has just died stays around for a certain time and requires help to pass on its journey. Yet if this is the child's soul leaving its body, it is not obvious why John should be the one to help it on its way. After all, he is a man not given to such belief, or to reflection on spiritual matters of this kind.

In my own practice I have come across comparable experiences. On at least three occasions I have met people who, in a dream, have seen someone suddenly lose energy. Later they discovered that the person fell ill, or died. But here John actually meets the child, holds it, cares for it briefly.

Once again, there seems to be no rational explanation. The stillborn baby was the son of John's wife's brother, so logically we might expect that if anyone was to dream of the baby it would be Joan.

WAKING THE BODY

His friends assembled at the wake
And Mrs Finnegan called for lunch,
First they brought in tay and cake
Then pipes, tobacco and whiskey punch . . .

Whack fol the da, oh dance to your partner
Round the floor, your trotters shake;
Wasn't it the truth I told you
Lots of fun at Finnegan's wake!

(Traditional, 'Finnegan's Wake')

In Ireland, north and south of the border, as soon as the news of a death is known, the house is open for three days: family and friends come and go – or stay – right up until the funeral takes place. Nowadays the dead person may not be physically present, but still the house is never left unattended and is rarely empty. Ireland is a land of stories, and it's a land of memories, tales, drink, and even dancing and singing at wakes. This kind of celebratory activity fills the time when it is believed the person remains in body before preparing to move on in spirit. Constant talk and activity keep the deceased in mind and conjure up bright images of the good days. In a sense, the loved member of the family and community is, for this intervening time, both dead and alive.

It is thought that, in the past, there was a very good practical reason for the wake: to make absolutely sure the person really *was* dead. At the end of the song 'Finnegan's Wake', in the row and ruction Tim Finnegan is miraculously revived when a noggin of whiskey sprays over him; Joyce uses this to symbolize resurrection. Now, although fear of being buried alive is less of an issue, the tradition continues.

DANCING INTO THE NEXT WORLD

For centuries the Catholic Church in Ireland battled against the 'unchristian behaviour' – excessive drinking, dancing and bawdy songs – that inevitably went along with the ritual keening of the 'howling women'. But when death is seen as a beginning as well as an ending, we need to express more than grief and sorrow. The silent sadness of stopped clocks is counterbalanced by memory and celebration: of the life past and the life to come. Brendan Kennelly captures this perfectly, when remembering his father:

> You're buried now
> In Lislaughtin Abbey
> And whenever I think of you

I go back beyond the old man
Mind and body broken
To find the unbroken man.
It is the moment before the dance begins,
Your lips are enjoying themselves
Whistling an air.
Whatever happens, or cannot happen
In the time I have to spare
I see you dancing, father.

CANDLES, CLOCKS AND MIRRORS

Lead, kindly Light, amid the encircling gloom
Lead thou me on . . .

(J. H. Newman, 'Lead, Kindly Light')

Candles, as a focus for prayer and meditation, are used in most funeral rites to symbolize the spirit and the light that wards off darkness. The tradition of stopping clocks seems to survive only in the superstition that it is bad luck to have a ticking clock in the same room as the corpse; perhaps it reminds us too much of our own mortality. The song, 'My Grandfather's Clock', expresses a widespread idea that clocks and watches belonging to the person who has just died mark the time of death; for example, when Thomas Edison the inventor died on 19 October 1931, at 3.24 a.m., 'Three of his assistants reported that their clocks stopped precisely at 3.24 a.m. Three minutes later, the grandfather clock in Edison's laboratory also stopped.'

Many cultures have rituals concerning mirrors, some based on the belief that the soul extends beyond the body in the form of reflection. To prevent it from becoming trapped in the mirror, which would delay its passage to the next world, mirrors are covered or turned to the wall. Nowadays, like the stopped clocks, our uneasiness about spirits' reflections features mainly in ghost stories told by flickering candlelight.

Rituals accompany our transition from life to death, marking the time of our journey from one form of existence to another. Between our waking mind and our dreaming mind there lies a similar transitional area rather than a clear-cut borderline.

THE EDGE OF SLEEP

God . . . created man in such a way that the veil of the senses could be lifted through sleep, which is a natural function of man. When that veil is lifted, the soul is ready to learn the things it desires to know in the world of Truth . . . Clear dream visions are from God. Allegorical dream visions, which call for interpretation, are from the angels.

(Ibn Khaldun, *The Muqaddimah*)

In Chapter 5 we met Rachel, a prolific dreamer who provided illustrations of several distinct types of dream that had influenced her life in a constructive way. Rachel also talked about another experience that may, or may not, be classified as a dream. Here she is certainly not alone: many readers will have similar tales to tell and a great deal of anecdotal evidence confirms that this sort of dream is widely known.

Six months after my grandfather died I booked a package holiday to Ibiza for myself and my son. We'd just got there; it was very hot. We had a nice room, small but it overlooked the bay. It was very, very pretty.

I woke up – I'm telling you, I woke up, I was not asleep. That's as clear as anything. I was in that stage where you have just woken, that in-between stage when all the interesting things seem to happen . . . And there was my grandpa, at the bottom of my bed!

The night after I've arrived in Ibiza for a summer holiday I wasn't thinking of my grandpa. My grandpa's got to be the last thing on my mind.

I sat up. I was absolutely shocked, my heart was pounding. I turned round to look at my son to see if he saw Grandpa, but he was asleep. I admit that I wasn't fully awake, but I wasn't dreaming. Grandpa was suntanned, he looked as he did a while before he died, before he'd become ill.

I said, 'What are you doing here?'

He said, 'I came to see you.' And he smiled.

I reached out to him and he indicated, 'I'm going off to have a cup of tea now' – just as he would when alive – and he vanished.

I sat bolt upright and the tears were pouring down, I was so stunned.

To Rachel, who dreamed so much, the incident seemed odd but she didn't dwell on it. She wouldn't have remembered it, she said, had she not run into her cousin two weeks later at a yoga class. As they started to do their exercises, Rachel told him about her strange dream.

He said, 'Was it about Grandpa?' And he repeated to me word for word exactly the same thing that had happened to me. The same conversation – Grandpa was wearing the same clothes – and there was nothing more than this visit and 'I'm going now' and the cup of tea.

Rachel and her cousin were both close to their grandfather and they had seen him at exactly the same time, almost six months to the day after he died. To Rachel, this was the final proof that it was not a dream. It was a visitation.

MUTUAL DREAMING

'Now Kitty, let's consider who it was that dreamed it all. This is a serious question, my dear . . . You see, Kitty, it *must* have been either me or the Red King. He was part of my dream, of course – but then I was part of his dream, too! . . .'

Which do *you* think it was?

(Lewis Carroll, 'Which dreamed it?')

Rachel and her cousin both dreamed of their grandfather. What we don't know is whether *he* dreamed of them. This may sound odd; but almost as strange things have happened. Linda Magallon includes the following account in her book, *Mutual Dreaming*:

A young woman in central Florida dreams that her brother, a racecar driver, is working on a stock car when he forgets to rehook a rod and spring. She yells at him but is unable to make herself understood over the noise of the engine. The brother's wife dreams of seeing her sister-in-law's face over the bed and knows something is wrong. She wakes the brother, and he reports he's just had a dream his sister is yelling, but he can't understand her. After contacting his sister and hearing her dream, the brother checks out his car and finds that the cable connecting the brake pedal is broken. If driven in that condition, the car would have surely crashed.

Another dream recorded by Magallon is that of an eighteen-year-old girl, her mother and her best friend, all of whom dreamed about a younger girl who was pregnant. None of them knew who the girl was. Within a week, the girl's fourteen-year-old sister came and told her older sister that she was pregnant. A friend of mine told me of an experience that to me seems similar.

One morning, she woke out of a powerful dream in which she had found she had a breast lump. She does not like self-examination but, as a result of this dream, she overcame this and, to her horror, discovered that she did indeed have a big lump. Her GP referred her for a mammogram. The weekend before she saw the specialist who was to give her the result, she was phoned by an old friend, who needed to talk to her. She was too pre-occupied really but sensed the urgency of her friend's request, so asked if it was important. It was, but the friend did not want to tell her over the phone. When they met, she said she had just been diagnosed with breast cancer and had a year to live. It was hardly encouraging news for my friend to hear at that moment, but luckily her own diagnosis was better. The lump turned out to be no more than cysts. I had already known that my friend was phenomenally intuitive, but this time it was not until later that she realized that the dream had actually been about her friend.

In the earliest times dreams seem to have been more of a social phenomenon than purely personal. Perhaps this just reflects the stage of development of the ego, of the sense of individuality we have so acutely refined in modern people. Ordinary dreams are valueless simply because they concern themselves with the mundane and the personal. As our consciousness moves to a deeper level in dreaming we grow closer to the collective level where other realms become more accessible.

HYPNAGOGIC HALLUCINATIONS

For a long time I used to go to bed early . . . And half an hour later the thought that it was time to go to sleep would awaken me; . . . I had gone on thinking, while I was asleep, about what I had just been reading, but these thoughts had taken a rather peculiar turn; it seemed to me that I myself was the immediate subject of my book: a church, a quartet, the rivalry between François I and Charles V.

(Marcel Proust, *Remembrance of Things Past*)

As we fall asleep, the mind passes from a relaxed state to stage 1 of non-REM. Usually this is followed by a gradual descent in the early part of the night until we reach stage 4, the deepest phase of sleep.

Along with waking we leave behind both the external world – which disappears, to be replaced by another landscape – and logical thought. In stage 1 sleep there is a period of imagery: a single static image or short sequence occurs which is quite different from the activity characteristic of an REM dream. Such images may be related to what we were thinking about prior to falling asleep; if woken, dreamers will describe a picture rather than the typical NREM thinking. These are hypnagogic hallucinations: vivid pictures that arise in this specific situation. When you ask someone to explain a *dream*, the typical REM imagery is described. If you ask what the dreamer was thinking *when they wake*, many describe a kind of circular mentation about a subject that does not lead anywhere, just goes round and round with no imagery.

GAMBOLLING ATOMS

... the central mystery itself, the elusive brightness that shines from the edges of certain dreams; the brightness which, when we awaken, is already fading from our minds, and which we rise in the hope of finding, perhaps today, this new day in which anything might happen, anything at all ...

(Michael Cunningham, *The Hours*)

Perhaps the most famous example of a hypnagogic hallucination, and the one that appears in nearly every book on dreams, is that of Friedrich August Kekulé, the German chemist.

In 1853 Kekulé was living in London and working at St Bartholomew's Hospital. On the last bus home one night through the deserted city streets he drifted into a reverie and saw atoms whirling around in a dance, with larger atoms dragging the smaller ones at the end of a chain.

'The cry of the conductor "Clapham Road" awakened me from my dreaming,' he said; nevertheless, that night he made sketches of the forms that had danced in his dreams.

By 1864 Kekulé was Professor of Chemistry in Ghent. His visions of these 'diminutive beings' had led to his discovery of the ability of carbon atoms to form chains. In the intervening years he had published his influential textbook on organic chemistry and initiated the First International Congress of Chemists. Sadly, he also became a widower.

Kekulé's current research was an attempt to determine the structure of benzene and he had spent a great deal of time working on it. Although he knew the formula, he still could not visualize it; he was assuming a straight chain molecule.

I lived in elegant bachelor quarters in the main thoroughfare.

My study, however, faced a narrow side-alley and no daylight penetrated it . . . I was sitting writing on my textbook, but the work did not progress; my thoughts were elsewhere. I turned my chair to the fire and dozed. Again the atoms were gamboling before my eyes. This time the smaller groups kept modestly in the background. My mental eye, rendered more acute by the repeated visions of the kind, could now distinguish larger structures of manifold conformation; long rows sometimes more closely fitted together all twining and twisting in snake-like motion. But look! What was that? One of the snakes had seized hold of its own tail, and the form whirled mockingly before my eyes. As if struck by lightning I awoke; and this time also I spent the rest of the night in working out the consequences of the hypothesis . . .

Kekulé had been studying benzene for many years but the crucial breakthrough had eluded him. Still – as with Schatzman's riddles which we met in Chapter 1 – the dream seemed to know the answer. Perhaps the relaxed dream state allows answers to drift to the surface of our consciousness when there is nothing to stand in their way. Yet this on its own does not answer the key question of what solved the problem. It is not that consciousness blocks the solution, though that may be partly true, it is really that the solution is found somewhere below consciousness. How it arrives in our mind – whether via a sudden 'flash' or in a dream – is the result of the work of the underlying mind.

OUROBOROS

Old Sages (by the Figure of the Snake
Encircled thus) did oft expression make
Of Annual-Revolutions; and of things,
Which wheele about in everlasting-rings;
There ending, where they first of all begun . . .
. . . These Roundells, help to shew the Mystery
of that immense and blest Eternitie,
From whence the CREATURE sprung, and into whom
It shall again, with full perfection come . . .

(George Wither, A Collection of Emblemes, 1635)

The Ouroboros – the snake that devours its own tail – is one of the oldest symbols in the world, often representing the encircling waters of the universe. This symbol of the Great World Serpent is engraved on a bronze receptacle dating from around 1200 BC, from the Chou dynasty in China, while its literary history is as old as the Greek *Oneirocritica*, or dream-book, of the diviner Artemidorus of the second century. Over 3,000 years later, the Ouroboros was still alive in Kekulé's dream.

Ouroboros has been seen as a visualization of the cycle of the seasons; as time and the continuity of life on earth; as completion, totality, perfection and eternity, 'Alpha and Omega, the beginning and the ending'.

THE LIGHT OF COMMON DAY

Returning each morning from a timeless world,
the senses open upon a world of time . . .

(W. H. Auden, 'The Dark Years')

As we've just seen, hypnagogic hallucinations are at times more than just static images, and indeed can be quite complex. They are generally convincing, appearing to be more substantial than dreams. Enid Blyton, when analysing the sources of her inspiration, noted that she heard noises along with the hypnagogic imagery: 'They have always seemed to me to be too *real* to be imagined – they must come from *outside* me, not inside my mind.'

Images that we experience as we emerge from sleep in the morning – usually from REM – are called hypnopompic hallucinations. The longest period of REM occurs in

211

the last hour or two of sleep, shortly before we wake. This may be the origin of the widespread Muslim belief that dreams appearing just before waking are more truthful than dreams that we have at earlier times of the night.

Writers seem to be very alert to these, for the images and ideas that remain with us as we wake can be more easily captured before they fade away. Henry Perowne, the neurosurgeon hero of Ian McEwan's novel *Saturday*, enjoys 'the luxury of being half asleep, exploring the fringes of psychosis in safety'. But more often the return to waking reality suggests sadness, the evanescence of the ideal, the cold light of our daytime responsibilities and demands. In *Dream Days* and *The Wind in the Willows* Kenneth Grahame, lamenting that 'hard, cold waking and all its penalties', conjured up a magical, mythical sunny world that vanished in the bleak light of the Great War. Just so did Jay Gatsby's haunting, impossible dream fade into the reality of modern America:

> And as I sat there brooding on the old, unknown world, I thought of Gatsby's wonder when he first picked out the green light at the end of Daisy's dock. He had come a long way to this blue lawn, and his dream must have seemed so close that he could hardly fail to grasp it. He did not know that it was already behind him . . . where the dark fields of the republic rolled on under the night.
>
> (F. Scott Fitzgerald, *The Great Gatsby*)

'BRIGHTNESS FALLS FROM THE AIR'

> Deep peace of the running wave to you,
> Deep peace of the flowing air to you,
> Deep peace of the quiet earth to you,
> Deep peace of the shining stars to you . . .
>   Until we meet again,
> May God hold you in the hollow of His hand.
>
> (Anon, 'A Celtic Blessing')

Some dreams are intensely poignant and clear, while also providing deep reassurance. In 'Dreams after Childhood Trauma', Kathleen Nader describes a five-year-old boy with leukaemia who relapsed after a bone marrow transplant. He 'began to dream of spacemen coming to take him to their planet. In his early dreams he was afraid of the spacemen. In later dreams he found them to be friendly, and decided it was safe to go with them. He died a few months after befriending them.'

The death of a child is especially painful and it is hard for us to see beyond our grief. People do their best to help; and perhaps dreams do too. However sad we are, it is comforting to believe that the child felt safe and was happy to travel with the friendly spacemen when he had to leave this world.

In *On Dreams and Death* von Franz discusses the dream of an old woman reported by Dr Jay Dunn:

She sees a candle lit on the window sill of the hospital room and finds that the candle suddenly goes out. Fear and anxiety ensue as the darkness envelops her. Suddenly, the candle lights on the other side of the window and she awakens.

On the same day, the woman died, 'completely at peace', says von Franz. Like the boy, who was afraid of the space-men at first, she had felt anxious. The return of the light calmed her fears and it becomes, for her, a reassuring image – the constant candles that light the path through the shadows into the next life.

THE 'REAL' DEAD

The dead are always looking down on us, they say,
while we are putting on our shoes or making a sandwich,
they are looking down through the glass-bottom boats of
heaven
as they row themselves slowly through eternity . . .

(Billy Collins, 'The Dead')

We will end with another account of a married couple; this time it is the husband who tells the tale. Mark's wife had been ill for two and a half years before she finally died of ovarian cancer. She was only fifty and had been very healthy and fit before the illness. They were very close, and Mark found her physical deterioration distressing, but they had had time to sort things out between them, although they had hoped to have longer.

Three days before she died she said she had 'to walk away now': that was the last they spoke.

Mark was not a dreamer, and neither was his wife, but three nights after she died, Mark dreamed she was there in bed beside him. She was exactly as she had been in life; it was a completely real experience. Lying next to him, she was no longer wasted away but restored to her

214

former robust health and beauty.

'I'm perfectly all right,' she said. That was all; the whole experience was very brief.

Mark shot up in bed, wide awake. He felt that 'It was more than a dream, more like a physical encounter.' He could not explain it any further. It had been comforting – but only in a way.

Perhaps, then, we should not 'rage against the dying of the light', as Dylan Thomas insists, but should 'go gentle into that good night'. Elsewhere Thomas asserts that 'death shall have no dominion', and in this he echoes the certainty of writers throughout the ages; for example John Donne –

> One short sleep past, we wake eternally,
> And Death shall be no more: Death, thou shalt die.

9

THE RIVER OF LIFE

Five miles meandering with a mazy motion
Through wood and dale the sacred river ran,
Then reached the caverns measureless to man
And sank in tumult to a lifeless ocean . . .
And 'mid this tumult Kubla heard from far
Ancestral voices prophesying war!

(Samuel Taylor Coleridge, 'Kubla Khan')

John's dream, along with the others we examined in Chapter 8, focused attention on the presence of dead people in our dreams. It seemed that John was chosen to play a role in the baby's journey from one world to another, for reasons that were obscure. Rachel's grandfather – like Mark's wife, and the mothers who appeared in the dreams of Irene's mother and Ethel – conveyed a sense of reassurance or protection. Although their purposes may have been different, all of these figures were once members of the dreamer's family. In this chapter

Patrick's dream, while similar in some respects, broadens the picture.

'THE GATE OF DEATH, THE GATE OF BIRTH'

In my pursuit after Truth I have discarded many ideas and learnt many new things. Old as I am in age, I have no feeling that I have ceased to grow inwardly, or that my growth will stop with the dissolution of the flesh.

(Mahatma Gandhi)

Through the collective unconscious we are connected to all of humanity; to a multitude of minds, a vast unknown community. Many ancient cultures, from the Celtic lands to Siberia, set out to explore the furthest reaches of this world. Dreams, the ancient Egyptians believed, were the gateway to eras beyond our current life; their trained dreamers, who acted as seers as well as advisers to the state, travelled to a deeper level of reality in search of spiritual knowledge. As Robert Moss writes, the Pharaoh also visited other worlds:

In the *heb sed* festival . . . the king was required to journey beyond the body, and beyond death, to prove his worthiness to continue on the throne. Led by Anubis, Pharaoh descended to the Underworld. He was directed to enter death, 'touch the four sides of the land', become Osiris, and return in new garments – the robe and spiritual body of transformation.

It was in Egypt that Orpheus, whom Apollo taught to

play the lyre, extended his knowledge of the gods and their initiatory rites, bringing back to Greece many mystic ceremonies, as well as the tale of his descent into the Underworld.

Patrick, who had several very intuitive relatives, was alert to the mysteries and ambiguity of dreams. He had been impressed by the almost documentary quality of the dream he recounted, but was not surprised by the wider frame of reference it implied.

Patrick

'I can only assume somehow the future has happened and it's coming backwards,' Patrick concluded, after admitting he'd discarded a raft of theories. He had told me his dreams were Jungian, symbolic, and all in colour; clearly he was familiar with the territory. Still, this one had startled him. 'It's probably the most powerful dream I've ever had,' he said. As we talked, he outlined the events that led up to it.

He had been about to join his wife, Sheila, who had taken their young daughter to Florida to convalesce after a serious illness. First of all, Patrick thought, he should visit his parents; they too had been unwell. When he arrived, his father was out with his cronies in the pub, so Patrick and his mother sat talking in the kitchen. Unexpectedly, she produced a bottle of fine malt whisky that a friend had given her. Patrick was surprised, for she rarely drank alcohol.

I watched as she splashed two liberal measures into cheap tumblers and added tap water. 'A parting glass, my son,' she said. She smiled. 'I'm very tired, and I won't be here when you get back.'

I was visibly upset, but she lifted her glass. 'God bless, my son. I'll always be watching out for you. Like your grandmother watches out for me.'

After dealing with business in Chicago and New York, Patrick arrived at Marco Island in Florida and slowed down to holiday speed. It was nearly time to return home when, one night, he woke abruptly at 3 a.m. and sensed his mother's presence in the room. He drifted off to sleep again, and had a remarkable dream.

I was near Ludlow in Shropshire, the town my grandmother lived and worked in, and to which my mother took me many times when I was a small boy.

It was a midsummer Sunday. On the sloping grassy banks of the river an evening service was under way in the open air. There was a large congregation, all of whom I knew. Some were dead, and others were then alive; a few are still alive as I write this. Leading the singers was an ancient white-haired clergyman, the Reverend Ellis Rees-Jones, who had been dead for many years. He had come to my childhood home just before my mother's mother was taken away to the Infirmary to die.

I looked at the faces of the singers and recognized them all. Among the dead were my Grandmother Emma, Uncle Sonny and Aunt Liz, Ida and Lily, Elsie and Gibbo, Uncle Bill, Sam junior and Uncle Ted. Weirdest of all, I recognized – from old photographs – my Grandfather Samuel, the piano tuner. All of my living relatives were there: my sister, Aunt Edie, Uncle Cliff and their daughter Janice. Interestingly, there was not a soul from the

Hall tribe, not even my father. The congregation consisted only of my mother's tribe.

The singing was inspired and all the hymns were tuneful. They began with 'When I survey the wondrous Cross' and closed with 'The old rugged Cross', my mother's favourite.

The service ended, old Rees-Jones raised his hand in blessing, and the crowds began to drift away. I watched the summer dusk fall on the river as I stood between my mother and Aunt Edie.

Edie said to me, 'We have to go before we see the white dog of Saint Cadoc.'

'What white dog?' I asked her. 'What are you talking about?'

My mother said, 'Only those who pass on ever see the white dog.'

Even as she spoke, a white boat glided around the river bend. It moved silently and slowly, and the only occupant was a large white dog that sat unmoving in the prow.

The remnants of the crowd fled back up the grassy slope, until only my aunt, my mother and myself remained. Edie gripped our arms.

'We have to go!' she insisted. 'If you see the white dog, you die.'

Edie and I turned away, but then, to my horror, I saw my mother break free and run forward past me, down towards the boat and the river. I shouted to her to come away, but she ignored my shouts, and then I saw her eyes. She was blind.

In a panic, I woke up.

Patrick was distraught: the dream was so real and disturbing. Sheila opened her eyes and told him to write it down, so he found a pen and some hotel notepaper and recorded every detail while it was still vivid. 'Sleep was impossible after that,' Patrick said. 'So I pulled on a T-shirt and shorts and walked along the Gulf shore. As the sky rapidly lightened, I remember seeing the pelicans fishing in the shallows.'

Back at the hotel, Patrick and his family had an early breakfast and returned to their room. As they walked through the door, the telephone was ringing. It was Patrick's sister; she told him their mother had suffered a severe stroke and had been taken to hospital, only to have a second stroke there.

'Edie was with her,' my sister said. 'Edie told her she would be OK. But she shook her head, smiled, pointed heavenwards and died.'

I don't know why I asked the question, but I did. 'Was she blind?'

My sister replied, 'How could you possibly know that?'

She was! The first stroke had blinded her.

Patrick and his sister compared notes and found that, allowing for the transatlantic time difference, their mother had died at the precise moment when Patrick had awoken and sensed her presence in the room.

INTERPRETATION

The shores of Styx are lone for evermore,
And not one shadowy form upon the steep
Looms through the dusk, as far as eyes can sweep,
To call the ferry over as of yore . . .

221

> For in the world of Life strange rumours run
>   That now the Soul departs not with the breath,
> But that the Body and the Soul are one;
>   And in the loved one's mouth, now, after death,
> The widow puts no obol, nor the son,
>   To pay the ferry in the world beneath.
>
> (Eugene Lee-Hamilton, 'Idle Charon')

Patrick knew without doubt that the dream was about his dying mother. Her behaviour at their final meeting had led him to expect her death, even if consciously he had not accepted the fact. In saying goodbye to him she had unequivocally predicted her own end; she knew she was not going to see her son again. I have frequently heard similar accounts from relatives who are trying to come to terms with loss.

This dream has a profoundly mythological feel. There are echoes of Tennyson's 'Lady of Shalott', dying as the river carries her boat down to Camelot; or of the River Styx in the Underworld, across which the souls of the dead are ferried. Rivers are often dangerous crossings and mark a clear boundary between one land and another, a border that must be crossed in the transition from life to death. If we let our imagination take flight, we are in the old world of the Egyptians and the Greeks. Patrick's dream speaks of the mystery of life and the ultimate question of a life after death. Yet any simple explanation is confounded by the foreknowledge of blindness that is revealed only at the climax of the dream. Here we have almost a repeat of John's dream, which enabled him to say in advance that the baby had been a boy. Whoever or whatever entered Patrick's dream, it was already known that his mother was blind as she approached death.

Blindness is beyond prediction. Of course, it could be argued that it is a symbolic loss, just as Oedipus was blinded psychologically by his sin. Equally, it is physical. It is the blindness of the life force evaporating, the shutting down of the nervous system as it fades away. Central to accounts of the Near Death Experience is the tunnel: this is usually explained as resulting from reduction in the supply of oxygen to the brain, which leaves only the central visual area still working. The entire peripheral field is lost, and then central vision disappears. Reduction in the supply of oxygen to the brain causes random firing of nerves in the retina. This gives rise to flashes of light which are more intense in the centre because this area is so much more densely populated, hence the light surrounded by relative darkness. As we die, so we lose sight.

I prefer Patrick's explanation: that the future has already happened and is coming backwards. According to modern physics, in theory this idea is less extraordinary than it may sound even if – in relation to the larger objects of our everyday world, not to mention common sense – it seems unimaginable. Unfortunately, the world of the very small – of subatomic particles – and the ordinary world seem to be very different. It would be fascinating to know how many people sensed the 2004 tsunami before it happened; there is much anecdotal evidence of precognitive dreams relating to the World Trade Center disaster. Of course, it is impossible to research such events accurately, as they cannot be looked at before they happen.

As Patrick's mother moved beyond life it was made clear to him that he should not look too closely. The dead have always been surrounded by taboo, for the very reason that the energy tied up in them – energy that cannot be lived, feelings that can no longer be expressed – can fall back into the bereaved individual's unconscious and create trouble. Say farewell and don't look back or you may be turned into a pillar of salt like Lot's wife, or trapped in the Underworld like Eurydice when Orpheus could not resist a backward glance. It is as if Patrick walked to the edge of this dangerous territory – this other world – but absolutely must go no further. Here he saw his mother, partly mortal still, not yet crossing to the other side.

THE WHITE DOG OF SAINT CADOC

A man with a hazel wand came without sound,
He changed me suddenly; I was looking another way;
And now my calling is but the calling of a hound;
And Time and Birth and Change are hurrying by.

(W. B. Yeats, 'He mourns for the change that has come upon him . . .')

The night before his mother's death Jung also had a frightening dream, which bears a resemblance to Patrick's. 'I was in a dense, gloomy forest; fantastic, gigantic boulders lay about among huge jungle-like trees. It was a heroic, primeval landscape,' he wrote.

Suddenly I heard a piercing whistle that seemed to resound through the whole universe. My knees shook.

Then there came crashings in the underbrush, and a gigantic wolfhound with a fearful, gaping maw burst forth. At the sight of it, the blood froze in my veins. It tore past me, and suddenly I knew: the Wild Huntsman had commanded it to carry away a human soul. I awoke in deadly terror, and the next morning I received news of my mother's passing.

Her death, he continued, had come with 'unexpected suddenness'.

Returning to Patrick, once we move beyond consideration of his mother, other aspects of his dream are more difficult to fathom. Patrick was able to trace certain links with his family: for example, his grandmother came from a village near Ludlow on the border between Wales and England, as did all of her family. Yet despite his extensive knowledge of Celtic mythology, the identity of the white dog eluded him.

Saint Cadoc is easier to pin down, but fact must be disentangled from fiction in the accounts of his life. The historical Cadoc lived in Wales in the sixth century and founded the great church and abbey of Llancarfan, west of Cardiff. One of the leading Welsh saints, he later became a bishop and met a martyr's death in Italy. The legend that he was transported there on a white cloud may not be entirely reliable. A highlight of his spiritual life was the conversion of his parents to Christianity. For many years he had prayed that his father, King Gwynllyw, would see the light and abandon his violent ways, until

One night, Gwynllyw had a dream in which an angel of God appeared and told him he would find a rare and valuable white ox on Stow Hill. When he found the beast the next day, the King was so impressed that the vision had come true that he allowed his son to baptize him . . . It was a happy day when he made public profession of his faith and was baptized at the river's edge.

Perhaps Saint Cadoc's ox had somehow transformed into the white dog of Patrick's dream. Such dogs do appear in Celtic tales, often with ominous overtones, and of course Patrick may have been aware of this. In 1899, W. B. Yeats was evidently familiar with these uncanny creatures; when trying to work out the source of his inspiration for his poem 'He mourns for the change . . .' he wrote:

> The hound is certainly related to the Hounds of Annwoyn or of Hades, who are white, and have red ears, and were heard, and are, perhaps, still heard by Welsh peasants, following some flying thing in the night winds; and is probably related to the hounds that Irish country people believe will awake and seize the souls of the dead if you lament them too loudly or too soon.

The legendary Welsh *cwn annwfn* are the hell hounds of *annwfn*, the magical pre-Christian Otherworld. Their association with death is clear. For Jung, the Wild Huntsman in his dream was Wotan, who had taken his mother. He was a Mercury or Hermes figure, according to Jung, later to transmute into the devil in the Christian world-view. Of course neither Patrick nor Jung had come across these hounds in daily life; we can only speculate on whether their emergence at this very specific time is co-incidental. Here then is another aspect of the collective unconscious, a timeless contemporary of David's panther. Curiously, Freud too described a dream relevant to Patrick's experience.

'LIKE A BIRD TO AN UNSEEN SHORE'

To die will be an awfully big adventure.

(J. M. Barrie, *Peter Pan*)

The brief yet moving dream that Freud describes is one that he uses to illustrate his theory of dreams as wish-fulfilment:

A father had been watching beside his child's sick-bed for days and nights on end. After the child had died, he went into the next room to lie down but left the door open so that he could see from his bedroom into the room in which his child's body was laid out, with tall candles standing round it. An old man had been engaged to keep watch over it, and sat beside the body murmuring prayers. After a few hours' sleep, the father had a dream that *his child was standing beside his bed, caught him by the arm and whispered to him reproachfully: 'Father, don't you see I'm burning?'* He woke up, noticed a bright glare of light from the next room, hurried into it and found the old watchman had dropped off to sleep and that the wrappings and one of the arms of his beloved child's

227

body had been burned by a lighted candle that had fallen on them.

Freud's explanation of the dream is simple and rational: the father would have noticed the glare from the next room; and before he fell asleep he may have been worried about the competence of the old man. Freud, who believed that nothing new could be found in dreams, explained that the son could have spoken these words before his death – the burning would then refer to the fever, and '*Father, don't you see?* may have been derived from some other highly emotional situation of which we are in ignorance'.

The father's fulfilled wish was obviously that the child was still, for a moment, alive.

Freud's explanation, while possible, is unlikely. Here is a man who has had very little sleep for days, has fought for the life of his son, and has lost him. His sleep would probably have been deep; external stimuli, as we saw in Chapter 2, would be shut off. Unless they are very powerful, they will not disturb the dreamer – a fact Freud was unaware of. If the light from the candles did not waken the watchman, it is not likely to have intruded into the father's dream.

To the hunter-gatherer, indeed to almost every society apart from modern western society, this dream would simply have been proof of the soul or spirit passing from the boy. As noted earlier, many peoples believe the souls of the dead are around for a period of time after death and need help on their onward journey.

While Jung's example shows a parallel with the dog,

here we have a different kind of association, this time with the dead person. Patrick's mother was blind as she died; the boy here has a burning arm, post-mortem. Neither of these could have been known to the dreamer. Although Freud gives a scientific explanation, this feels like the rational left hemisphere of the split-brain patients making something up in order to defend the status quo. Is it too fanciful to point out that the child had caught his father by the arm in the dream when it was his arm that was burning? Perhaps no explanation will satisfy as we are moving into the complete unknown.

OTHER VOICES

The river is within us, the sea is all about us;
The sea is the land's edge also, the granite
Into which it reaches, the beaches where it tosses
Its hints of earlier and other creation . . .

(T. S. Eliot, 'The Dry Salvages')

The river is a highly charged symbol. It runs through not only imaginative writing but the customs and beliefs of most cultures. In the Punjab in north-western India, for example, it is believed that the dead must cross a wide river, the borderline between worlds. Before this, the ceremony of Deeva Batti is performed. A lamp made from flour dough is lighted and placed near the head or on the right palm of the dead person and a gift is made on their behalf. A cow given away at this time is considered the best form of charity among the Hindus, for it is thought that in crossing the river to the next world, the journey of the dead is made easier if they hold on to the tail of this cow.

The funeral procession makes its journey to the cremation ground, and on their way back mourners bathe at a pond or well, wash all their clothes and perform another farewell ritual. Each one sits on the ground, bends forward, lifts a blade of grass and after the priest has chanted a verse, breaks it into two and throws it back behind their head, thus severing all worldly relations with the dead person. The bones are later taken to be immersed in the Ganges, the most sacred river.

PASSING THROUGH

In a Wonderland they lie,
Dreaming as the days go by,
Dreaming as the summers die:

Ever drifting down the stream –
Lingering in the golden gleam –
Life, what is it but a dream?

(Lewis Carroll, *Through the Looking-Glass*)

The evening service conducted on the grassy river bank that Patrick describes is undoubtedly Christian, despite the Celtic overtones of the dream as a whole. In addition to its meaning as a boundary, in Christianity the river symbolizes the river of life: the course of our life as 'an ever rolling stream' that bears us through the earthly world and on to meet our Maker; via St Peter with his keys to the kingdom of Heaven, we hope. The faithful 'gather at the river', whose crystal tide flows right up to the throne of God. The river is at the same time the River Jordan, the 'streams of living water' that bring the spiritual resurrection expressed in the sacrament of baptism when the soul is washed clean of the sin that is already within us when we are born.

The river of life flows through this world, carrying us towards old age and death. But the journey does not begin when we take our first breath as a newborn child; nor does it end when we breathe our last. We are constantly in transit, travelling from a world we cannot see, and leaving our present reality to move on to another that is also unknown to us. In the Christian tradition, many thinkers have explored the idea that we travel from another world and are merely given to our earthly parents to look after before we move on to our destiny. Man's life is like the swift flight of a sparrow through a bright room, wrote Bede, a monk living in Jarrow in the eighth century. The bird flits in from the rain or snow to a hall warmed by a good fire then almost at once vanishes out into the wintry storms from which it emerged: 'So this life of man appears for a short space, but of what went before, or what is to follow, we are completely ignorant.'

We may assume our current life *is* life, but it can also be seen as part of a continuum – life once again as an unending circle, not a finite chain. When Keats died at the age of just twenty-five, Shelley, though mourning the loss of his friend, envisaged him not as coming to the end of life but as waking from the earthly *dream* of life, a dream that Robert Browning later described as 'insane' compared to the true eternal life into which we enter on our death.

Wordsworth, writing on immortality, agrees: life flows with us and through us from a world that was once as real to us as our present existence:

> Our birth is but a sleep and a forgetting:
> The Soul that rises with us, our life's Star,
> Hath had elsewhere its setting.
> And cometh from afar:
> Not in entire forgetfulness,
> And not in utter nakedness,
> But trailing clouds of glory do we come
> From God, who is our home:
> Heaven lies about us in our infancy!
> (William Wordsworth, 'Intimations of Immortality')

Throughout ancient Celtic lands too there was the belief that life continued after death of the body; the soul passed on to an immortal Otherworld outside time. It is not the precise equivalent of the kingdom of Heaven, for the dead had power to return to the land of the living from their own world which was parallel to earthly life. Mortals could be invited into it, though it was a fearful realm and one encircled by rules and taboos. Poets – whose role included healing and divination – were thought to have a special gift of clairvoyance and prophecy gained from visions and dreams in which they could gain access to ancestors' knowledge. The worlds of the living and the dead were intertwined, just as Patrick's living and dead relatives joined forces to take part in the evening service by the river.

SOCRATES AND THE SLAVE-BOY

It is wonderful that five thousand years have now elapsed since the creation of the world, and still it is undecided whether or not there has ever been an instance of the spirit of any person appearing after death. All argument is against it; but all belief is for it.

(James Boswell, *The Life of Samuel Johnson*)

In the *Meno*, one of Plato's most famous dialogues, Socrates argues that within themselves people have knowledge that they could not have acquired in their present lifetime. To prove this, he says, he will show that one of Meno's slave-boys can work out Pythagoras' theorem.

Using his question-and-answer method, Socrates elicits the boy's opinion on a series of statements, insisting that he is not 'teaching', simply drawing out the boy's 'recollection', which must be his memory of knowledge from a previous existence – unless, of course, he has been taught geometry? Meno confirms that he has not. Since the boy was born and bred in his house, he is certain of this.

Socrates: And yet he has the knowledge?
Meno: The fact, Socrates, is undeniable . . .
Socrates: And if there have been always true thoughts in him . . . which only need to be awakened into knowledge by putting questions to him, his soul must have always possessed this knowledge . . . And if the truth of all things always existed in the soul, then the soul is immortal. Wherefore be of good cheer, and try to recollect what you do not know, or rather what you do not remember.

233

The arguments put forward in *Meno* are much debated and analysed, with not all commentators finding them convincing. Nevertheless, the slave-boy dialogue reinforces the idea that the soul contains knowledge from a time beyond the individual's own life.

SYNCHRONICITY

> Or say that the end precedes the beginning,
> And the end and the beginning were always there
> Before the beginning and after the end,
> And all is always now.
>
> (T. S. Eliot, 'Burnt Norton')

Just as dogs appear to know the moment when their owners are setting off to return home to them, both Patrick and John – who, as we saw earlier, was handed a baby to take care of – seemed to be aware of the precise time of a spirit's passing on. The idea of time radiating from both present (telepathy) and future has a somewhat causal ring to it, as if a signal from the future is being sent to the present and can be picked up by the brain acting as a receiver.

Jung's concept of synchronicity concerns the types of event that may strike us as more than just coincidence. Here he describes what happened when one of his patients was telling him of a dream she had had at a critical point in her therapy. In it, she was given a golden scarab:

> While she was telling me this dream I sat with my back to the closed window. Suddenly I heard a noise behind me,

234

like a gentle tapping. I turned around and saw a flying insect knocking against the window-pane from outside. I opened the window and caught the creature in the air as it flew in. It was the nearest analogy to a golden scarab that one finds in our latitudes, a scarabaeid beetle, the common rose-chafer, which contrary to its usual habits had evidently felt an urge to get into a dark room at this particular moment.

Although he admitted that nothing similar had happened to him before or since, Jung considered that two such events occurring together were connected by meaning. In contrast to Newtonian physics, which dealt with causality, quantum mechanics – like synchronicity – relates to acausality. Just as the world is full of causality – one thing makes another happen, one billiard ball hits another – it is also full of acausal events. The phone rings and it is someone you have just thought of but not heard from in many years. To call this synchronicity does not explain it; it does suggest that such events are connected in the unconscious, but that we cannot see beneath the surface.

UNUS MUNDUS: ONE WORLD

The psychologist Anthony Storr writes:

Jung, in common with other thinkers at different periods of history, believed in an ultimate unity of all existence. Using the terminology of medieval philosophy, he referred to this as the *unus mundus*. This unity is outside the human categories of space and time, and beyond our separation of reality into physical and mental.

Spirituality, as Deepak Chopra reminds us, 'is based on the idea that there's more to life than meets the eye'. The so-called material world is in fact made up of energy vibrating on different wavelengths. There is no sharp division between the observer and the observed: we are all connected in a unity beyond the concepts of 'space and time'. Already we know we can perceive some phenomena (such as the colours red and violet) but not others (infrared and ultraviolet); nevertheless, all are real. If, as exponents of String theory propose, an unimaginable eight to thirteen dimensions exist, surely there are other rules of the universe we cannot yet comprehend.

10

THE WOUNDED HEALER

What is precious, is never to forget.
The essential delight of the blood drawn from ageless springs
Breaking through rocks in worlds before our earth.
Never to deny its pleasure in the morning simple light
Nor its grave evening demand for love.
Never to allow gradually the traffic to smother
With noise and fog, the flowering of the spirit.

(Stephen Spender, 'The Truly Great')

Dreams can help us to fight against an illness we didn't know we had. They can reveal what will happen in the future. They can console us and reassure us in the presence of death. They can save lives. But that isn't all they can do. As well as saving lives, they can make them worth living.

We will look at this in relation to Vicky, whose dream was so forceful that, as she told me, 'I think about it almost every day. Ten years later it hasn't gone away. It's given me another dimension that wasn't there before.' When we say 'It changed my life' it is often no more than a cliché. For Vicky, it was the truth.

Vicky

At the end of the 1980s, Vicky was having a rough time. Within just two years her mother, sister and husband died. Then, in May 1990, her car was written off when someone drove into her at a red light. She was left with severe whiplash; and the day before, she had been tested for cancer. Three months later she got a positive diagnosis. Coping with the children on her own wasn't easy, especially when the house was being extended and every room was in chaos.

After surgery and radiotherapy, Vicky found it very hard to go on – and the biggest fight, she found, was the mental and emotional battle of believing she would get well and could resume a normal life. 'This ambivalence about living lasted for several years,' she said. 'I felt totally exhausted and in some ways I wanted to give up. It was only because I had to stay alive for my children that I knew I needed to find the resources within me to overcome the disease.'

From day to day she felt she was doing no more than staggering on, when out of the blue she had one of the most powerful and vivid dreams she had ever experienced.

I was in a car, driving down a sloping country lane. In the distance I could see a motorway. I was very anxious, asking myself, 'Is this the right road?' There was a road on my left but it was facing the wrong way – the information was on the reverse of the sign. As I passed it I glanced back, but it was completely unhelpful. Not for the first time in my life, I felt lost.

Suddenly, I was out of the car and standing in bushland. It looked like Australia (although I have never been there). As I stood in the very hot sun, an extremely tall, young black male came towards me. He was Aboriginal and was in some sort of full ceremonial dress. He wore a head-dress and his skin glistened. He looked extremely healthy – he literally shone and he was upright and muscular. He was holding a spear but I was not afraid of him.

He stopped in front of me, looked at me and said, 'It's good to be alive.' Then he strode off into the bush, occasionally waiting for me to catch up with him.

Eventually, he stopped and showed me two large earthenware containers on the ground. One contained fresh drinking water; the other was full of grain. Still not speaking, he led me to a vast, round lake, almost encircled by mountains. The sun was shining and a breeze was making the water dance. Although remote and spartan, it was incredibly beautiful. I had a sense that the lake was bottomless.

When Vicky woke up she felt immediately that she knew what the dream meant. The sense that something had actually *happened* to her was overwhelming: 'I understood that wanting to die was the wrong road for me to take and that the road sign had been the wrong way round to emphasize this – I was not meant to die at this time.'

INTERPRETATION

Energy is the only life . . . Energy is Eternal Delight.
(William Blake, *The Marriage of Heaven and Hell*)

Looking back to Vicky's life before her dream, we find one of those awful situations where everything appears to be going wrong. Not only the loss of three of her family, but a car crash and further injury, then cancer. It must have seemed to Vicky that her world was disintegrating.

In order to live, we need the support of the unconscious mind – although we are seldom aware of it. Often it appears consciously as a certain energy or determination helping us to work hard and live a full life and it is very easy for us to identify with this drive and think it is ours. It is only when the energy suddenly disappears, as in a period of illness or depression, that we begin to realize we cannot always control everything. In retrospect, Vicky saw this: 'I got into a whole load of coping strategies – but I think I was acting out coping, rather than coping. On the surface it looked as if I was OK, but I wasn't. I *had* to be OK, because I couldn't afford to fall apart.' As if she is being tested, Vicky is assaulted from all sides; confronted with a very profound questioning as to whether she really wants to live.

It is the dream – and in particular the figure of the Aborigine – that quite unexpectedly comes to her aid. It is impressive, and the symbols within it are extraordinarily strong. It was far more than 'just a dream', as Vicky so vehemently points out. Such dreams speak of other dimensions, of mysteries, of meaning.

THE WISDOM OF THE AGES

To see a World in a Grain of Sand
And a Heaven in a Wild Flower,
Hold Infinity in the palm of your hand
And Eternity in an hour.

(William Blake, 'Auguries of Innocence')

Why an Aborigine? Vicky had no links with Australia. She described this figure – male, black, young, healthy – as her alter ego, meaning the exact opposite of herself. In Jung's terms, he is the animus, or masculine principle in the female unconscious. (A man thus has an anima, or female principle.) For Vicky, living in Britain, Australia, representing the opposite end of the earth, seems to confirm this. Vicky was sure she knew the meaning of the dream the instant she woke: the spear and ceremonial clothes were signs of the man's authority, his right to take control and lead her in the right direction. The distant motorway was the road she should travel in the future: 'and which I am now, metaphorically, travelling', she added. The water and grain that the Aborigine pointed out she took as an indication that she should live simply; she is now vegetarian. Water, of course, symbolizes life. Vicky also linked it with the sheer wonder of living. And the lake to which she was led was a deep one – there was more here than she could ever need. 'It was a joyous day, with the

241

sun and wind, these mountains and the blue sky and the reflection in the water . . .'

The symbols of the dream remained alive in her conscious life, warming and comforting her as if she was seated by a fire in the cool of the evening. Such images are not simple signs; they are suffused with layers of richness that change as the symbols live on in that person, altering their life 'like wine through water'.

Once he has made his life-affirming statement – 'It's good to be alive' – which could hardly be more direct, the Aborigine imparts no more wisdom in words. He is more an image of health, though for Vicky he was very real. 'It sounds crazy,' she said. 'But he was a three-dimensional person.' We spent some time analysing the nature of this figure who continued to exert a strong influence. Although she felt his presence, he did not appear again and she could not talk to him. His existence was ambivalent: 'He is separate but he is also integral to me. I have almost integrated him into my permanent self. In some ways I feel androgynous these days. I feel a lot of male qualities come from him: they balance me and I draw on them.'

This 'Aborigine within' knows what to do, just as the dream figure knew where to take Vicky: 'It was very simple, it wasn't complicated or difficult. I just had to follow him.

'I cannot really explain this,' Vicky said in a recent letter: 'except to say that this dream person feels like a "building block" within me, representing a solid foundation that has strengthened and enabled me to cope since I was ill – and in a strange sort of way, aids me in the business of being well.' So in a certain sense Vicky has assimilated the energy of this strong, powerful and youthful character to gain deeper sources of strength and inspiration.

ALCHEMY

Are you willing to be sponged out, erased, cancelled,
made nothing?
Are you willing to be made nothing?
dipped into oblivion?

If not, you will never really change.

The phoenix renews her youth
only when she is burnt, burnt alive, burnt down
to hot and flocculent ash.
Then the small stirring of a new small bub in the nest
with strands of down like floating ash
shows that she is renewing her youth like the eagle,
immortal bird.

(D. H. Lawrence, 'Phoenix')

Vicky's life can be seen as illustrating aspects of the alchemical process. Jung was fascinated with alchemy for practical reasons. Through the physical experiments a parallel process was being lived; matter was a metaphor for psyche, and by working on chemicals the alchemists were really struggling with the deeper layers of the unconscious. It was an allegorical journey, and there was no magical philosopher's stone. Base lead was the human condition, and gold the divine state: the transformation of Adam to Christ. This was a process that occurred within each person. It was not a question of imitating some ideal being; instead, each individual had to struggle with their own nature and all its imperfections. God was to be liberated from within, rather than discovered as external.

In the alchemical work, the nigredo, or blackening, is the first stage of the labour, which involves the burning off of all impurities. In psychological terms, it is a period of darkness and loss prior to the start of an easing of negativity and the move towards the more hopeful stages of growth and positive change. It is, in fact, a remarkably apt description of what happened to Vicky.

Where the alchemist has to isolate the chemicals, place them in a container, seal it and then heat the mixture, a similar process is occurring in the psyche. In his book *Dreams and Nightmares*, the psychiatrist Professor Ernest Hartmann – an expert on sleep and dreams as well as trauma – argues that dreams reflect the emotional concerns of the dreamer. This is most obvious in dreams that occur after acute trauma. By following a dream series, he shows how the emotional disturbance can be integrated and smoothed by the weaving in of material from other situations via analogy or metaphor, the predominant mode of thinking in dreams. This provides a broader context for the trauma and helps the individual overcome it.

In general then, the emotion of a problem that confronts us generates a tension within. This is the heating of the chemicals and if the vessel is sealed – that is, the tendency to project the problem on to someone else or simply to run away into alcohol or drugs or whatever is avoided

– we experience the full impact ourselves. As Kekulé was going crazy trying to figure out the structure of benzene, sufficient heat seems to have been generated in the unconscious to produce the dream of the Ouroboros, as we saw in Chapter 8. In Vicky's case, her suffering was the energy that finally caused the Aborigine to appear.

After her dream she experienced a dynamic shift within herself. Some deep battle had been won and she knew she was going to be all right:

> I feel I have been to hell and back but in some mysterious, incomprehensible way, it was all for my own good. With this comes a sense that I have completed my journey and yet am just starting it – a sort of cosmic knowledge, for want of a better expression. Now I just *know* who I am. I am still well, there is no sign of a return of the cancer. My career is expanding and, despite everything, I feel happier and more integrated than at any time in my life.

LIFE IN PROGRESS

> Look to your health; and if you have it, praise God, and value it next to a good conscience; for health is the second blessing that we mortals are capable of; a blessing that money cannot buy.
>
> (Izaak Walton, *The Compleat Angler*)

Vicky found that her dream opened up the wider issue of healing and intrigued her; she wanted to work out how it had turned her life round. At first she saw it as relating only to her cancer but after several years decided it was holistic: it affected her whole being – physical, spiritual, emotional and mental. The dream figure was the ideal, healthy person that Vicky now wanted to be. Paradoxically, she felt that already she had more or less attained this goal by adopting a positive view of life.

The Aborigine proved more helpful than some of the doctors Vicky had encountered. She couldn't stand the consultant, she said, because 'nothing nasty has ever happened to him in his life and I can't talk to him. I would much rather deal with a person who has had an awful time themselves. It feels much more comfortable.' This is the idea of the wounded healer, that only through one's own suffering can one understand the suffering of others.

In Greek mythology, Chiron the centaur was the wounded healer. Half man, half horse, he was the son of the Titan Cronos and therefore immortal. Whilst the rest of the centaurs – no relations – were wild and drunken followers of Dionysus, Chiron was famous for his wisdom and healing abilities. He was the tutor of many Greek heroes, including Asclepius, Achilles, Jason and Heracles. Among the skills he taught them were music and medicine.

In a fight with the other centaurs, Heracles accidentally wounded Chiron with a poisoned arrow. To escape an eternity of pain, Chiron gave his immortality to Prometheus. Chiron's descendants are the wise centaurs that feature in tales such as C. S. Lewis's chronicles of Narnia, where they are star-gazers who see into the future.

JUNG'S PSYCHOSIS

(*Query*: Does not modern psychology teach that definite danger attaches to deliberate stifling of any impulse, however unhallowed? Answer probably Yes. Cannot, however, ignore the fact that even more definite danger probably attached to encouragement of unhallowed impulse. Can only conclude that peril lies in more or less every direction.)

(E. M. Delafield, *The Provincial Lady Goes Further*)

Both Freud and Jung understood the concept of the wounded healer, for each of them had a 'creative illness' – Freud suffered from depression before he came up with his first major paper 'The Aetiology of Mental Illness' in 1896, and in the years following 1913 Jung had an illness closer to a psychosis. However, as it was not severe in outcome, he could probably best be categorized as 'pseudo-psychotic'. In a sense, healers need to stay ahead of whoever they are treating; as long as they understand things a bit better, they can be of use. Sometimes both healer and patient may be completely lost. Jung once famously opened an interview with 'So you're in the soup too!'

Although it is true that the more of life you experience the better able you will be to empathize and help, as a therapist you don't have to have resolved all of your own problems entirely. However, in order to help your patient with a specific problem you must be aware of it and working on it yourself. If you do not see it as having any relevance to you then you will be unaware of how it is interfering with the treatment.

After the publication of *The Psychology of the Unconscious*, later to become *Symbols of Transformation*, in 1911 had led to the break with Freud, Jung was effectively isolated. The following year he began to have visions of rivers of blood, and of floods across Europe: he had entered a dark phase. In 1914, he had three dreams of the world being frozen and all living green things being killed. Fortunately, the last of these had an optimistic ending:

> There stood a leaf-bearing tree but without fruit (my tree of life, I thought), whose leaves had been transformed by the effects of the frost into sweet grapes full of healing juices. I plucked the grapes and gave them to a large waiting crowd.

Jung was to undergo another five years of struggle with the visions and powerful emotional states that erupted from deeper layers of the unconscious. His isolation was paralleled by the destructive havoc of the Great War, and the connection of his early dreams and visions with the war is obvious. It was not until 1927 that a crucial dream came to lead him out of the wilderness. In this dream, he was with colleagues in Liverpool. The atmosphere was dark, dirty and depressing. Climbing higher, he found the city was arranged radially around a central square:

> In the centre was a round pool, and in the middle of it, a small island. While everything round about was obscured by rain, fog, smoke, and dimly lit darkness, the little island blazed with sunlight. On it stood a single tree, a magnolia,

in a shower of reddish blossoms. It was as though the tree stood in the sunlight and was at the same time the source of the sunlight.

For several years Jung had spontaneously been drawing mandalas – designs symbolizing the universe – in order to cope with his inner turmoil, and his dream was the culmination of this process.

Although he had found comfort and refuge in drawing the mandalas, it was only later, when Richard Wilhelm sent him his work on Eastern mysticism, *The Secret of the Golden Flower*, that he both understood the universal importance of the mandala and also began to move out of his profound isolation. In his autobiography he stresses its significance to him: 'I saw that everything, all paths I had been following, all steps I had taken, were leading back to a single point – namely, to the mid-point . . . the mandala is the centre. It is the exponent of all paths. It is the path to the centre, to individuation . . . in finding the mandala as an expression of the self I had attained what was for me the ultimate.'

THE MANDALA OF TIBETAN BUDDHISM

The nature of God is a circle of which the centre is everywhere and the circumference is nowhere.

(Anon, possibly Empedocles)

The mandala – which in Sanskrit means 'whole world' or 'healing circle' – is an ancient symbol. The word is also said to mean 'centre of the Universe in which a fully awakened being abides'. A legend relates that the founder of Tibetan Buddhism, Padmasambhava (Guru Rinpoche) was born at the centre of a lake, in a lotus blossom. The clear blue lake named after him is believed to have great healing power. Circles – like the Ouroboros – represent unity, eternity and wholeness.

Mandalas are used as a focus for meditation, and there is an immense variety of them. Designed as intricately detailed imaginary palaces, most contain a host of images of deities and earthly objects, each of which represents an aspect of wisdom or a spiritual principle. Everything in the palace has special significance in the pattern and teaches a particular lesson. Mandalas can be created in media such as fabrics or paper; they can also be three-dimensional. The sand mandala developed by Tibetan monks is constructed using sand that is first of all dyed and then placed on a large table. Despite the meticulous work that has gone into it, this mandala exists for a short time. As artist and counsellor Clare Goodwin explains:

> The design is ritually prepared over a period of days, then blown away to represent the impermanence of life. The sand, which has been blessed throughout the process, is seen to benefit the lands and rivers it comes in contact with. Tibetans believe that a sand mandala contains the knowledge [needed] to achieve enlightenment in this lifetime.

Native American medicine wheels and sand paintings adopt similar symbolism, as do the rose windows of Gothic cathedrals. Like the mandala, these circular windows of radiant coloured glass are intended to inspire awakening of the spirit. In the twenty-first century, as in medieval times, 'Sitting in the earthly darkness, contemplating the light pouring through the inspired designs prompts a powerful experience.'

SHAMANIC DREAMING

An explosion of infra-red shoots the colours of the spectrum from the horizon to the heavens and a surreal Tibetan sunrise greets me, from far below . . . The true test in life comes after Everest. We cannot survive on top for long anyway, and surely it is the people and the valley below which sustain us. As our Sherpa friends say, 'When you get to the top, keep climbing!'

(Dave Rodney, Canadian climber, in *Everest*)

In Chapter 3 we looked at lucid dreams: those in which we are able to direct the course of events. Tibetan Buddhism, along with Hindu transcendental meditation and shamanism throughout both Americas, contains numerous accounts of this. Some individuals seem to be unusually gifted, and the descriptions of their dream journeys hint at an experience we can barely contemplate. Dreaming lies at the centre of these cultures, and is taken for granted in a way that is alien to the western world.

In an article on interpreting dreams in the Amerindian nations, Barbara Tedlock, Professor of Anthropology at the State University of New York, gives an account of a Cahuilla shaman, Ruby Modesto, who dreamed so deeply that often she could not find her way back to consciousness; eventually her uncle, also a shaman, had to be called in and he managed to bring her out of the dream. 'When I was about ten years old I dreamed to the 13th level,' she explains:

> the way you do that is by remembering to tell yourself to go to sleep in your 1st level ordinary dream. You consciously tell yourself to lie down and go to sleep. Then you dream a second dream. This is the 2nd level and the prerequisite for real Dreaming . . . You can tell yourself ahead of time where you want to go, or what you want to see, or what you want to learn . . . On the 3rd level you learn to see unusual things, not of this world. The hills and terrain are different.

Lucid dreaming here is highly developed, with the dreamer scaling unknown heights while constantly controlling the ability to think and dream simultaneously. The dream world is suffused with energy and power, which is why it made such an impact on Vicky. It is not without risk, and must be treated with respect. Ruby's distressed father made her promise not to explore these distant levels until she knew how to return from them without help.

SPIRITUAL GUIDES FROM OTHER REALMS

Who had uttered these words? . . . They came from deep inside me, from my soul. Never before had I believed or suspected that I had a soul but just then I knew I had. I knew also that my soul was friendly, was my senior in years and was solely concerned for my own welfare. For convenience I called him Joe. I felt a little reassured to know that I was not altogether alone. Joe was helping me.

(Flann O'Brien, *The Third Policeman*)

Our dreams are sometimes crowded: overrun by people we meet in daily life who come and go less predictably than usual and behave erratically and fantastically. Still, most of the time we know who they are and their activities are no more peculiar than we would expect, for a dream. But there are dream figures who make more of an impact. Either the circumstances are remarkable – as when Rachel and her cousin simultaneously dreamed of their grandfather a few months after his death – or the figures themselves command our attention, like the Aborigine in Vicky's dream.

Some of them have a very definite spiritual purpose. Since ancient times, dreams have been viewed as an authentic means of divine communication. The Old Testament makes this explicit:

the Lord came down in the pillar of the cloud, and stood in the door of the tabernacle, and called Aaron and Miriam: and they both came forth.

And he said, Hear now my words: If there be a prophet among you, I the Lord will make myself known unto him in a vision, and will speak unto him in a dream.

(Numbers 12: 5–6)

In the Bible, God speaks to his people in dreams either directly or through angels: 'In a dream, in a vision of the night ... he openeth the ears of men.' God orders

Abraham to offer his son Isaac as a sacrifice, as a test of faith; and in the New Testament Gospels angels are kept busy conveying divine warnings and advice to Joseph and Mary: the Holy Family are instructed not to return to Herod; to flee into Egypt; and are then directed, again by an angel, to move on to Israel.

Somewhat confusingly, the Israelites are also warned *against* listening to their dreams:

> If there arise among you a prophet, or a dreamer of dreams, and giveth thee a sign or a wonder,
>
> And the sign or the wonder come to pass, whereof he spake unto thee, saying, Let us go after other gods, which thou hast not known, and let us serve them;
>
> Thou shalt not hearken unto the words of that prophet, or that dreamer of dreams: for the Lord your God proveth you, to know whether ye love the Lord your God with all your heart and with all your soul . . .
>
> And that prophet, or that dreamer of dreams, shall be put to death.
>
> (Deuteronomy 13: 1–5)

Clearly, some judgement was required in the interpretation of dreams.

DANCING TO THE RHYTHM OF THE SONG

Spiritual guidance in dreams is found in many of the major religious traditions, including Judaism and Islam; the Qur'an is traditionally held to have been revealed to Muhammad in a dream by the angel Gabriel.

Hindu gods and goddesses too appear in dreams. Prahlad Chandra Bramachari, a poor Indian, who worked as a sweeper and dish-washer, said that in his dreams the goddess Kali visited him and instructed him in meditation and yoga. Bramachari, a devotee of the goddess, experienced trance states and visions throughout his life. He spent his later years as a Kali priest in Ramnathpur, West Bengal, where his goddess worship celebrations attracted thousands of visitors. His followers spoke of the intensity and power of his gaze, and there were even claims that Bramachari himself could enter their dreams:

I once had a dream of Baba before I met him, in which I was playing a guitar and singing spiritual songs. He appeared in a loincloth, dancing with one arm up in the air, his legs moving rapidly, stomping to the rhythm of the song. Suddenly, the scene changed, and he was staring at me, six inches from my face, his eyes focused intently on me. A strange power radiated from his eyes. I felt myself expand inwardly, and my heart was full of a bliss that spread through my body. Later I learned that one of his devotees had given him a picture of me. When I met him months later, as soon as I walked into the room his translator told me that Baba wanted to know if I remembered him, that he had visited me.

As we have seen, divine figures enter dreams for a variety of reasons – to give comfort and reassurance; to offer advice (often firmly); to warn of danger; and to reveal glimpses of the future. Here the reason for the visit appears to have been conversion to the faith. Occasionally these figures seem to have quite down-to-earth, practical reasons for their intervention. However, it may not always be possible to pin down the identity of the helpers, as one baffling case reveals.

HELPING VOICES

It is the province of knowledge to speak and it is the privilege of wisdom to listen.

(Oliver Wendell Holmes, *The Poet at the Breakfast Table*)

Throughout this book we have wondered why dreams are not more specific and verbal and do not simply state their meaning in words. Vicky found the key to her healing in a numinous figure. However, the hearing of voices while awake has a long and important tradition in all major religions. Is there a connection between waking hallucinations and dreaming? The following fascinating case history, which is summarized from the *British Medical Journal*, illustrates this issue.

A middle-aged previously healthy woman was at home reading in the winter of 1984 when she heard a 'distinct voice inside her head'. It said, 'Please don't be afraid. I know it must be shocking for you to hear me speaking to you like this, but this is the easiest way I could think of. My friend and I used to work at the Children's Hospital, Great Ormond Street, and we would like to help you.'

The woman had heard of Great Ormond Street Hospital, but had never been there. Her children were well, so that was not it. She felt very frightened. Then the voice spoke again: 'To help you see we are sincere, we would like you to check out the following,' it said – and gave her three separate pieces of information which she did not possess at the time. She checked them out and found they were true, but this did not help: already she had concluded that she had 'gone mad'. Her GP referred her urgently.

She saw the author of the *BMJ* piece, a psychiatrist, who diagnosed functional hallucinatory psychosis and offered counselling and anti-psychotic medication. After a couple of weeks' treatment the voices disappeared, and the woman went on holiday. But while she was abroad they returned and told her to go home immediately for treatment as there was something wrong with her.

The voices told the woman to go to the scanning department of a large London hospital; they even gave her its address. The voices told the woman she had a tumour and that her brain stem was inflamed. They had been right before, so she was very distressed when she saw the psychiatrist the next day. He referred her for a scan to reassure her, although he had found no indication of any problem. The request was initially rejected, but finally the hospital agreed to the scan and a tumour was indeed found, despite the puzzling lack of symptoms. An immediate operation was the surgeon's recommendation. The voices were in agreement.

When the woman recovered consciousness after the operation the voices said, 'We are pleased to have helped you. Goodbye.'

She recovered and her medication stopped. Twelve years later she remained well. The voices have never returned.

When the case was presented, the doubters had a simple explanation: manipulation of the British health service by a woman who had come to the UK from abroad, already knowing she had a tumour. The author points out that she had arrived fifteen years earlier, was therefore entitled to NHS treatment, and in any case had no symptoms. Another explanation was that she had sensed something wrong, and this led her to fear she had a brain tumour. Her unconscious knowledge of hospitals manifested itself in the form of auditory hallucinations; the disappearance of the voices after the operation showed they were probably related to the tumour itself.

The final explanation was the psychic one: she was being helped by thought transference from people with psychic abilities who had intuited her problem. None of the above seems to provide much of an answer.

In my own clinical practice I have worked with people who have had such voices. In the case of one woman, they were multiple and she heard them on both sides of her head telling her what to do and what not to do. Slowly, over many years, they seem to have guided her to a place of tranquillity but it has not been an easy journey. This woman does not suffer from a psychiatric illness; where the voices came from and why they are there remain a mystery.

Jung described a similar case: a woman who was schizophrenic and had 'voices' throughout her body. One, in the centre of her chest, she called 'God's voice', and Jung told her to take notice of it. 'As a rule this voice made very sensible remarks,' he wrote, 'and with its aid I managed very well with the patient. Once the voice said, "Let him test you on the Bible!"' So Jung set her a chapter to read, and over seven years he tested her every two weeks. Eventually, after six years, the right side of the woman's body was entirely free of the voices while there had been no increase in their intensity on the left side. Jung described this as a half-cure.

While we do not understand the nature of hallucinations and their relation to the underlying activity of the brain, including dreaming, it seems likely that they are interconnected. Not all voices can be helpful or trusted but some appear to be of value; just as not all dreams appear of value but some most certainly are.

SUFI SAINTS AND MODERN EGYPTIANS

In the 1990s, Valerie Hoffman was working on the role of visions in modern Egyptian life. In her research she found that people often listened to their dreams and acted on them. One visitation, which had a valuable, and very practical, outcome, illustrates how dreams are accepted as an integral part of life in the contemporary Islamic world:

In two very similar cases, middle-class, college-educated women – whose families had no connections with Sufism and who claimed no previous knowledge of the major Sufi saints – were afflicted by physical and psychological illnesses that medical doctors seemed unable to cure, when suddenly they were visited in their dreams by great Sufi saints, both deceased and living. They found themselves propelled by these dreams to seek the solace of the shrines of the great deceased saints and to seek blessing, guidance and healing from specific living spiritual guides. Both of them found the guides they had seen in their visions, and one of them claimed that her dream had shown her the route and physical layout of the house of the woman who was to be her main spiritual guide.

Healing, to most of us, has an aura of calmness, serenity and caring: this is the 'blessing' these Egyptian women found from their spiritual guides. It suggests peace and the concentration of a Tibetan monk contemplating a mandala. This is one end of the spectrum. The face of healing shown in David Chetlahe Paladin's life is startlingly at odds with this.

KILL OR CURE

> But (when so sad thou canst not sadder)
> Cry; – and upon thy so sore loss
> Shall shine the traffic of Jacob's ladder
> Pitched betwixt Heaven and Charing Cross.
> (Francis Thompson, 'The Kingdom of God')

David Paladin was a Navajo Indian who grew up on a reservation, then was drafted into the American army in 1941 and sent on a secret operation behind enemy lines. The logic was that when the Germans intercepted messages transmitted in Native American languages they could not interpret them.

David was captured, tortured and spent years as a prisoner of war. When the camps were liberated, he was found unconscious and dying. Back in the United States, he spent over two years in a coma and when he finally awoke, he was so weakened by the injuries he had sustained in the camp that he could barely walk. He made up his mind to say a last goodbye to his people and then retire to a veterans' hospital.

At the reservation, his family and friends were horrified by his condition and they held a council to decide how to help him. The action they took was, to say the least, unexpected:

The elders approached David, yanked the braces off his legs, tied a rope around his waist, and threw him into deep water. 'David, call your spirit back,' they commanded. 'Your spirit is no longer in your body. If you can't call your spirit back, we will let you go. No one can live without their spirit. Your spirit is your power.'

It was the hardest thing he had ever done. 'I saw the faces of those Nazi soldiers,' David said. 'I lived through all those months in the prison camp. I knew that I had to release my anger and hatred. I could barely keep myself from drowning, but I prayed to let the anger out of my body. That's all I prayed, and my prayers were answered.'

David recovered. He learned to walk again and subsequently became a shaman, artist and Christian minister. Within himself, he had fought the darkness of Nazi power, overcome it and gained the strength to work as a healer. Now he could help others to 'call back their power' when their life force was threatened. Without his literal wounding, his skill in healing might never have awoken.

Vicky's experiences were less extreme than David Paladin's, but in the context of her life just as important. Her illness had drained her, made her feel old. 'It's one of the things that makes surviving difficult,' she said. 'You almost feel you've completed your life's course. But then you have to go on living. That was what I was wrestling with at the time.' Like David, she felt worn out; and although neither of them really contemplated taking their own life, they did think of just giving up; which was the same thing, Vicky said.

At the moment when she wasn't looking for help, the dream arrived. 'If anything, I had resolved with chaos that there wasn't an answer,' she told me. The dimension that was added to her life brought her a vitality that she thought had gone for ever. And the Aborigine was there to stay:

He's not ageing. But he is age itself. I'm sure he is a sage. He is timeless. He's like something that goes back thousands of years – almost a conduit for the wisdom of the ages. It's like having a staff. He gives me strength, he doesn't go away. He's not judgmental. Very affirming of me.

On just one occasion has Vicky felt especially close to her dream, although this time the landscape was quite different. She was at Crawford Lake in Ontario, a historic First Nations site. It is a quiet settlement in the woods by the edge of the water. 'There's a boardwalk and you can go right round the edge and there are turtles, and it was incredibly peaceful. I sensed that he was there as well; I was surrounded by the qualities that were in him.'

11

THE TREE OF LIFE

There were scraps of lime in the bin where I keep leftover bits. These neat blond pieces of wood had once been parts of trees with leaves that stirred in the wind. Trees are living things; they have souls, they have significances; Odin, hanging on his tree through days and nights, acquired wisdom; Absalom was caught in a tree by his hair and was killed; Christ was crucified on the tree of his cross. Walk into a wood and you can feel the trees listening.

(Russell Hoban, *The Bat Tattoo*)

Vicky's compelling dream of the hot sun and shining waters of the outback changed her whole outlook on life. Significant dreams can be like that: arriving unannounced, they baffle us with their apparent irrelevance to the aim and course of our existence. Not everyone is so disconcerted. For Anna, the final dreamer in this book, the concrete reality of daily life intertwines with dreaming; they weave together into a continuum where all events are equally valid.

Despite an idyllic childhood, Anna had always been troubled by images of mortality. 'In every paradise there is a snake, which must at some time surface,' she explained. 'In my case it was something like a foretaste of death, which has haunted my life ever since.'

Over the years, Anna said, her dreamscape fulfilled the function of preparing her for adverse events, as if intent on taking the sting out of them: when she was troubled, she found that her dreams would console and support her. Strangely, in happier, more positive times the opposite happened: they caused her unease. Her dreams seemed to be acting as a counterbalance to life on the surface. For most of her life, Anna had been aware of her dreams and reflected on their significance:

> My mother used to tell me that I had got out of bed the wrong side. It set me thinking, and I wonder if the trouble does not really begin long before then – when one first gets into bed and enters that other world. People talk about the small hours, but there is nothing small about them at all. They are the time when a lot of the real action of our lives takes place and the dream leaves its legacy.

When Anna's second pregnancy ended in miscarriage at eight weeks it was not entirely a surprise to her as her dreams had been, to her mind, clear warnings. Still, the event was no less distressing. Within two months, she discovered she was pregnant again. Now she was very nervous. Seven weeks into the pregnancy, she had a very strong dream:

I was in our bed, here in London. The floor was giving way beneath me — only the bare wooden floor joists were holding me up. There was water running down the walls into the drawing-room below. And then I realized that the water was sticky and glutinous and that in fact it was blood.

I was terrified that the floor would give way, but our builder — who was in reality working on the house at the time — was there. He pointed out that the main beam is under our bed, and told me not to worry. 'Look,' he said, 'this beam is solid oak.' And when I looked I saw that it was indeed a living tree, not just a piece of wood. In the moment of waking I understood that it was actually the Tree of Life.

The dream, Anna said, did not have a frightening feel to it, however shocking it sounds. Nevertheless, a few days later she had to be admitted to hospital with a severe haemorrhage; it seemed inevitable that she would miscarry again, and at the same stage of her pregnancy. She had a long wait through the night for a scan, during which time her condition seemed to improve. A nun visited the ward. 'You will be all right,' she told Anna.

Next morning, Anna was relieved to hear the electrical impulse of the baby's heart beating, and to make out the image of its head on the scan. But she wasn't in the clear yet. Five more times she had to return to the hospital, the latest time at nineteen weeks: 'I lost a massive amount of blood and was taken by ambulance on a drip,' she recalled. Against all expectations, the baby was still alive.

Then, on the night of 5 June 1995, some fifty-one years after my father landed on the beaches of Normandy, I understood that this unexpected survivor would arrive. There was controlled panic when, at 3.10 on the morning of the 6th, a baby presented itself as an undiagnosed breech into the world. The delivery room was suddenly filled with a crash team, but the small blue person of Victoria was safely – if strangely – delivered into the dawn. A day to remember.

INTERPRETATION

And he shewed me a pure river of water of life, clear as crystal, proceeding out of the throne of God and of the Lamb. In the midst of the street of it, and on either side of the river, was there the tree of life, which bare twelve manner of fruits, and yielded her fruit every month: and the leaves of the tree were for the healing of the nations.

(Revelation 22: 1–2)

Anna's dream of the Tree of Life is like Sally's dream of the scruffy man handing out bibles. It speaks of another reality underlying our version of life. Life, it suggests, is not so haphazard as we think. For Anna's child to survive one threatened miscarriage early in pregnancy is extremely fortunate, but to survive six is quite extraordinary. To 'know' this in advance, through her dream, is also remarkable. The builder seems, to my mind, to have a link with the bearded man in Sally's dream but he is more positive – possibly because his news is more positive. And there, holding Anna and her new baby, is life itself, solid and unshakeable.

CELTIC TREES OF POWER

Up the airy mountain,
  Down the rushy glen,
We daren't go a-hunting
  For fear of little men . . .
They stole little Bridget
  For seven years long;
When she came down again
  Her friends were all gone.
They took her lightly back,
  Between night and morrow,
They thought that she was fast asleep,
  But she was dead with sorrow.

(William Allingham, 'The Fairies')

As the quotation from Russell Hoban at the head of this chapter illustrates, trees are pervaded with spiritual meaning. This is true in Britain and Ireland as much as in shamanic cultures. From the yew, ash and birch to the hawthorn, holly, elder and oak, the trees of the British Isles are ringed with tradition. In the past, their strength and qualities were respected and they were used for many purposes. Protection against enchantment and the evil eye – which we might call negative energy – was one of them.

Two of the most potent trees in the Celtic tradition are the rowan and the hazel. Rowan was especially valuable in protecting against witchcraft and enchantment: rowan twigs bent into the form of a cross are still placed above doorways today, to ward off bad fortune. The small five-pointed star on each rowan berry resembles a pentagram, an ancient protective symbol, while the vibrant orange-red of the berries in autumn counters the dangerous green of the uncanny inhabitants of fairyland.

No relation whatsoever to the twentieth century's whimsical flower fairies, these 'little people' were far from lovable; they may have been angels who fell from heaven with Lucifer; or they may be spirits of the dead. Some said the fairies had been in the world since before Adam. Whatever their origin, it was known that they lacked souls and occupied themselves in attempts to steal human babies and replace them with changelings. Their fairy thorn trees must never be dug up. Vengeance could be swift: the modern use of the word 'stroke' for cerebral haemorrhage derives from the 'fairy stroke' that left its victim literally speechless. The honey taste of rowan was also believed to bring rejuvenation and its boughs were woven into roofs to shelter the 'happy dead'.

Sacred to poets, the hazels of wisdom grew at the heads of Ireland's seven great rivers. Hazelnuts dropping into the water caused 'bubbles of mystic inspiration' to form; the Salmon of Knowledge that swims through Irish legend gained wisdom by eating hazelnuts and rowan berries. The reason why the salmon has such power is unknown; one theory is that its ability to move between salt and fresh water suggests the passage from this world to the next.

To W. B. Yeats, the hazel was the Irish version of the Tree of Life: as well as giving rise to inspiration, hazel was used for the 'wishing rods' of diviners and it had a strong healing force. One story of Dian Cecht, the principal healing god of the ancient Irish, declares that his spring could cure every mortal wound except decapitation. Whether this is true or not, we will never know. But his fame is still alive today:

> In modern folklore Dian Cecht's porridge is a cure for
> colds, sore throat, phlegm, and worms: it is made of hazel
> nuts, dandelion, woodsorrel, chickweed and oatmeal.

THE TREES OF CALEDONIA

> I have dim mystic sympathies with tree and hill reaching
> far back into childhood . . . An old park is my delight and
> I could tumble about it for ever.
>
> (Alfred Tennyson, Letter to Emily Sellwood, 1838)

The Tree of Life is a symbol that lies at the heart of many cultures, and trees have been venerated since ancient times. How many more generations will be able to delight in the trees that grace the natural world and keep it alive?

All over the planet, humanity is going about its business: the rainforest falls, toxic chemicals run into the rivers, the air is polluted by industry, the whales and dolphins die; entire species become extinct. Nowadays, statements like this have lost their impact. Eco-fatigue has set in. But it's not all bad news. We can find some cause for optimism in Scotland.

To the Romans, Scotland was known as Caledonia, which means 'wooded heights'. Once, the Caledonian Forest stretched across the Highlands: today less than 1 per cent of the trees survive. The charity Trees for Life, which grew out of the Findhorn Foundation, is attempting not only to limit the damage to Scotland's trees, but to increase the diversity and vitality of the area; to help the

Earth heal itself. Impelled by the vision of an increasingly worn-out and impoverished world, Trees for Life's view is positive: 'People are learning to work with nature, rather than against her.' The need to do this is vital, for it is those of us alive now who 'will determine which of our fellow species and intact ecosystems survive into the future'. Despite the scare stories, it is not too late: the Tree of Life, in all its many manifestations, may remain alive for generations to come.

THE SHAMANIC PRAYER TREE

The Axis of the World has been concretely represented, either by the pillars that support the house, or in the form of isolated stakes, called 'World Pillars'. For the Eskimo, for example, the Pillar of the Sky is identical with the pole at the center of their dwellings.

(Mircea Eliade, *Shamanism*)

The River of Life and the Tree of Life are symbiotically linked. As the course of the River of Life runs from birth onwards, so Yggdrasil, the World Tree of Norse mythology, has its roots in the past, lives in the present and stretches its branches towards the future. It nourishes all life, both spiritual and physical. It sustains us in the way that the beam of solid oak underpinned Anna's bed in her dream. The Tree has many varieties, from the shamanic world tree to the True Cross on which Christ was crucified, his atonement for mankind's sins bringing eternal life. In essence, they are all the same.

Ragged pieces of material tied to thorn trees near

healing springs in Ireland are evidence of prayer and hope. In a far distant part of the world the intentions and reverence are the same, even if the prayers are directed to different gods.

In central Russia live the Buryat Mongolians, a shamanic people. In the Buryat Republic the environment contains thousands of species of animal and plant, as well as forests even bigger than the rainforests of South America. Here Father Sky and Mother Earth are revered, and trees are the homes of powerful spirits. Each tree symbolizes the centre of the world, the place where heaven and earth touch and time and place converge, the 'still point of the turning world'.

The *barisaa*, or prayer tree, is an important site of worship in Siberian and Mongolian shamanism. One ritual is designed to bring peace and spiritual cleansing and is often performed at the site of a massacre or battle. Here, it is believed, the restless souls of those whose lives have ended abruptly continue to spread confusion, misery and despair, so their evil and vengeful thoughts need to be calmed. The 'peace tree' ritual is also carried out in violent inner-city areas. An array of items is used – from salt, sand and juniper to vodka and wooden spoons.

At prayer trees, Buryats also make offerings of tobacco, or tie ribbons to the branches in honour of the spirits. The tying on of the ribbons must be done with a specific intention, for example to bring peace, healing or luck.

According to the Geser Fund, whose aim is to promote preservation of the ecology of Siberia and to share its ancient wisdom with the outside world, the region is still relatively untouched by the modern industrial way of life but there are ominous signs that this is changing. As in Scotland, the demands of industry are threatening both the forests and *tegsh* – the shamanic way of living in balance and in consciousness of one's true nature and purpose. Bennie LeBeau, whose Medicine Wheel ceremony in Yellowstone Park was described in Chapter 7, is a spiritual relation of those who carry out prayer tree rituals to cleanse the world of evil and violent thoughts and draw calm out of chaos.

THE WORLD'S RIM

Give me my Scallop shell of quiet,
My staffe of Faith to walke upon,
My Scrip of Joy, Immortall diet,
My bottle of salvation:
My Gowne of Glory, hopes true gage,
And thus Ile take my pilgrimage.

('The Passionate Mans Pilgrimage')

The idea that life is a journey from the cradle to the grave and then beyond is an obvious and an old one. Often, as noted in Chapter 9, our journey is imagined as a voyage along a river. Our life's odyssey – defined as a 'long, eventful journey' – can also be a pilgrimage or search. In the fifteenth-century play *Everyman*, God sends Death to order Everyman to go on just such a pilgrimage; he is not permitted to escape, or to 'defer this matter to another day', as he hopefully suggests. He even fails to bribe Death with £1,000 (a vast amount in those days). Like the rest of us, he complains that he isn't ready yet. But there's no getting away from it: he has to go. Confident at first, Everyman calls on his friends – Fellowship, Kindred, Beauty, Strength and Goods among them – but when they find out what's involved, each makes his excuse and Everyman must travel on alone. 'I have the cramp in my toe,' his cousin explains. Guided by Knowledge, in the end it is only Good Deeds that can speak for him. Socrates, according to Plato's *Phaedo*, had similar views – moderation, justice, courage, freedom and truth were, he thought, the qualities needed for 'the journey to the world below'.

John Bunyan's *Pilgrim's Progress*, originally published in 1678, is one of the best-known allegories of human life as a journey. An itinerant tinker, Bunyan was a man with a mission; viewed as a subversive and ridiculed as a 'pestilent fellow' at his trial, he was convicted of preaching without a licence and eventually spent twelve years or so in Bedford Jail. His hero, Christian, along with Mr Worldly Wiseman and Giant Despair, would have seemed like family to most children in Britain until at least late Victorian times, for *Pilgrim's Progress* was one of the few books thought moral enough for them to read on the Sabbath. From it they would have learned that each of us is on a pilgrimage 'from This World to That Which Is to Come'. More than 300 years later we are less confident. 'I try to see the line which leads through my life into the world, and out of the world again,' Jung wrote. But is the world which is to come the Celestial City?

A NEW LEVEL OF BEING

Has anyone supposed it lucky to be born?
I hasten to inform him or her it is just as lucky to die,
   and I know it.
I pass death with the dying, and birth with the
   new-washed babe
. . . and am not contained between my hat and boots.

(Walt Whitman, 'Song of Myself')

Marie-Louise von Franz, reflecting on life after death, points out that the problem is that we find it difficult to imagine our self continuing in any kind of afterlife without our body: we identify almost completely with the physical body. This is a very western standpoint. Opinions on what happens after death are certainly different in the shamanic world picture.

From his research in shamanic communities, Mircea Eliade discovered much about the 'beyond': the world of the dead visited by shamans in their ecstatic journeys. On their return, the shamans describe in minute detail the lands and the 'wondrous forms and figures' they have encountered; the result, says Eliade, is that this 'unknown and terrifying' world gains a structure, is organized into specific patterns and over time grows familiar. Its inhabitants become 'visible', with their own personalities and life stories, which helps to make death acceptable.

As Eliade stresses, there is a crucial difference in attitude between western and other cultures. 'Anguish before Nothingness and Death seems to be a specifically modern phenomenon,' he notes:

In all other, non-European cultures, that is in the other religions, Death is never felt as an absolute end or as Nothingness: it is regarded rather as a rite of passage to another mode of being; and for that reason always referred to in relation to the symbolisms and rituals of nitiation, rebirth or resurrection.

Non-Europeans do of course feel anguish when faced with death, Eliade goes on to say. However, death for them is not terrifying. Its existence does not make human life appear absurd or futile, for 'it is accorded the highest value as an experience indispensable to the attainment of a new level of being'.

Death is the great Initiation. But in the modern world Death is emptied of its religious meaning; that is why it is assimilated to Nothingness; and before Nothingness modern man is paralysed.

John's dream, in Chapter 8, seemed to relate to the transitional stage between life and a new stage of being, just as Patrick, in Chapter 9, may be seen as approaching his mother as she was passing through an unstable border-land around the time of her death. In *Memories, Dreams, Reflections*, Jung commented that although it is impossible to produce proof of the continuance of the soul after death, there are nevertheless 'hints', or 'experiences that make us thoughtful'. Some of these, as we know, take the form of dreams.

THE STRANGE CASE OF MARGARET McQUEEN

The sky whitens as if lit by three suns.
My mother shades her eyes and looks my way
Over the drifted stream. My father spins
A stone along the water. Leisurely,

They beckon to me from the other bank.
I hear them call, 'See where the stream-path is!
Crossing is not as hard as you might think.'

I had not thought that it would be like this.

(Charles Causley, 'Eden Rock')

Jeff Zaslow of the *Chicago Sun-Times* published an article based on my idea of dreams as expressing the physical state of the body, not just psychological ideas. In his article he asked readers if they had any examples. This story was among the replies, which were forwarded to me.

About twenty-five years ago, my mum found my dad sitting on the steps of our back porch. He was crying. She asked him what was wrong and he said he had had a very vivid dream.

In the dream, his mother and father were standing with their arms outstretched towards him. They were very clear in the dream but there was an older woman behind them who was very hazy — 'smoke-like', he said. He did not know who she was. I must tell you now, Mum and Dad were from Ireland. Mum told him, 'Aw Tim, it was just a dream' and they both continued their day.

He had the dream two more times, but, strangely, the woman became clearer and his parents became more smoke-like in the background. She now was in front. A final dream came on Sunday and Dad asked her who she was. She told him 'Margaret McQueen'. Dad did not know who she was; the name meant nothing to him.

On Tuesday, my mother called and told me Dad was in the hospital — in a coma. He died the following Saturday. He never woke up.

At the wake, my sister was telling some of my parents' friends about the dream, and a very old woman from the 'old country' said, 'Margaret McQueen was the name of the midwife that brought your father into this world.' I nearly passed out. She brought him into this world and then led him home.

This dream and Anna's appear to agree with Jung's idea of a greater reality underlying our conscious experience. The Tree of Life may remind us of those ads where a man walks on water. We know he is on some solid surface but because it is just under the water we can't see it. That is like life, sometimes. To us it seems as if we are making it up as we go along, that there is no plan. Could it be that a path is mapped out and we are walking along it, with support that we cannot see?

When we see the world as external to us, as 'out there', we will always find it hard to integrate the dream world into everyday life. By contrast, the shaman seems to be able to live in harmony with his dreams, and throughout the ages dreams have informed the life of many cultures. From a modern western perspective, tribal communities are 'primitive' cultures. But looked at from a different angle they may appear more, not less, advanced.

'MORE THINGS IN HEAVEN AND EARTH'

'Amanda,' Hotchkiss said, 'the crane didn't exist in Ancient Egypt. There wasn't a crane until someone invented it.'

'That's just what I'm saying,' she said. 'You don't pay attention. It's always been there, in people's minds, waiting for them to discover it. The crane was sitting there all along. They just refused to see it. It's a question of how you look at things.'

(Carol Hill, *Amanda & the Eleven Million Mile High Dancer*)

Shakespeare, speaking through Hamlet, acknowledges that different philosophies exist. Horatio didn't have all the answers and today we are no better at accounting for 'wondrous strange' phenomena. One of them is REM: the rapid eye movements that occur during sleep. In Chapter 2 it was noted that although REM is clearly very old developmentally, we still have at best only tentative ideas of its function. Of course, it may have none, but that seems most unlikely because of its widespread occurrence in nature. The paralysis that accompanies REM appears to put mammals at a disadvantage, which adds to the feeling that it must have an important role to play.

In the nineteenth century, Alfred Russel Wallace, the Welsh naturalist, was puzzled. A pioneer in the field of evolution by means of natural selection, Wallace sent Darwin a memoir in 1858 that forced him to modify and hasten publication of *The Origin of Species*. Wallace, of course, knew nothing of REM; what *he* couldn't understand was the surprising mental ability of an early type of *Homo sapiens*:

> The aborigine or Cro-Magnon possesses a potential intelligence that vastly exceeds anything that he might need for coping with his natural environment . . . But why the devil did this potential evolve? It couldn't have arisen for learning Latin in English schools.

Ramachandran and Blakeslee discuss this in their book, *Phantoms in the Brain*, focusing on a really crucial point that Wallace makes: 'An instrument has been developed in advance of the needs of its possessor . . . Here is an instance in which evolution appears to have foreknowledge.'

The brain of Cro-Magnon man was capable of doing much more than was ever likely to be required of it: there was no obvious need for its large size. It may be that REM too – closely associated with dreaming – has a higher function, of little value until the further development of human consciousness. As humanity becomes more highly developed and 'intelligent', will the dream come into its own? Or has it guided us all along?

AYAHUASCA

Where the bee sucks, there suck I:
In a cowslip's bell I lie;
There I couch when owls do cry.
On the bat's back I do fly . . .

(William Shakespeare, Ariel's song)

Another puzzle relates to the complex brew *ayahuasca*, used throughout the Amazonian region as a consciousness-altering drug. *Ayahuasca* (which has many other names) has been known for hundreds of years, but how it was discovered remains a mystery to western investigators. In his book *The Cosmic Serpent*, Jeremy Narby explains the problem:

> Here are people without electron microscopes who choose, among 80,000 Amazonian plant species, the leaves of a bush containing a . . . brain hormone, which they combine with a vine containing substances that inactivate an enzyme of the digestive tract, which would otherwise block the effect. And they do this to modify their consciousness. It is as if they knew about the molecular properties of plants and the art of combining them, and when one asks them how they knew these things, they say their knowledge comes directly from [the] plants.

Stanley Krippner cites this in a study of shamanic states of consciousness and confirms that he can illustrate it from his own experience. For thirty years he worked with a shamanic healer called Rolling Thunder who often used plants medicinally even when he could not logically have known their properties. How could he be sure they were safe?

Rolling Thunder told him:

> 'I ask the plant what it is good for. Some plants are only meant to be beautiful. Other plants are meant for food.

Still others are to be used as medicine. Once a healing plant has spoken to me, I ask its permission to take it with me and add it to my medicine pouch.'

In the West, we cannot return to shamanism: that unified view of the world is long gone. We have freed ourselves from a vast amount of primitive superstition, which often manifests itself as obsessive behaviour, but in doing so have lost our inner relationship with the old mind. Now we have global pharmaceutical giants instead of an instinctive understanding of the plants and creatures that live on the same planet as us.

Freedom from faith is more than the abandonment of superstition. As Eliade points out, it produces a world-view in which death is no more than the end of life. It is a high price to pay for progress.

ON THE TRACK OF LIFE

Every funeral may justly be considered as a summons to prepare for that state into which it shows us that we must some time enter; and the summons is more loud and piercing as the event of which it warns us is at less distance. To neglect at any time preparation for death is to sleep on our post at a siege; but to omit it in old age is to sleep at an attack.

(Samuel Johnson, in the *Rambler*)

Jung devoted his life to working on meaning and religion and how they relate to psychology. On the subject of life after death, he has very important things to say. From analysis of his own dreams and those of others, over the years he shaped and revised his views. To an ageing person in particular, he states, death is a momentous issue: like Everyman, he is faced with an imperative question and he cannot avoid answering it:

> To this end he ought to have a myth about death, for reason shows him nothing but the dark pit into which he is descending. Myth, however, can conjure up other images for him, helpful and enriching pictures of life in the land of the dead. If he believes in them, or greets them with some measure of credence, he is being just as right or just as wrong as someone who does not believe in them. But while the man who despairs marches towards nothingness, the one who has placed his faith in the archetype follows the tracks of life and lives right into his death. Both, to be sure, remain in uncertainty, but the one lives against his instincts, the other with them.

CONCLUSION

Legend has it that when the gods made the human race, they fell to arguing where to put the answers to life so the humans would have to search for them.

One god said, 'Let's put the answers on top of a mountain. They will never look for them there.'

'No,' said the others. 'They'll find them right away.'

Another god said, 'Let's put them in the centre of the earth. They will never look for them there.'

'No,' said the others. 'They'll find them right away.'

Then another spoke. 'Let's put them in the bottom of the sea. They will never look for them there.'

'No,' said the others. 'They'll find them right away.'

Silence fell . . .

After a while another god spoke. 'We can put the answers to life within them. They will never look for them there.'

And so they did that.

(Marie-Louise von Franz, *The Way of the Dream*)

Just eleven main dreams have been presented in this book. Each one could be dismissed as a one-off, a coincidence that is inevitable, given the huge number of dreams each night and the enormous possibility of a chance overlap with some disastrous life event.

Yet these few are no more than the clearest dreams in a much larger sample of 400. As we have seen throughout this book, many people have experienced the power of dreams that contain a message. An important body of dreams exists, from primitive societies onwards. Again and again, we find significant dreams recorded in literature and in life – from the earliest Native American and Mongolian tribes to Delta Goodrem's warning dream, which is very much of our own time. Any conversation that opens with this subject almost invariably leads into discussions of people's own experience, all of it adding to the whole.

Examples of dreams related specifically to illness – which have formed the core of our book – seem to be less common; in general conversation precognitive dreams are more often described. However, many books on dreams contain a chapter on dreams and illness, as throughout the centuries the value of dreams in diagnosis and treatment has been recognized. It is likely that the Egyptian and Greek civilizations, among others, were simply building on the foundations of the world of the shaman. We may think of shamanism as far in the past, but there are still societies where the bond with nature and the spirit world is alive, if under threat. In 2005, for the BBC2 series, *The Tribe*, Bruce Parry spent a month in a village high in the Himalayas. Here he met a female shaman who continues the old traditions in the face of pressure from the twenty-first century. Using leaves, she searches the future to predict the outcome of the next day's hunt. And although the young people are drawn to the magic of movies and TV, they also participate in the equally powerful animal sacrifice: the spirits do, after all, still have to be appeased, for if they are offended they can cause illness, or even death. Perhaps it is felt that western materialism on its own cannot bring prosperity to the village.

IN A STRANGE LAND

What is the source of the shaman's knowledge? This is where it gets difficult. It is as if it is 'hardwired' into the brain. So many ideas appear to come from the depths, whether scientific theories or premonitions of danger, artistic creations or the solution to a trivial puzzle. There is a large amount of evidence of this, some of which we have examined. Modern science has revealed that our consciousness lies on top of a vast array of brain functions and we are still aware of just a small fraction of what goes on in our mind – or in the outside world. According to scientists, about 85 per cent of the matter in the universe is missing.

'So there's a great deal more to discover; we're nowhere near the end of the mystery,' said Philip Pullman, author of the trilogy *His Dark Materials*. He had been invited to the Rutherford Appleton Laboratory, where he learned of the real-life search for dark matter that bears a striking similarity to the Dust he invented: matter that can understand itself. The borders of scientific knowledge are inhabited by a strange anti-gravity force called dark energy, and even by the controversial suggestion of mathematician Roger Penrose that there may be a link between human consciousness and quantum gravity.

We thought we were excavating a personal pond until Jung described it as an ocean. To our PC we have added the Internet. Beneath our surface differences we are all, perhaps, connected by the psyche.

STREAMS FULL OF STARS

What is this life if, full of care,
We have no time to stand and stare . . .
No time to see, in broad daylight,
Streams full of stars, like skies at night.
No time to turn at Beauty's glance,
And watch her feet, how they can dance . . .
A poor life this if, full of care,
We have no time to stand and stare.

(W. H. Davies, 'Leisure')

We are acutely aware of the loss of our fundamental relationship with nature. In pursuit of a materialistic utopia, or just trying to keep our head above water, we seem to lack the time to consider moving into a slower lane. The ancient way of living with the world has been disregarded; life is out of balance. To quote Yeats, 'Things fall apart; the centre cannot hold; Mere anarchy is loosed upon the world.' Inevitably, a prosperous standard of living has to be paid for: in money, in damage to the air we breathe, the water we drink, the quality of the soil in which we grow our food. Oil stocks will run out, pollution continues to spread, and genetic modification is a two-edged sword. Global warming, caused by environmental pollution in Europe, is now thought to be the cause of drought in Africa.

Scientific advances have added immeasurably to our lives, but the rational side of our nature must be held in balance with our older, less ambitious side. Both are essential to our material and spiritual health. As the camerlengo asks, in Dan Brown's best-selling novel *Angels and Demons*, 'who is more ignorant? The man who cannot define lightning, or the man who does not respect its awesome power?'

The smaller, more intimate and close a group is, the more likely it is to sense things about its own members. In a family the mother may intuit a problem in one of the children, or a partner pick up something the other had not been aware of. Primitive groups, living in close communion and surrounded by nature, with no television or other means of getting away from immediate reality, must rely on nature for food, shelter and medicine, and in these close groups an acuteness of listening may develop. They will hear their instincts in a way we probably cannot. Nevertheless, above the noise of our busy lives, as we have seen in this book, the unconscious dream *can* still occasionally make itself heard, bursting through our comfortable belief that we are in charge of reality. There are times when our dreams insist that we listen – usually for good reason.

Jung felt that if enough people were able to integrate the conflict within themselves, humanity could avoid disaster. Listening is the key. Just as doctors advise us to slow down, to avoid the stress that is damaging our health, we must slow down our exploitation of the planet if it, too, is not to die.

Listening to our dreams and aiming for balance are as crucial today as they have always been in the shaman's world. There are so many decisions that can only be made instinctively, just as there are so many decisions that can only be made intellectually. As a psychiatrist I have to rely on my training and knowledge of disease and drugs, but I could not function if I did not also use my instinct and the instincts of close colleagues whose intuition I have learned to trust. In this sense we form a small primitive group whose area of emotional concern is the person we are trying to help. Sometimes a dream or idea may give us a clue to a way forward. Most of the time this is unnecessary; occasionally only a sixth sense will be of any value.

We will never stop searching for the meaning of dreams, or indeed of life. At times we will find the answers we look for; but we cannot expect to know everything. Part of what this book shows is that we need to accept that at the heart of life is mystery. Albert Einstein, one of the foremost scientific explorers, knew this:

The most beautiful experience we can have is the mysterious. It is the fundamental emotion that stands at the cradle of true art and true science. Whoever does not know it and can no longer wonder, no longer marvel, is as good as dead, and his eyes are dimmed. It was the experience of mystery – even if mixed with fear – that engendered religion. A knowledge of the existence of something we cannot penetrate, our perceptions of the profoundest reason and the most radiant beauty ... it is this knowledge and this emotion that constitute true religiosity. In this sense, and only this sense, I am a deeply religious man ... I am satisfied with the mystery of life's eternity.

While Jung was in Africa he spent several months living with the Elgonyis in Uganda. They would meet in the morning and Jung would discuss their dreams. At one meeting the Laibon, the old medicine man, 'appeared in a splendid cloak made of the skins of blue monkeys – a valuable article of display', Jung wrote. He then asked him about his dreams, and the Laibon answered with tears in his eyes: '"In old days the Laibons had dreams, and knew whether there is war or sickness or whether rain comes and where the herds should be driven." His grandfather, too, had still dreamed. But since the whites were in Africa, he said, no-one had dreams any more. Dreams were no longer needed because now the English knew everything!'

Jung was aware that a vital relationship with the natural world had been lost, and that the loss would affect not only the Laibon and his tribe, but all of humanity:

His reply showed me that the medicine man had lost his *raison d'être*. The divine voice which counselled the tribe was no longer needed because 'the English knew better'. Formerly the medicine man had negotiated with the Gods or the power of destiny and had advised his people. He exerted great influence ... Now the medicine man's authority was replaced by that of the DC (District Commissioner). The value of life now lay wholly in this world ... Far from being an imposing personality, our Laibon was only a somewhat tearful old gentleman. He was the living embodiment of the spreading disintegration of an undermined, outmoded, unrestorable world.

Without the aura of power conferred by his spiritual role, it is sad to think of the Laibon as just a 'tearful old gentleman'.

But we should not lose hope. The primitive or archaic mind is still with us and it makes itself known to us in the type of dreams we have met in this book. Underlying our consciousness, it remains a source of inspiration and wisdom, as well as a source of destructiveness and madness. It is important to understand this relationship as fully as we are able. The dream world is capable of knowing things of which the dreamer is unaware. If the unconscious is an orchestra, many dreams reflect individual instruments playing solos. Perhaps the conductor is absent or they are tuning up before performing. For some reason known only to the conductor, they will play together for us at times. The music may consist of small, hardly discernible snatches or it may be a whole symphony. It may have little or no impact or it may stay with us all our lives.

GLOSSARY

Active imagination. Jung's method of talking to the unconscious, allowing the image to speak back.

Alchemy. An early form of chemistry, in which the aim was to try to turn base metals such as lead into gold, and to find the elixir to achieve eternal life.

Alpha waves/rhythm. EEG waves that are found when the brain is in a relaxed state.

Analytical psychology. Jung's method of psychological treatment, so named to differentiate it from Freudian psychoanalysis.

Anima/Animus. Personification of the feminine nature of a man's unconscious; and the masculine nature of a woman's.

Archetypes. Jung's fundamental elements of the collective unconscious. The shadow, the anima and the Self are examples. These pre-existent primordial images take on a specific form only when manifested in consciousness. They are inherited along with the instincts and have a biological basis.

291

Attachment theory. Developed by Bowlby and Ainsworth, this theory defines the quality of the early relationships between child and main carer, usually the mother.

Axis mundi. The axis of the world. An ancient symbol, referring to that which all things revolve around; the support of all things. One manifestation is the cosmic tree which the shaman climbs or descends in his flight.

Beta waves/rhythm. EEG waves that occur in the brain when we are wide awake, with our eyes open.

Blindsight. The ability to locate objects in the visual field without having any visual awareness. This can occur after some forms of brain damage.

Brain scan: CT and MRI. Modern techniques for studying brain structure.

Collective unconscious. Jung's concept of the inherited psyche laid down by all the experiences of the development of the species. Contains the archetypes. Each individual inherits this but it is far beyond the limits of one individual just as the ocean is far more than each ship that sails on it.

Complexes. Fragments that have split off from consciousness due to traumatic or incompatible aspects. Complexes influence consciousness and behave as if they have a consciousness of their own, showing up, for example, in slips of the tongue (parapraxes).

Corpus callosum. The band of nerves crossing from one half of the brain to the other. This is far the biggest connection between the two sides and cutting it is called a **corpus callosotomy.**

Cortex (occipital/temporal/parietal). Regions on the outer surface of the brain that deal with incoming sensations, integrate this information and generate conscious images and action responses.

Dream incubation. The generation of tension around a subject of importance to the individual. The undertaking of incubation has physical aspects such as travelling, hardship, the location of the place itself, and mental aspects, including concentrating, praying and suffering. This process is also referred to as a dream quest.

Electroencephalograph (EEG). Electrical recording taken from the scalp showing underlying brain (cortical) activity.

False awakening. The sensation of waking in one's normal environment but realizing one is still asleep due to some inconsistencies; or fully waking and only then realizing that it was a dream.

Frontal lobes. The cortex at the front of the brain especially concerned with executive actions of the brain as a whole. The cortex can direct attention to certain tasks while ignoring other brain actions: so, for example, you may hear a far-off noise while ignoring something much louder close by. Essential for motivation and moral control.

Functional hallucinatory psychosis. Hallucinations (auditory, visual, etc.) due to a mental illness rather than brain injury or disease.

Hippocampus. Brain structure shaped like a sea-horse essential for making or retrieving new memories.

Hypnagogic hallucinations. Visual images experienced as we fall asleep and pass into light sleep stages 1 or 2 of non-REM.

Hypnopompic hallucinations. Visual images that arise as we emerge from sleep, usually from REM.

Individuation. Jung's concept of the journey through life, with the ego gradually integrating the unconscious to create a new centre for consciousness.

Limbic system. Primitive centres below the level of the cortex dealing with emotional expression. Closely related to the hippocampus and therefore memory.

Lucid dreaming. The awareness that we are dreaming while we are still in the dream.

Malignant melanoma. A cancerous skin tumour, usually black.

Mandala. Magic symbol of the universe, of very ancient origin. In Jung's view, mandalas 'usually appear in situations of psychic confusion and disorder'. Most often a circle, but can also be a square or quaternity.

Mythopoetic function. Myth-producing aspect of the unconscious. Presumably has a biological basis.

Narcolepsy. First described in 1880, a state of consciousness characterized by abnormal sleep tendencies, including excessive daytime sleepiness. Often REM occurs immediately on going to sleep, accompanied by muscle paralysis (cataplexy), hypnagogic hallucinations and sleep paralysis.

Non-REM sleep (NREM). The major sleep stage separate from REM (rapid eye movement) sleep. Usually the first stage of sleep at night. Has four stages, depending on depth of sleep. The deeper stages (3 and 4) occur early in the night and REM is more in evidence towards the morning. The body is not paralysed, hence sleepwalking and talking occur during NREM.

Objective dreams. Dreams that refer to external events of everyday life.

Ouroboros (or Uroboros). Ancient symbol of a snake biting its own tail. In many myths it encircles the world and represents the waters surrounding the earth.

Persona. The mask that everyone wears in society. Behind it is the true personality. It is very marked in some, hardly at all in others.

Personal unconscious. Freud did not elaborate on the unconscious so Jung needed to differentiate the personal from the collective unconscious. The personal unconscious consists of the contents of consciousness that are capable of being made conscious: for example, you may know the name of the capital of Great Britain but it will probably not be in your mind at any given time. In that sense it is not conscious but can easily be made so. The personal unconscious also contains all the facts of the individual life that are relatively forgotten or unacceptable.

Phases of sleep. Non-REM sleep stages 1 to 4. See **Non-REM.**

Precognitive dreams. Dreams that tell of future events.

Prodromal dreams. Dreams that are to do with physical illness, before it is manifest.

Projection. The tendency to see faults in others that are really our own.

Psyche. Encompasses all mental processes, conscious and unconscious.

Psychiatrist. Medical practitioner who treats mental illness and is qualified to prescribe and administer drugs, unlike a psychologist. Only a few psychiatrists are also trained psychotherapists.

Psychoanalyst. Uses Freud's theories in the practice of psychotherapy.

Psychology. Scientific study of human and animal behaviour. Many psychologists (called 'Doctor' if they have a Ph.D. degree) work in clinical settings in various capacities, including psychotherapy of many varieties.

Psychosexual. Psychological aspects of sexual activity as opposed to physical.

Psychosis/pseudo-psychosis. Loss of contact with reality, usually with delusions (firmly held but false beliefs) and hallucinations, most often auditory. In pseudo-psychosis the symptoms merely *resemble* psychotic phenomena.

Psychotherapy. Generic term for talking treatment. There are many different types of psychotherapist.

PTSD (Post-traumatic stress disorder). First defined in 1980, a condition caused by an overwhelming trauma. Sufferers re-experience the trauma in nightmares, ruminations and flashbacks, and also exhibit anxiety and a tendency to avoid situations that act as reminders.

Rapid Eye Movement sleep (REM). A specific period of sleep occurring regularly through the night every 90 minutes to 2 hours and lasting 90 minutes or so. The EEG shows that the brain is as active in REM sleep as in consciousness, and during REM phases the muscles are paralysed to prevent acting out of the associated dreams.

Self. Jung's term for the central core of the unconscious which contains the archetypes. The Self is also the central archetype and is symbolized by the mandala.

Shaman. A doctor-priest or medicine man and master of the ecstatic in many primitive tribes and indigenous peoples. There are also female shamans.

Subjective dreams. Dreams that refer to inner aspects of the dreamer, such as fantasy, emotions and wishes.

SWS (Slow wave sleep). The deeper stages of non-REM, 3 and 4.

Synchronicity. Meaningful coincidence; two events connected by meaning but without one having caused the other.

Tegsh. The shamanic way of living in balance and harmony and in consciousness of one's true nature and purpose.

Thalamus. A large brain structure, the relay station for incoming sensation from the body, with nerves taking the information on to the cortex.

Thick-boundaried/thin-boundaried. Ernest Hartmann's theory of individual variations in access to fantasy and imagination. If the boundary is thin, access is relatively easy.

Unihemispheric sleep. Found in birds and aquatic mammals where just one side of the brain sleeps at a time: 'sleeping with one eye open'.

Unus mundus. A single unitary world.

HOW TO RECORD AND ASSESS YOUR DREAMS

'Aha,' said the king. 'So, you go to sleep, in the morning and dream all day that you are at the office and that you work, work, work. And at night, as soon as you've gone to bed, you wake up and all night you are what you really are. Sometimes a pilot, sometimes a rower, and sometimes an I-don't-know-what. Don't you think it's better that way round?'

'I don't know. How is that better?' I said.

'It's more varied,' the king explained. 'And the night becomes more important. The day is just a dream . . .'

(Axel Hacke, *Little King December*)

Sometimes we remember our dreams; sometimes we don't. As we have seen, a dream that has something to tell us will not follow rules. There are no magic spells to ensure that we have creative and valuable dreams. Nevertheless, there are some techniques we can adopt in order to enhance our ability to recall the dreams we do experience.

Go to bed early. Getting a good rest means you won't be tired in the morning and so will find it easier to recall your dreams. It may help if you avoid alcohol. Some people find it better to keep a low light on at night, rather than searching for a switch if they wake in the dark. Others find that any light disrupts their sleep.

Before falling asleep, repeat to yourself: 'When I wake up I will remember my dreams.'

When you wake up, lie quietly for a few minutes and allow images and memories to surface. Once the outside world floods back in, it is very hard to retrieve the dream. If you can postpone this, any hypnopompic images may be clearer. It is important to focus on the dream as you waken, but do not make demands. Allow it to speak when it is ready.

KEEPING A RECORD

Always remember: record your dreams now – analyse them later.

Concentrate on getting down as much information as possible, as quickly as possible, while the dream is still with you. The more you stop to think, or to search for the perfect words to describe it, the less time you have to capture the dream and the more chance it has to escape.

Next to your bed keep **a notebook**. Next to it there will of course be **a pen or pencil**: every night, check that no one has borrowed it. (There is no reason why random scraps of paper can't be used, except that they are easier to mislay, or may end up being used as bookmarks or shopping lists.) For some people, the style of notebook is important. It's up to you whether to mark your dream book 'Private'. What is important is that you should not have to censor this record of your dreams; if you are worrying about what other people might think, you will feel anxious about writing uninhibitedly.

Write down everything you can recall, without trying to edit or organize the material: a few images or phrases, a mood, how you felt on waking – keep a record of all of these, whether they seem to make sense or not. Don't stop to work anything out. What you have written may later prove unexpectedly illuminating, as Nancy (in Chapter 1) found to her surprise: 'I rummaged through my papers to find my record of the dream and was astounded to see the imagery in the dream and think of its connection to my current reality.'

An alternative is to use **a tape recorder or minidisc player**: again, this must be next to the bed and set up ready to record. Many people may find talking into a machine quicker than writing in a notebook, especially in the middle of the night. And when you play it back later, you could pick up clues to your feelings at the time of the dream.

Occasionally it is helpful to **make a rough sketch** of images that arise in the dream – for example buildings or road layouts. Do not be tempted to turn these into artistic creations; by the time you are satisfied with the likeness, the rest of the story will probably have vanished.

State the date and time at the start of each notebook entry or recording. Later, this will enable you to trace any emerging patterns and themes, or to follow the development of a story through time. It also means that at the interpretation stage you can relate the dream world to all that is going on in your waking life. Giving each dream a title may help – but don't try to shape it into a coherent story.

Recording your dreams in **the present tense** can aid clarity: 'I am swimming in the sea at Brighton when I notice that a party is taking place on the beach.' Not only does this recreate the immediacy of the dream – the sense that you are there now, in the middle of it – but it helps avoid confusion when something has happened in the past in the dream itself : 'I am swimming in the sea and thinking about a party that I once went to on the beach.' But don't worry about this if you would find it distracting. Tenses are not crucial; you can always spend time disentangling them later.

INTERPRETATION

You should not try to force the dream too much; nor should you be lazy, and expect the meaning just to come to you. Balance is the key.

The aim is to discover the associations between the dream elements and your life. No single image is universal: fire, for example, may represent rage, hunger, passion – or just fire. It may be positive and warming: it may be negative and destructive. What it means to you will depend entirely on your associations with the image. *Recent events and problems are likely to surface in your dreams, or cast a shadow over them, as our mind tries to work through these situations.*

Working with the records you have kept – however fragmentary – take each aspect separately and consider what comes to mind: does a house in the dream evoke memories of somewhere you once knew, even if the appearance is quite different? Perhaps it is more a question of atmosphere than appearance. A stranger in your dream may remind you of someone in your everyday life; again, it could just be an aspect of their behaviour. If you dream of a celebrity, think of what that person means to you: do they represent a particular quality? Figures who represent authority may relate to our parents. More complex is their possible relation with our own inner authority figures, who will be reflected in many external situations. Thus police, the Queen, teachers and so on may all reflect a certain type of authority for the individual. They may still be like Mum or Dad even if the dreamer is an adult.

Associate the elements with as much real-life background as you can, gradually building up a picture of the dream in relation to you, and to the events and preoccupations of your life. From this, clues to what the dream is really about may emerge. As will have become clear from this book, it is difficult to be sure of the meaning of every aspect of a dream, and it is even more difficult to interpret your own dreams. As Marie-Louise von Franz, an expert in this area, said:

Dreams . . . never tell us what we already know. They tell us what we don't know. But when people interpret their own dreams they tend to say, 'Yes, I know what that means.' And then they project what they already know into the dream . . . they give a completely banal explan-ation of something they've known for years about themselves. And then I say, 'Wait, wait, wait, let's take the dream as it is, slowly, from beginning to end.' And it comes out quite differently and surprisingly . . .

The trouble with interpreting your own dreams is that you can't see your own back. If you show it to another person, he can see it, but you can't. And dreams point to your back, to what you don't see.

In the morning, or later, you may want to talk to other people about your dream. Going over what happened helps to fix it in your mind and can shed light on events that seem bizarre. It's the same idea that inspired 'brain-storming' – everyone has their own angle; the comments and questions of your friends may suddenly make a string of odd and unrelated fragments fall into place. And often your friends won't even realize what it was they said. However, do bear in mind that the content may be more revealing than you think, and this could strike you as you're in the middle of describing the dream. It may be awkward if your unconscious thoughts turn out to be antagonistic to the very friends who are listening to you; or you could find yourself telling them more than you want them to know.

If you wish to pursue this in a systematic way, consider going to a dream therapist or joining a dream group. Various organizations dedicated to dream interpretation can be found on the Internet.

Dream on!

NOTES

INTRODUCTION

13: 'I've dreamt in my life': Emily Brontë, *Wuthering Heights* (London, T. C. Newby, 1847), Chapter 9.

15: '"We will speak to the people"': Ted Hughes, *What Is the Truth? A Farmyard Fable for the Young* (1984); reprinted as *Collected Animal Poems Volume 2* (London, Faber & Faber, 1995), p. 2.

15: The molecular biologist ... Francis Crick: see Transcript of a visit with Francis Crick, Carolina Biological Supply Company, *www.accessexcellence.org*, the National Health Museum website.

16: In January 1994 ... research study: The first article to deal with my work was by Victoria Macdonald, in the *Sunday Telegraph* on 13 February 1994, with a follow-up on 19 January 1997 which featured some examples supplied by readers. It included David's dream (discussed in Chapter 4), which he had sent in response to a piece in the now defunct UK paper, *Today* ('Sweet dreams and how the subconscious can help', *Today*, 1 March 1994). An article appeared in *The Times* (2 June 1997), and further, shorter pieces in many other magazines, including *She*, *Good Housekeeping*, *Zest* and *Top Santé*.

17: 'Bagpipes': see *The Victorian Book of Dreams, including signs, auguries, divination by cards and prognostics from the physiognomy and moles, &c, &c*, ed. Marion Giordan (n.d.; repr. London, Hugh Evelyn, 1964).

20: 'Can't you see . . .': Anne Sexton, 'Old' from *All My Pretty Ones* (1962), in *The Complete Poems* (Boston, Houghton Mifflin, 1982), p. 69.

23: 'All nature is but art': Alexander Pope, *An Essay on Man* (London, 1773–4), lines 289–92.

24: 'The grant of shamanic powers': Mircea Eliade, *Shamanism: Archaic Techniques of Ecstasy*, trans. Willard R. Trask (London, Routledge, 1964, 1968); Princeton, NJ, Bollingen Foundation/Princeton University Press, 1972; 1974 Bollingen edn, p. 101.

24: As Igjugarjuk . . . explains: Joseph Campbell, *The Masks of God*, 4 vols, 1959–68. Vol. 1: *Primitive Mythology* (1959), Harmondsworth, Penguin, 1976, p. 54.

25: 'We . . . are the first race': Niall Ferguson, *Empire: How Britain Made the Modern World* (London, Allen Lane, 2003), p. 228.

25: In just twenty empire-building years: ibid., p. 223.

25: 'Our meddling intellect': William Wordsworth, 'The Tables Turned', in Wordsworth and Samuel Taylor Coleridge, *Lyrical Ballads with a Few Other Poems* (London, 1798).

26: 'The dull catalogue': John Keats, 'Lamia', lines 229–34, in *Lamia, Isabella, The Eve of St Agnes, and Other Poems* (1820).

CHAPTER 1: THE RIDDLE

27: 'What shall I say they are': Robert Louis Stevenson, *Across the Plains: Leaves from the Notebook of an Emigrant between New York and San Francisco* (London, Chatto & Windus, 1892), p. 73.

28: Dr Morton Schatzman's research: see Alfred Alvarez, *Night: An Exploration of Night Life, Night Language, Sleep and Dreams* (New York, W. W. Norton; London, Jonathan Cape, 1995), pp. 165–7.

30: 'a riddle': Winston Churchill, broadcast talk, 1 October 1939.

31: 'Jacques Lacan once said': Alvarez, *Night*, pp. 167–8.

31: 'I shall tell you how': Talk given by Gaston Leroux in Nice, quoted in Leroux, *The Mystery of the Yellow Room* (1908; Sawtry, UK, Dedalus, 2nd edn, 2003), Afterword by Terry Hale, pp. 235–6.

32: 'a basic foundation of our thought' and **'Metaphor is learned':** Ernest Hartmann, *Dreams and Nightmares: The New Theory on the Origin and Meaning of Dreams* (New York, Plenum, 1998), p. 108.

33: One classic example: Plutarch (AD *c*.50–*c*.125), biography of Alexander in *Parallel Lives* (Loeb Classical Library, 1919). The text can also be found online; see *http://-penelope.uchicago.edu/ Thayer/E/Roman/Texts/Plutarch/Lives/Alexander*/4.html*.

33: 'The best songs': John Lennon, quoted in Frederic

Seaman, *The Last Days of John Lennon* (New York, Random House, 1996), p. 171.

34: 'Almost all my mathematical thinking': Roger Penrose, *The Emperor's New Mind* (Oxford, Oxford University Press, 1989; London, Vintage, 1990), pp. 549–54.

34: 'mathematical landscape': Francis Galton, in Rupert Sheldrake, *The Sense of Being Stared At and Other Aspects of the Extended Mind* (2003; London, Arrow, 2004), p. 33.

35: 'Last night I dreamt': Daphne du Maurier, *Rebecca*, 1938; Hitchcock film, 1940.

35: 'I had long been trying': Stevenson, *Across the Plains*, p. 73.

35: 'Jekyll was conceived': in *The Letters of Robert Louis Stevenson*, ed. Bradford A. Booth and Ernest Mehew, 8 vols (New Haven and London, Yale University Press, 1994–5), quoted in Claire Harman, *Robert Louis Stevenson: A Biography* (London, HarperCollins, 2005).

36: 'Night waned': Mary Shelley, Preface to the 1831 edition; in *Frankenstein, or The Modern Prometheus*, ed. J. M. Smith (Basingstoke, Macmillan; Bedford, St Martin's, 2000).

37: 'One night I had a dream': Dedication of a 1903 volume of his plays to Lady Gregory. For Cathleen, see W. B. Yeats, *The Countess Cathleen* (1892) and *Cathleen ni Houlihan* (1902).

38: '"Make way, please"': Enid Blyton, *Five Go to Demon's Rocks* (London, Hodder & Stoughton, 1961), p. 183.

38–9: 'I shut my eyes' and 'my conscious mind': Enid Blyton, correspondence with psychologist Peter McKellar,

1953–7, in Barbara Stoney, *Enid Blyton: A Biography* (London, Hodder & Stoughton, 1974), pp. 216, 220.

39: 'It is common practice': John Steinbeck, cited in Deirdre Barrett, *The Committee of Sleep*, New York, Crown Publishers, 2001.

40: 'one of the most instinctive songs': Paul McCartney, quoted in Bill Harry, *The Paul McCartney Encyclopedia* (London, Virgin Books, 2002), p. 926.

40: Frank Gehry: Terry Kirby, 'The world-famous architect, the cancer victim and the dream that turned into a glittering prize', *Independent*, Friday, 11 June 2004, pp. 14–15; see also 'Let me be Frank', *Scotsman*, Friday, 19 September 2003, *www.arcspace.com* and *Studio International*, 14 October 2003.

41: 'It faded': William Shakespeare, *Hamlet*, I. i. 157.

41: 'No bird soars too high': William Blake, *The Marriage of Heaven and Hell*, *c.*1790–93, in *Blake: Complete Writings with variant readings*, ed. Geoffrey Keynes (London, Oxford and New York, Oxford University Press, 1966, 1969).

41: anonymous 'person from Porlock': see Coleridge's note in *Christabel and Other Poems* (1816).

45: James Joyce's ... concept of epiphany: see *James Joyce: Poems and Shorter Writings*, ed. Richard Ellmann, A. Walton Litz and J. W. Ferguson (London, Faber & Faber, 1991).

47: 'In my dreams': Carlos Ruiz Zafón, *The Shadow of the Wind*, trans. Lucia Graves (London, Phoenix, 2004), p. 287.

47: 'a solemn phantom': Charles Dickens, *A Christmas Carol* (1843), end of Stave 3: 'The Second of the Three Spirits'.

48: Delta Goodrem: in *Glamour*, 2004.

49: 'A 6-year-old girl dreamed': Fraser Boa, *The Way of the Dream, Conversations on Jungian Dream Interpretation with Marie-Louise von Franz* (Boston and London, Shambhala, 1988), 1992 edn, p. 31.

51: 'I dreamed this story': W. B. Yeats, note to 'The Cap and Bells', from *The Wind among the Reeds* (1899); reprinted in *The Collected Poems of W. B. Yeats* (London, Macmillan, 1933).

52: 'Was it a vision': John Keats, 'Ode to a Nightingale', written 1819; in *Lamia, Isabella, The Eve of St Agnes, and Other Poems* (1820).

52: 'dreaming may occur': Louis Jolyon West, quoted in M.W. Mahowald, S.R. Woods and C. H. Schenck, 'Sleeping Dreams, Waking Hallucinations and the Central Nervous System', *Dreaming, Journal of the Association for the Study of Dreams*, vol. 8, no. 2 (June 1998), pp. 89–103 (published by Human Sciences Press, New York).

CHAPTER 2: 'THIS LIFE'S A FICTION'

54: 'This Life's a Fiction': William Blake, *The Everlasting Gospel* (*c.* 1818), in *Blake: Complete Writings*, ed. Geoffrey Keynes (London, Oxford and New York, 1966; 1969 edn).

54: 'Just like the digital codes': Ian McEwan, *Saturday* (London, Jonathan Cape, 2005), pp. 254–5.

55: Rupert Sheldrake's theory: see *The Sense of Being Stared At and Other Aspects of the Extended Mind* (2003; London, Arrow Books, 2004).

56: 'I am a Bear': A. A. Milne, *Winnie-the-Pooh* (London, 1926), Chapter 4.

57: 'We can become so caught up': quotation from the website of the Christian Millennial Fellowship: *www.cmfellowship.org*.

58: 'When in that House': W.S. Gilbert, *Iolanthe; or, The Peer and the Peri* (1882), in *The Savoy Operas* (London, Macmillan; New York, St Martin's Press, 1954).

59: 'I have come to the borders': Edward Thomas, 'Lights Out', in *The Collected Poems of Edward Thomas* (Oxford, Clarendon Press; New York, Oxford University Press, 1978).

60: 'My simile of a "private cinema screen" ': Enid Blyton, correspondence with Peter McKellar, 1953–7, in Barbara Stoney, *Enid Blyton* (London, Hodder & Stoughton, 1974), p. 220.

61: 'In the real dark night': F. Scott Fitzgerald, *The Crack-Up; with other uncollected pieces, note-books . . . etc.*, ed. E. Wilson (New York, New Directions, 1945), p. 75.

61: In 1953 a postgraduate student: In 1953 Eugene Aserinsky and Nathaniel Kleitman reported the discovery of REM sleep in the journal *Science*. Aserinsky was a medical student at the University of Chicago where Kleitman, an international sleep expert, was his professor. See R. L. van de Castle, *Our Dreaming Mind* (London, Aquarian, 1994), p. 228.

61: 'paradoxical sleep': M. Jouvet, *The Paradox of Sleep: the Story of Dreaming*, trans. Laurence Garey (Cambridge, Mass., MIT Press, 1993).

62: In an experiment on cats: ibid.

63: 'Those who have likened': *The Essays of Montaigne*, trans. E. J. Trechmann, 2 vols (Oxford, Oxford University Press, 1935).

64: 'For you dream you are crossing': Gilbert, *Iolanthe*, Act II.

65: '"Now, what I want"': Charles Dickens, *Hard Times* (London, 1854), Chapter 1.

65: 'Imagination is more important': Albert Einstein, 'What Life Means to Einstein', originally published in *Saturday Evening Post*, 26 October 1929, reprinted in 'On Science' in *Cosmic Religion*, p. 97.

66: 'The left brain may see 132 trees': R. Joseph, *The Right Brain and the Unconscious: Discovering the Stranger Within* (New York, Plenum, 1992), p. 35.

67: 'Do what you will': Blake, *The Everlasting Gospel*.

67: Roger W. Sperry: see *www.rogersperry.info*.

68: 'The Atoms of Democritus': William Blake, 'Poems and Fragments from the Note-Book' (1800–1803), in *Blake: Complete Writings*, ed. Keynes.

71: 'The Imagination may be compared': John Keats, letter of 22 November 1817 to Benjamin Bailey, in *The Letters of John Keats*, ed. Maurice Buxton Forman (4th edn, 1952).

72: In the late 1970s: Robert Bosnak, *Tracks in the Wilderness of Dreaming* (New York, Delacorte Press, 1996).

72: '. . . the time will come': Benjamin Disraeli, maiden speech, Houses of Parliament, 1837.

74: 'He often went out alone': J. M. Barrie, *Peter Pan*, Chapter 7.

74: There is evidence . . . non-REM sleep: Jacob Empson, *Sleep and Dreaming*, 1989 (2nd revised edn, New York, London, Harvester Wheatsheaf, 1993), pp. 171–3.

CHAPTER 3: MIND INVADERS

77: 'Where do people go': Jeanne Willis, 'Inside Our Dreams', in *Toffee Pockets* (London, Bodley Head, 1992).

77: Ernest Hartmann: In *Dreams and Nightmares: The New Theory on the Origin and Meaning of Dreams* (New York, Plenum, 1998), pp. 49–50 and 220–29.

79: 'If a man could pass thro Paradise': Samuel Taylor Coleridge, Notebook entry, 1815–16, published in *Anima Poetae* (1895).

80: 'I dreamt that I was lying in the garden': Frederik van Eeden, 'A Study of Dreams', *Proceedings of the Society of Psychical Research*, vol. 26 (1913).

81: 'Man's earliest conception of dreams': A. J. J. Radcliffe, *A History of Dreams* (London, Grant Richards, 1923; London, Senate, 1966), p. 17.

81: 'Up by 4 a-clock': Samuel Pepys, *Diary*, 15 August 1665.

83: one person 'woke from dreams': Mark Solms, *The Neuropsychology of Dreams: A Clinico-Anatomical Study* (Mahwah, NJ, Lawrence Erlbaum, 1997), p. 194.

83: A good illustration: Linda Caine and Robin Royston, *Out of the Dark* (London, Bantam Press, 2003), p. 312.

85: 'You are not a human being': Teilhard de Chardin, French geologist, priest, philosopher and mystic (1881–1955). Quoted on *en.thinkexist.com*.

85: As Radcliffe noted: see Radcliffe, *History of Dreams*, p. 17.

86: 'We can understand': C. G. Jung, 'Basic Postulates of Analytical Psychology' (1934), para. 672, in *The Structure and Dynamics of the Psyche, Collected Works*, Vol. 8.

86: 'The Indians of Guiana': Radcliffe, *History of Dreams*, p. 24.

87: 'Toward the end of the thirty days': Joseph Campbell, *The Masks of God*, 4 vols (1959–68), Vol. 1: *Primitive Mythology* (1959; Harmondsworth, Penguin, 1976), p. 244.

87–8: 'A shaman's instruction' and 'The available documents': Mircea Eliade, *Shamanism: Archaic Techniques of Ecstasy*, trans. Willard R. Trask (London, Routledge, 1964, 1968; Princeton, NJ, Bollingen Foundation/ Princeton University Press, 1972; 1974 Bollingen edn, pp. 103 and 13).

88: 'If the Sun & Moon': 'Auguries of Innocence', in 'Poems from the Pickering Manuscript' (c. 1803) in *Blake: Complete Writings*, ed. Geoffrey Keynes (Oxford University Press, London, Oxford and New York, 1969).

89: The Andaman Islanders (Ongees) believe: Vishvajit Pandya, 'Forest Smells and Spider Webs: Ritualized Dream Interpretation among Andaman Islanders', *Dreaming: Journal of the Association for the Study of Dreams*, vol. 14, nos. 2–3 (June–September 2004), pp. 136–50.

90: 'Open wide': John Keats, 'Fancy', written 1818, published 1820. Copied into letter of 2 January 1819 to George and Georgiana Keats. See *The Letters of John Keats*, ed. Maurice Buxton Forman, 4th edn (London, Oxford University Press, 1952, 1960).

90: 'Protons, neutrons and electrons': Ernesto Cardenal, 'The Music of the Spheres', trans. Dinah Livingstone (London, Katabasis, 1990).

90: 'merely toys with the wooden jigsaw pieces': Basil Willey, *Samuel Taylor Coleridge* (London, Chatto & Windus, 1972), p. 201.

91: 'How do you know': Blake, 'A Memorable Fancy', *The Marriage of Heaven and Hell*, in *Blake*, ed. Keynes.

91: 'in one dream I can compose': Sir Thomas Browne, *Religio Medici* (1642), in *The Works of Sir Thomas Browne*, Vol. 1, ed. Geoffrey Keynes (London, Faber & Faber, 1928, 1964).

91: In 1891: Ambrose Bierce, 'An Occurrence at Owl Creek Bridge', in *Tales of Soldiers and Civilians* (1891).

93: '"You still haven't proved you're real"': Audrey Niffenegger, *The Time Traveler's Wife* (London, Vintage, 2004), p. 70.

95: 'I do not know': H. A. Giles, *Chuang Tzu: Mystic, Moralist and Social Reformer*, trans. from the Chinese (1889).

97: 'but only a beautiful flower arrangement' and 'A butterfly is a symbol': Fraser Boa, *The Way of the Dream, Conversations on Jungian Dream Interpretation with Marie-Louise von Franz* (Boston and London, Shambhala, 1988), 1992 edn, p. 30.

98: 'About ten days or so': Thom Gunn, 'The Reassurance', in *Collected Poems* (London, Faber & Faber, 1993).

100: 'I . . . was once asked': Marie-Louise von Franz, *On Dreams and Death* (1984 in German); trans. E. Xipolitas Kennedy and Vernon Brooks (Boston and London, Shambhala, 1986, 1987), Introduction, p. xv.

102: Haruki Murakami: see Murakami, *Norwegian Wood*, trans. Jay Rubin (London, Vintage, 2003), p. 360.

CHAPTER 4: THE PANTHER'S PARTING GLANCE

103: 'IDIOT': *The Victorian Book of Dreams, including signs, auguries, divination by cards and prognostics from the physiognomy and moles, &c, &c*, ed. Marion Giordan (n.d.; repr. London, Hugh Evelyn, 1964).

107: 'As is generally known': Marie-Louise von Franz, *On Dreams and Death: A Jungian Interpretation* (1984 in German); trans. E. Xipolitas Kennedy and Vernon Brooks (Boston and London, Shambhala, 1986, 1987), Introduction, p. vii.

110: 'Each outcry of the hunted Hare': William Blake, 'Auguries of Innocence', in 'Poems from the Pickering Manuscript' (*c.* 1803), in *Blake: Complete Writings*, ed. Geoffrey Keynes (Oxford University Press, London, Oxford and New York, 1969).

111: 'The Buryat (Siberians) say': for this story, see *http://www.angelfire.com/ca/Indian/TotemAnimals.html*.

113: 'Man has no Body': William Blake, *The Marriage of Heaven and Hell* (*c.* 1790–93), in *Blake*, ed. Keynes.

114: 'Strange how things in the offing': Seamus Heaney, 'Squarings', xlviii, in *Seeing Things* (London, Faber & Faber, 1991), p. 108.

119: 'Several things dovetailed': John Keats, letter to George and Thomas Keats, 21 December 1817, in *The Letters of John Keats*, ed. Maurice Buxton Forman, 4th edn (London, Oxford University Press, 1952, 1960), letter 32, p. 71.

120–1: an experiment by Colin Martindale and 'Their frontal lobes': for Martindale's research, see Guy Claxton, *The Wayward Mind: An Intimate History of the*

Unconscious (London, Time Warner UK, 2005), pp. 266–8.

120–1: Hartmann's thin boundaries: *Dreams and Nightmares: The New Theory on the Origin and Meaning of Dreams* (New York, Plenum, 1998).

122: 'that untravelled world': Alfred Tennyson, 'Ulysses' (1842).

122: 'The materialist ideologies': Kathleen Raine speaking in BBC Radio 4 programme 'The Sacred'; cited in *Something Understood*, introduced by Mark Tully, compiled by Beverley McAinsh (London, Hodder & Stoughton, 2001).

CHAPTER 5: THE ENERGY WITHIN

124: '. . . angels in some brighter dreams': Henry Vaughan (1621–95), 'Beyond the Veil'.

125: 'Yes, sir, we practise Necromancy': W. S. Gilbert, speech of John Wellington Wells (of J. W. Wells & Co. Family Sorcerers), from *The Sorcerer* (1877), Act I, in *The Savoy Operas* (London, Macmillan; New York, St Martin's Press, 1954).

126: 'Be silent': Edwina Gateley, 'Let Your God Love You', from *Psalms of a Laywoman* (Lanham, Maryland, Sheed & Ward, 2000), in *Something Understood: An Anthology of Poetry and Prose*, introduced by Mark Tully; compiled by Beverley McAinsh (London, Hodder & Stoughton, 2001).

128: 'We have moved away': Oonagh Shanley-Toffolo, *The Voice of Silence: A Life of Love, Healing and Inspiration* (London, Rider, 2002), p. 132.

129: the prophet Samuel: 1 Samuel 3: 3–4.

129: 'lonely caverns': A. J. J. Radcliffe, *A History of Dreams* (1923; London, Random House/Senate, 1966), p. 60.

129: 'To enter the precinct': Anthony Shafton, *Dream Reader: Contemporary Approaches to the Understanding of Dreams* (New York, SUNY Press, 1995), p. 408.

133: 'A general anarchy': Samuel Johnson, in Mme D'Arblay, *Diary and Letters* (1891 edn), Vol. I, Chapter 3, September 1778.

136: In Dublin: John Waters interviewed by Emily O'Reilly for *Veronica Guerin: The Life and Death of a Crime Reporter* (London, Vintage, 1998), p. 185. Guerin's story is also told in a 2003 film starring Cate Blanchett.

138: 'We affirm that the world's magnificence': Filippo Marinetti, 'Founding Manifesto of Futurism' (1909), in U. Appolonio (ed.), *Futurist Manifestos* (London and New York, 1973).

139: 'And now some one here may say': 'A Sermon Delivered on Sabbath Morning, August 9th, 1857, by the Revd. C. H. Spurgeon at the Music Hall, Royal Surrey Gardens [London]'. For more of the Revd Charles Haddon Spurgeon's sermon, see *www.spurgeon.org.*

141: 'On Christmas Day 1911': Frederik van Eeden, 'A Study of Dreams', *Proceedings of the Society of Psychical Research*, vol. 26 (1913).

143: 'Presently Ethel came back': Daisy Ashford, *The Young Visiters, or Mr Salteenas Plan* (1919; London, Chatto & Windus, 1973), pp. 18–19.

145: 'O body swayed to music': W. B. Yeats, 'Among School Children', from *The Tower* (1928); reprinted in

The Collected Poems of W. B. Yeats (London, Macmillan, 1933).

146: '. . . the initiation dreams': Ted Hughes, *Winter Pollen: Occasional Prose* (London, Faber & Faber, 1994), p. 58.

147: 'passes through an "opening"': Mircea Eliade, *Shamanism: Archaic Techniques of Ecstasy*, trans. Willard R. Trask (London, Routledge, 1964), pp. 259, 261.

147: 'All things began': Sir Thomas Browne, *The Garden of Cyrus* (1658), in *The Works of Sir Thomas Browne*, Vol. 1, ed. Geoffrey Keynes (London, Faber & Faber, 1928, 1964).

147: Srinivasa Ramanujan: see Robert Kanigel, *The Man Who Knew Infinity* (New York, Scribner's, 1991), pp. 36, 66–7.

149: 'But man, the two-fold creature': Elizabeth Barrett Browning, *Aurora Leigh* (1857), Book 7, lines 802–4.

149: 'For it is the function': C. G. Jung, *The Structure and Dynamics of the Psyche*, in *Collected Works*, Vol. 8, para. 342, p. 158.

CHAPTER 6: 'THE WHITE FLAME OF LIFE'

150: 'The White Flame of Life': J. B. Priestley, *Rain upon Godshill: A Further Chapter of Autobiography* (London, Macmillan; New York, Harper & Bros, 1939).

150: 'Listen': Flann O'Brien [Brian O'Nolan], *The Third Policeman* (1967; London, Flamingo, 1993), pp. 123–4; italics in the original.

151: In 1865 Abraham Lincoln: For details of Lincoln's prophetic dream, and background information, see Troy Taylor, 'History and Hauntings of Illinois: The Haunted

President' (2002) on *http://www.prairieghosts.com/lincoln2.html*. The site also gives sources for Troy's article.

154: 'No man is an Island': John Donne, Meditation XVII, in *Devotions upon Emergent Occasions* (1624).

154: publication of his study: Carl Jung, *The Psychology of the Unconscious* (1911–12), in *Collected Works* [CW] Vol. 5: *Symbols of Transformation*; present revised edition, *Symbols of Transformation*, 1956, 1966.

155: 'the profundity and richness': Carl Jung, *General Aspects of Dream Psychology*, in CW, Vol. 8: *The Structure and Dynamics of the Psyche*, para. 498, p. 260.

155: 'every man, in a sense': ibid., para. 483, p. 250.

155: 'an ever-widening spiral': O'Brien, *Third Policeman*, p. 123.

155: 'Time present and time past': T. S. Eliot, 'Burnt Norton' (1935), lines 1–3, in *Four Quartets* (New York, 1943). See *The Complete Poems and Plays of T. S. Eliot* (London, Faber & Faber, 1969).

157: 'That has puzzled me too': Marie-Louise von Franz, in Fraser Boa, *The Way of the Dream, Conversations on Jungian Dream Interpretation with Marie-Louise von Franz* (Boston and London, Shambhala, 1988; 1992), p. 217.

157: 'When I go to bed': Enid Blyton, correspondence with Peter McKellar, 1953–7, in Barbara Stoney, *Enid Blyton: A Biography* (London, Hodder & Stoughton, 1974), p. 217.

158: 'I was in a house': Carl Jung, *Memories, Dreams, Reflections*, recorded and edited by A. Jaffé, trans. R. and C. Winston, from a manuscript Jung left on his death in 1961 (1962; London, Collins Fount Paperbacks, 1977), p. 182.

159: 'The deeper I went': ibid.

160: he was digging a burial mound: ibid., p. 104.

160: 'The hours are suns': Stephen Spender, 'The Truly Great', in *Collected Poems 1928–1985* (London, Faber & Faber, 1985).

160: 'He whose face': William Blake, *The Marriage of Heaven and Hell* (*c*. 1790–93), in *Blake: Complete Writings with variant readings*, ed. Geoffrey Keynes (London, Oxford and New York, Oxford University Press, 1966, 1969).

161: 'Since the meaning of most dreams': Jung, *CW*, Vol. 8, para. 545, p. 287.

161: 'a steadily mounting sense' and **'I was walking along a country road':** Jung, *The Archetypes of the Collective Unconscious* (1917), in *CW*, Vol. 7: *The Psychology of the Unconscious*, Chapter VII, 'Two Essays on Analytical Psychology', 1977 edn, pp. 110–11.

165: 'Merlin departed': Sir Thomas Malory, *Le Morte D'Arthur* (finished 1470; publ. by Caxton 1485), Chapter XVII: 'Yet more of the same battle, and how it was ended by Merlin'.

166: 'I have said': Walt Whitman, *Song of Myself* (1855) in *Leaves of Grass* (Philadelphia, David McKay, 1891–2), section 48.

167: 'If . . . I make use of a God-concept': Jung, *General Aspects of Dream Psychology* (1948), in *CW*, Vol. 8: *The Structure and Dynamics of the Psyche*, 1977 edn, p. 278. (First published as 'The Psychology of Dreams', 1916.)

168: 'God's in his heaven': Robert Browning, *Pippa Passes* (1841), lines 228–9.

168: 'passing through nature': Gertrude, Queen of Denmark, *Hamlet*, I. ii. 72.

168: The 'Great Chain of Being': see E. M. W. Tillyard, *The Elizabethan World Picture* (1943; London, Chatto & Windus, 1966).

168: 'Whatever IS': Alexander Pope, *An Essay on Man* (London, 1733–4).

169: 'The rich man in his castle': Mrs Cecil Alexander, 'All Things Bright and Beautiful', in *Hymns for Little Children* (1848). Mrs Alexander also wrote the words of 'Once in Royal David's City' and 'There is a Green Hill Far Away'.

169: 'I am maker of a dream': Vishvajit Pandya, 'Forest Smells and Spider Webs: Ritualized Dream Interpretation among Andaman Islanders', *Dreaming*, vol. 14, nos. 2–3 (June–September 2004), pp. 136–49. The quotations in the following lines are from the same source.

170: 'We think in eternity': Oscar Wilde, *De Profundis, being the first complete and accurate version of 'Epistola: in Carcere et Vinculis' the last prose work in English of Oscar Wilde* (London, Methuen, 1949), p. 91.

170–1: 'a living whole' and 'must be aware': T. S. Eliot, 'Tradition and the Individual Talent' (1919), in *Selected Essays* (London, Faber & Faber, 1932).

171: When *Finnegans Wake* was published: *Finnegans Wake* appeared on 2 February 1939, Joyce's fifty-seventh birthday. Before that it was known as 'Work in Progress' and various sections had appeared in avant-garde magazines since 1924.

171: 'Essentially *Finnegans Wake*': For Dr Mary E. Aldridge, see the website of Mesa Community College, Arizona: *http://www.mc. maricopa.edu/~maldridg/joyce. html*.

172: 'I dreamt I was standing': J. B. Priestley wrote about his dream in *Rain upon Godshill*, pp. 304–6.

CHAPTER 7: A MATTER OF LIFE AND DEATH

174: 'For this dream of being awake': Laurens van der Post, *The Face beside the Fire* (London, Hogarth Press, 1953), pp. 191–2.

174: At high noon: for information on Bennie LeBeau see Steven McFadden, 'Native American Spirituality: Native American Medicine Wheel Ceremony on May 8th 2004', found on *http://www.experiencefestival.com/ a/Native_American_Spirituality/id/5056*. Bennie LeBeau's homepage is *http://www.shrinesandsacredsites.com/teton/*.

176: 'The afternoon had been stormy': Reverend Francis Kilvert, *Diary*, Tuesday, 14 March 1871, in *Kilvert's Diary 1870–79. Selections from the Diary of the Rev. Francis Kilvert*, ed. William Plomer (1944; Harmondsworth, Penguin, 1977), p. 120.

176: Van der Post knew nothing about camels: for information on van der Post see Petri Liukkonen's 'Authors' Calendar', on *http://www.kirjasto.sci.fi/calendar.htm*, and *The Oxford Companion to Twentieth Century Literature in English*, ed. Jenny Stringer (Oxford, Oxford University Press, 1996).

176: 'If we could but make friends': van der Post, *The Dark Eye in Africa* (1955), cited in Liukkonen, 'Authors' Calendar'.

179: 'I saw Eternity': Henry Vaughan (1621–95), 'The World'.

180: 'If a man will begin': Francis Bacon, *The Advancement of Learning* (1605), Book I, v, no. 8.

181: In his excellent book: Guy Claxton, *The Wayward Mind: An Intimate History of the Unconscious* (London, Time Warner UK, 2005).

181: 'The great Fangio': ibid., p. 208.

182: '"We're looking at Andromeda's history"': Carol Hill, *Amanda & the Eleven Million Mile High Dancer* (1985; London, Bloomsbury, 1988), p. 91.

Quantum theory tells us: see Rupert Sheldrake, *The Sense of Being Stared At and Other Aspects of the Extended Mind* (2003; London, Arrow, 2004), p. 271, and references to P. Davies and J. Gribbin (*The Matter Myth*, London, Viking, 1991), Chapter 7. Thanks also to Alan Hale for further information.

183: David Deutsch, the quantum physicist: quotations from '"It's a much bigger thing than it looks": A talk with David Deutsch' of the Centre for Quantum Computation, Clarendon Library, University of Oxford (20 November 2000). For the text of this talk see *http://www.edge.org/3rd_culture/deutsch/deutsch_p2.html*, and for Deutsch's theories, *The Fabric of Reality: The Science of Parallel Universes – and its Implications* (London, Allen Lane, 1997).

184: 'When an individual': John Bowlby, *A Secure Base: Parent–Child Attachment and Healthy Human Development* (London, Routledge; New York, Basic Books, 1988), p. 121.

185: 'In the old days': J. M. Barrie, *Peter Pan* (1911), Chapter 4.

186: In 1971, Dr Mary Ainsworth: Dr Ainsworth's work

on attachment behaviour is reported in Bowlby, *A Secure Base*, pp. 46–8.

187: Sheldrake's work: Rupert Sheldrake, *Dogs That Know When Their Owners Are Coming Home: And Other Unexplained Powers of Animals* (New York, Crown, 1999; London, Arrow, 2000).

187: 'At all events': Carl Jung, *Four Archetypes: Mother, Rebirth, Spirit, Trickster*, trans. R. F. C. Hull (London, Routledge & Kegan Paul, 1972), p. 136.

188: One early radioactive hero: information on superheroes and their history can be found on many websites. The official Marvel website is a good starting point: *http://www.marveldirectory.com*.

189: 'dream-analysis deserves': Carl Jung, in 'The Practical Use of Dream Analysis', lecture at the 6th General Medical Council Congress for Psychotherapy, Dresden, April 1931. In Carl Gustav Jung, *Dreams*, trans. R. F. C. Hull (1974; London and New York, Routledge, 2002 edn), pp. 87, 98.

189: In 1959, Rita Dwyer: Rita's story is told in Patricia Garfield, *The Healing Power of Dreams* (London, Simon & Schuster, 1991), pp. 87–9. See also *http://www.geocities.com/asdreams_2000/members/rita_dwyer.htm*.

190: Revonsuo's 'threat simulation theory': A. Revonsuo, 'The Reinterpretation of Dreams: An Evolutionary Hypothesis of the Function of Dreaming', *Behavioral and Brain Sciences*, no. 23 (2000), pp. 877–901.

190: 'Listen with a compassionate heart': Oonagh Shanley-Toffolo, *The Voice of Silence: A Life of Love, Healing and Inspiration* (London, Rider, 2002), p. 132.

190: 'If a form should appear': Dr Samuel Johnson,

quoted in James Boswell, *The Life of Samuel Johnson Lld* (1791).

191: 'In August I received word': Shanley-Toffolo, *The Voice of Silence*, p. 56.

CHAPTER 8: RITES OF PASSAGE

192: 'A death-blow': Emily Dickinson, in *The Complete Poems of Emily Dickinson*, ed. Thomas H. Johnson (London, Faber & Faber, 1970).

194: 'the Brown Scapular': see *http://www.ocarm.org/eng/index.php*, the website of the Carmelite Order.

194: 'A bridge, now nearing': Walter de la Mare, 'The Bridge', from *Memory and Other Poems* (1938), in *The Collected Poems of Walter de la Mare* (London and Boston, Faber & Faber, 1979), p. 255.

194: 'Peace, peace!': Percy Bysshe Shelley, *Adonais*, an elegy on the death of Keats (1821), XXXIX, in *Selected Poems*, ed. Timothy Webb (London, Dent, 1977).

198: '*Angel*': John Henry (Cardinal) Newman, *The Dream of Gerontius*, Fourth Phase. The poem – later set to music by Elgar – first appeared in the *Month* in 1865, then was published as a book in 1866.

201: 'You're buried now': Brendan Kennelly, 'I See You Dancing, Father', in *A Time for Voices: Selected Poems 1960–1990* (Bloodaxe Books, 1990).

202: 'Lead, kindly Light': John Henry (Cardinal) Newman, 'Lead, kindly Light', composed in 1833, in *Lyra Apostolica* (1836).

202: 'Three of his assistants': Paul Blosser, 'Communication with the Afterlife', *Thresholds*, vol. 11, no. 3 (1993); reprinted *http://www.som.org/5A&S/afterlife.htm*.

203: 'God . . . created man': Ibn Khaldun, *The Muqaddimah*, trans. Franz Rosenthal (Princeton, Princeton University Press, 1967), pp. 80–81, 83, cited in Kelly Bulkeley, 'Reflections on the Dream Traditions of Islam', *Sleep and Hypnosis*, vol. 4, no. 1 (2002), pp. 4–14.

205: '"Now Kitty"': Lewis Carroll, *Through the Looking-Glass and What Alice Found There* (London, Macmillan, Christmas 1871), Chapter XII: 'Which dreamed it?'

205: 'A young woman': from Time Life Books (ed.), *Dreams and Dreaming* (Alexandria, Virginia, Time Life Books, 1990), p. 152; cited in Linda Lane Magallon, *Mutual Dreaming* (New York, Pocket Books, 1997), p. 15.

206: an eighteen-year-old girl: Magallon, *Mutual Dreaming*, p. 46.

207: 'For a long time': Marcel Proust, *Remembrance of Things Past* (1913–27), trans. C. K. Scott Moncrieff and Terence Kilmartin (Chatto & Windus, 1981; Harmondsworth, Penguin 1989), p. 3. These are the opening lines of the book.

208: 'the central mystery': Michael Cunningham, *The Hours* (London, 4th Estate, 1998; 1999), p. 210.

209: 'The cry of the conductor' and 'I lived in elegant bachelor quarters': Kekulé quoted in Royston M. Roberts, *Serendipity: Accidental Discoveries in Science* (New York, John Wiley & Sons, 1989), pp. 75–81. The article 'Friedrich August Kekulé, a Scientist and Dreamer' by William Jensen, University of Cincinnati, which discusses this story, can be found at *www.woodrow.org/teachers/chemistry/institutes/1992/Kekulé.html*.

210: 'Old Sages': George Wither, *A Collection of Emblemes, Ancient and Moderne* (London, 1635), emblem 3.23.

211: 'Returning each morning': W. H. Auden, 'The Dark Years', in *Collected Shorter Poems 1927–1957* (London and Boston, Faber & Faber, 1966; 1969), '1939–47', p. 176.

211: 'They have always seemed to me': Enid Blyton, correspondence with psychologist Peter McKellar, 1953–7, in Barbara Stoney, *Enid Blyton: A Biography* (London, Hodder & Stoughton, 1974), p. 224.

212: 'the luxury of being half asleep': Ian McEwan, *Saturday* (London, Jonathan Cape, 2005), p. 57.

212: that 'hard, cold waking': Kenneth Grahame, *The Wind in the Willows* (1908; London, Methuen, 1973), p. 137. See also Grahame's *The Golden Age* (1895) and *Dream Days* (1898).

212: 'And as I sat there': F. Scott Fitzgerald, *The Great Gatsby* (1926; Harmondsworth, Penguin, 1971), p. 188.

213: 'Brightness falls from the air': Thomas Nashe, 'A Litany in Time of Plague', from *Summers Last Will and Testament* (1592–3; published 1600).

213: 'Deep peace of the running wave': Anonymous, 'A Celtic Blessing', reprinted in *Do Not Go Gentle: Poems for Funerals*, ed. Neil Astley (Tarset, Bloodaxe Books, 2003), p. 87.

213: He 'began to dream of spacemen': Kathleen Nader, 'Dreams after Childhood Trauma', cited in D. Barrett (ed.), *Trauma and Dreams* (Cambridge, Mass., Harvard University Press, 1996), p. 12.

213: 'She sees a candle lit': Jay Dunn in Marie-Louise von Franz, *On Dreams and Death: A Jungian Interpretation* (1984 in German); trans. E. Xipolitas Kennedy and

Vernon Brooks (Boston and London, Shambhala, 1986; 1987), p. 64.

214: 'The dead are always looking down on us': Billy Collins, 'The Dead', in *Taking Off Emily Dickinson's Clothes: Selected Poems* (London, Picador, 2000).

215: Dylan Thomas: 'Do not go gentle into that good night' and 'Death shall have no dominion', in Dylan Thomas, *Collected Poems 1934–1952* (London, Dent, 1952), pp. 68 and 116. See also the New Testament, Romans 6: 9: 'Knowing that Christ being raised from the dead dieth no more; death hath no more dominion over him.'

215: 'One short sleep past': John Donne, 'Death Be Not Proud' (1633/35).

CHAPTER 9: THE RIVER OF LIFE

216: 'Five miles meandering': Samuel Taylor Coleridge, 'Kubla Khan: A Vision in a Dream', in *Christabel and Other Poems* (1816).

217: 'The gate of death': from Arthur Symons, 'Credo', in *The Oxford Book of Victorian Verse*, ed. Arthur Quiller-Couch (Oxford, Clarendon Press, 1912; 1971).

217: 'In my pursuit after Truth': Mahatma Gandhi in *Harijan* [an English-language journal founded by Gandhi], 29 April 1933, p. 2. Cited in *Something Understood: An Anthology of Poetry and Prose*, introduced by Mark Tully; compiled by Beverley McAinsh (London, Hodder & Stoughton, 2002), p. vii.

217: 'In the *heb sed* festival': Robert Moss, 'Dreaming like an Egyptian' (2002): see *www.mossdreams.com/egyptian.htm*.

221: 'The shores of Styx': Eugene Lee-Hamilton, 'Idle Charon', in *Victorian Verse*, ed. Quiller-Couch.

223: the Near Death Experience: For a review, see P. and E. Fenwick, *The Truth in the Light: An Investigation of over 300 Near-death Experiences* (1995; London, Headline, 1996), pp. 93–4.

224: 'A man with a hazel wand': W. B. Yeats, 'He mourns for the change that has come upon him and his beloved, and longs for the end of the world', from *The Wind among the Reeds* (1899), in W. B. Yeats, *The Collected Poems of W.B. Yeats* (London, Macmillan, 1933).

224: 'I was in a dense, gloomy forest': Carl Jung, *Memories, Dreams, Reflections*, recorded and edited by A. Jaffé, trans. R. and C. Winston (1962; London, Collins Fount Paperbacks, 1977), p. 344.

226: 'One night, Gwynllyw had a dream': from the website of All Saints Parish of Brookline, Massachusetts: *http://www.allsaintsbrookline.org/celtic/saints/cadoc.html*. Also see Donald Attwater with Catherine Rachel John, *Penguin Dictionary of Saints*, 3rd edn (1995).

226: 'The hound': *Collected Poems of W. B. Yeats*, 1982 edn, p. 525, note to p. 68.

227: 'Like a bird': William Cosmo Monkhouse, 'A Dead March', in *Victorian Verse*, ed. Quiller-Couch.

227: 'To die ... adventure': J. M. Barrie, *Peter Pan* (1911), Chapter 8.

227: 'A father had been watching': Sigmund Freud, *The Interpretation of Dreams* (1900; Harmondsworth, Penguin, 1991), p. 652.

228: *'Father, don't you see?'* : ibid., p. 653.

229: 'The river is within us': T. S. Eliot, 'The Dry

Salvages' (1941) from *Four Quartets* (New York, 1943), in *The Complete Poems and Plays of T. S. Eliot* (London, Faber & Faber, 1969), p. 184.

229: In the Punjab: for information on customs in India see *http://www.webindia123.com/punjab/People/death.htm*.

230: 'In a Wonderland they lie': 'A boat, beneath a sunny sky', verse following final chapter in Lewis Carroll, *Through the Looking-Glass and What Alice Found There* (London, Macmillan, Christmas 1871).

230: 'an ever rolling stream': Isaac Watts (1674–1748), 'O God, our help in ages past', verse 5.

230–1: The faithful 'gather at the river': Robert Lowry (1826–99), 'Shall we gather at the river'.

231: 'streams of living water': Sir Henry W. Baker (1821–77), 'The King of love', verse 2.

231: 'So this life of man': 'The Venerable Bede', *Historia Ecclesiastica Gentis Anglorum* (731); translated into Old English in the 890s.

231: the earthly *dream* of life: Shelley, *Adonais* (1821); Robert Browning, 'Easter Day', in *Christmas-Eve and Easter-Day* (1850); William Wordsworth, 'Intimations of Immortality from Recollections of Early Childhood' (1807).

233: 'It is wonderful': Dr Johnson quoted by James Boswell in *The Life of Samuel Johnson Lld* (1791).

233: 'Socrates': the dialogue can be found on the website of Professor George Boeree, of the Psychology Department, Shippensburg University, Pennsylvania: *http://www.ship.edu/~cgboeree/ meno.html*.

234: 'Or say that the end precedes': T. S. Eliot, 'Burnt Norton' (1940) from *Four Quartets* in *Complete Poems . . . of T. S. Eliot*, p. 175.

234: 'While she was telling me this dream': Carl Jung, in *The Structure and Dynamics of the Psyche*, VII, 'Synchronicity: An Acausal Connecting Principle', *Collected Works*, Vol. 8, para. 843, p. 438.

235: The psychologist Anthony Storr: in *Jung: Selected Writings* (London, Fontana, 1983, 1986), p. 331.

236: Spirituality . . . 'is based on the idea': Deepak Chopra writing on 'Science, Spirit & Synchronicity' on *http://www.meaningoflife. i12.com/Technology.htm*.

CHAPTER 10: THE WOUNDED HEALER

237: 'What is precious': Stephen Spender, 'The Truly Great', in *Collected Poems, 1928–1985* (London, Faber & Faber, 1985).

240: 'Energy is the only life': William Blake, *The Marriage of Heaven and Hell* (c. 1790–93), in *Blake: Complete Writings with variant readings*, ed. Geoffrey Keynes (London, Oxford and New York, Oxford University Press, 1966, 1969).

241: 'To see a World': William Blake, 'Auguries of Innocence', in 'Poems from the Pickering Manuscript' (c. 1803), ibid.

243: 'Are you willing': D. H. Lawrence, 'Phoenix', in *The Complete Poems of D. H. Lawrence*, ed. V. de Sola Pinto and W. Roberts, Vol. 2 (London, Heinemann, 1964), 'Last Poems', p. 728. Lawrence used the phoenix as his own symbol.

244: In his book, *Dreams and Nightmares*: Ernest Hartmann, *Dreams and Nightmares: The New Theory on the Origin and Meaning of Dreams* (New York, Plenum, 1998).

245: 'Look to your health': Izaak Walton, *The Compleat Angler* (1653), Chapter 21.

247: '*Query*': E. M. Delafield, *The Provincial Lady Goes Further* (London, Macmillan, 1932; 1939), p. 85.

248: 'There stood a leaf-bearing tree': Carl Jung, *Memories, Dreams, Reflections*, recorded and edited by A. Jaffé, trans. R. and C. Winston (1962; London, Collins Fount Paperbacks, 1977), p. 201.

248: 'In the centre': ibid., p. 223.

249: Richard Wilhelm sent him his work: Wilhelm, *The Secret of the Golden Flower: A Chinese Book of Life*, trans. R. Wilhelm with a European commentary by C. G. Jung; trans. from German by Cary F. Baynes (New York, Harcourt, Brace & World, 1962).

249: 'I saw that everything': Jung, *Memories, Dreams, Reflections*, p. 222.

250–1: 'The design is ritually prepared' and 'Sitting in the earthly darkness': see 'Meeting the Mandala' (1993) on Barbara Clare Goodwin's website, *http://www.abgoodwin.com/mandala/introduction-to-mandalas.shtml*.

251: 'An explosion of infra-red': Dave Rodney, Canadian climber, author and filmmaker, in *Everest: Reflections from the Top*, ed. Christine Gee, Garry Weare and Margaret Gee (London, Rider, 2003), p. 94.

251–2: the Amerindian nations . . . 'the way you do that': Barbara Tedlock, 'Sharing and Interpreting Dreams in Amerindian Nations', in *Dream Cultures: Explorations in the Comparative History of Dreaming*, ed. David Shulman and Guy Stroumsa (Oxford, Oxford University Press, 1999), pp. 95–6.

THE HIDDEN POWER OF DREAMS

252: 'Who had uttered these words?': Flann O'Brien [Brian O'Nolan], *The Third Policeman* (1967; London, Flamingo, 1993), p. 26.

255: 'I once had a dream of Baba': J. McDaniel, *Offering Flowers, Feeding Skulls: Popular Goddess Worship in West Bengal* (Oxford, Oxford University Press, 2004). For more information on Prahlad Chandra visit the Prahlad Foundation website: *www.prahlad.org*.

256: 'It is the province': Oliver Wendell Holmes, *The Poet at the Breakfast Table* (1872), Chapter 10.

256: A middle-aged previously healthy woman: Ikechukwa Obialo Azuonye, 'Diagnosis Made by Hallucinatory Voices', *British Medical Journal*, vol. 315 (December 1997), pp. 1685–6.

258: Jung described a similar case: Jung, *Memories, Dreams, Reflections*, p. 148.

259: 'In two very similar cases': Valerie J. Hoffman, 'The Role of Visions in Contemporary Egyptian Religious Life', *Religion*, vol. 27, no. 1 (1997), p. 48.

260: 'But (when so sad)': Francis Thompson, 'The Kingdom of God', in *The Oxford Book of English Mystical Verse*, ed. D. H. S. Nicholson and A. H. E. Lee (Oxford, Clarendon Press, 1917).

261: 'The elders approached David': Paladin's story is told by Caroline Myss in *Anatomy of the Spirit* (New York, Three Rivers Press, 1996), pp. 163–5.

CHAPTER 11: THE TREE OF LIFE

263: 'There were scraps of lime': Russell Hoban, *The Bat*

Tattoo (2002; London: Bloomsbury, 2003), p. 110.

267: 'Up the airy mountain': William Allingham, 'The Fairies', in *Poems* (1850).

269: 'In modern folklore': James MacKillop, *A Dictionary of Celtic Mythology* (Oxford and New York, Oxford University Press, 1998, 2004), entry for 'Dian Cecht'.

269: 'I have dim mystic sympathies': Alfred Tennyson, letter to Emily Sellwood, October/November 1838 in *Alfred Tennyson*, ed. Adam Roberts (Oxford, Oxford University Press, 2000), p. 495.

270: 'People are learning to work with nature': Trees for Life is based at Findhorn Bay. For information, see the organization's website, *http://www.treesforlife.org.uk/index.shtml*.

270: 'The Axis of the World': Mircea Eliade, *Shamanism: Archaic Techniques of Ecstasy*, trans. Willard R. Trask (London, Routledge, 1964), pp. 259, 261.

271: the Geser Fund: The Geser Fund takes its name from the Buryat heroic – and shamanist – epic, *Geser*. See *http://www.buryatmongol.com/geser.html*, and follow the link to 'The Geser Fund – Raising consciousness for the future'. The website *http://www.buryatmongol.com/peacetree.html* gives directions on how to create a prayer tree to act against violence in the modern world.

272: 'Give me my Scallop shell': 'The Passionate Mans Pilgrimage, supposed to be written by one at the point of death', often attributed to Sir Walter Ralegh (1554–1618). A manuscript of the poem is entitled 'Verses made by Sir Walter Raleigh the night before he was beheaded', which may refer to 1603, when he was sentenced to death. However, three weeks later he was reprieved. The scallop shell was worn by pilgrims returning from the Holy Land.

272: 'defer this matter': *Everyman* (*c.* 1509–19), in *Everyman and Medieval Miracle Plays*, ed. A. C. Cawley (London, Dent, 1956, 1974).

273: 'Socrates ... similar view': Plato, *Phaedo*, 114d; written 360 BCE, trans. Benjamin Jowett.

273: 'pestilent fellow': *Oxford Companion to English Literature*, 6th edn, ed. Margaret Drabble (Oxford, Oxford University Press, 2000).

274: 'Has anyone supposed': Walt Whitman, 'Song of Myself', in *Leaves of Grass* (1855).

274: Marie-Louise von Franz ... points out: in *On Dreams and Death: A Jungian Interpretation* (1984 in German); trans. E. Xipolitas Kennedy and Vernon Brooks (Boston and London, Shambhala, 1986, 1987): 'The Mystery of the Corpse and the Grave of Osiris'.

274: 'wondrous forms and figures': Eliade, *Shamanism*, p. 261.

274–5: 'Anguish before Nothingness' and 'Death is the great Initiation': Mircea Eliade, *Myths, Dreams, and Mysteries: The Encounter between Contemporary Faiths and Archaic Realities*, trans. P. Mairet (London, Harper & Row, 1975), pp. 235–6.

275: 'hints' and 'experiences': Carl Jung, *Memories, Dreams, Reflections*, recorded and edited by A. Jaffé, trans. R. and C. Winston (1962; London, Collins Fount Paperbacks, 1977), p. 343.

276: 'The sky whitens': Charles Causley, 'Eden Rock', in *Collected Poems 1951–2000* (London, Picador, 2000).

276: Jeff Zaslow: 'All That Jazz' column, *Chicago Sun-Times*, Thursday, 13 March 1997.

278: '"**Amanda,**" **Hotchkiss said**': Carol Hill, *Amanda & the Eleven Million Mile High Dancer* (1985; London, Bloomsbury, 1988), p. 76.

279: '**The aborigine or Cro-Magnon**': Wallace, quoted in V. S. Ramachandran and Sandra Blakeslee, *Phantoms in the Brain: Human Nature and the Architecture of the Mind* (London, Fourth Estate, 1998; 1999), pp. 190–91.

279: '**Where the bee sucks**': Shakespeare, *The Tempest*, V. i.

280: '**Here are people**': Jeremy Narby, *The Cosmic Serpent: DNA and the Origins of Knowledge* (New York, Jeremy P. Tarcher/Putnam, 1998), p. 11.

280: '"**I ask the plant**"': quoted in Stanley Krippner, 'The Epistemology and Technologies of Shamanic States of Consciousness', *Journal of Consciousness Studies*, vol. 7, nos. 11–12 (2000), pp. 94–118. Also available online at *http://www.stanleykrippner.com/papers/shamanic_epistemology.html*.

281: '**Every funeral**': Samuel Johnson, *Rambler*, no. 78 (15 December 1750).

282: '**To this end he ought to have a myth**': Jung, *Memories, Dreams, Reflections*, p. 337.

CONCLUSION

283: '**Legend has it**': Fraser Boa, *The Way of the Dream, Conversations on Jungian Dream Interpretation with Marie-Louise von Franz* (Boston and London, Shambhala, 1988; 1992), p. 218.

284: The BBC2 series, *The Tribe*: This episode was broadcast on 3 January 2005.

285: 'So there's a great deal more to discover': Philip Pullman, quoted in Roger Highfield, 'The Quest for Dark Matter', *Daily Telegraph*, 27 April 2005, p. 20. This article is also the source of the figure of 85 per cent.

286: 'What is this life': W. H. Davies (1870–1940), 'Leisure', in *Songs of Joy* (c. 1911).

286: 'Things fall apart': W. B. Yeats, 'The Second Coming', from *Michael Robartes and the Dancer* (1921), in *The Collected Poems of W. B. Yeats* (London, Macmillan, 1933; 1978), p. 210.

287: 'Who is more ignorant?': Dan Brown, *Angels and Demons* (London, Bantam Press, 2000), p. 423.

288: 'The most beautiful experience': Albert Einstein, 'The World as I See It', *Forum and Century*, vol. 84, pp. 193–4; reprinted in *Living Philosophies* (New York, Simon & Schuster, 1931), pp. 3–7.

289: While Jung was in Africa: Carl Jung, *Memories, Dreams, Reflections*, recorded and edited by A. Jaffé, trans. R. and C. Winston (1962; London, Collins Fount Paperbacks, 1977), p. 294.

BIBLIOGRAPHY

Alvarez, Alfred, *Night: An Exploration of Night Life, Night Language, Sleep and Dreams*, New York, W. W. Norton; London, Jonathan Cape, 1995. The edition cited is Vintage 1996.

Barasch, M., *Healing Dreams*, New York, Riverhead Books, 2000.

Barrett, Deirdre, *The Committee of Sleep*, New York, Crown Publishers, 2001.

Barrett, Deirdre (ed.), *Trauma and Dreams*, Cambridge, Mass., Harvard University Press, 1996.

Blake, William, *Blake: Complete Writings with variant readings*, ed. Geoffrey Keynes, London, Oxford and New York, Oxford University Press, 1966, 1969.

Boa, Fraser, *The Way of the Dream, Conversations on Jungian Dream Interpretation with Marie-Louise von Franz*, Boston and London, Shambhala, 1988, 1992.

Bosnak, Robert, *Tracks in the Wilderness of Dreaming*, New York, Delacorte Press, 1996.

Bowlby, John, *A Secure Base. Parent–Child Attachment and Healthy Human Development*, London, Routledge; New York, Basic Books, 1988.

Caine, Linda and Royston, Robin, *Out of the Dark*, London, Bantam Press, 2003.

Campbell, Joseph, *The Masks of God*, 4 vols, 1959–68. Vol. 1: *Primitive Mythology* (1959), Harmondsworth, Penguin, 1976.

Claxton, Guy, *The Wayward Mind: An Intimate History of the Unconscious*, London, Time Warner UK, 2005.

Do Not Go Gentle: Poems for Funerals, ed. Neil Astley, Tarset, Northumberland, Bloodaxe Books, 2003.

Eliade, Mircea, *Shamanism: Archaic Techniques of Ecstasy*, trans. Willard R. Trask, London, Routledge, 1964, 1968.

Eliot, T. S., *Four Quartets* (New York, 1943), in *The Complete Poems and Plays of T. S. Eliot* (London, Faber & Faber, 1969).

Fenwick, P. and E., *The Hidden Door*, London, Headline, 1997.

Fenwick, P. and E., *The Truth in the Light: An Investigation of over 300 Near-death Experiences*, 1995; London, Headline, 1996.

Ferguson, Niall, *Empire: How Britain Made the Modern World*, London, Allen Lane, 2003.

Freud, Sigmund, *The Interpretation of Dreams* (1900); trans. James Strachey, ed. James Strachey and Alan Tyson, revised by Angela Richards, Harmondsworth, The Penguin Freud Library, 1976, 1991.

Gilbert, W. S., *The Savoy Operas*, London, Macmillan; New York, St Martin's Press, 1954.

Harman, Claire, *Robert Louis Stevenson: A Biography*, London, HarperCollins, 2005.

Hartmann, Ernest, *Dreams and Nightmares: The New Theory on the Origin and Meaning of Dreams*, New York, Plenum, 1998.

Joseph, Dr R. *The Right Brain and the Unconscious: Discovering the Stranger Within*, New York, Plenum, 1992.

Jung, C. G., *The Collected Works of C. G. Jung*, ed. H. Read, M. Fordham and G. Adler, trans. R. F. C. Hull, London, Routledge & Kegan Paul, 1953–78.

Jung: Selected Writings, ed. Anthony Storr, London, Fontana, 1983, 1986.

Jung, Carl, *Four Archetypes: Mother, Rebirth, Spirit, Trickster*, trans. R. F. C. Hull, London, Routledge & Kegan Paul, 1972. Extracted from *The Archetypes and the Collective Unconscious*, Vol. 9, Part 1 of *The Collected Works of C. G. Jung*.

Jung, C. G., *Memories, Dreams, Reflections*, recorded and edited by A. Jaffé, trans. R. and C. Winston, 1962; London, Collins Fount Paperbacks, 1977. From a manuscript Jung left on his death in 1961.

Kanigel, Robert, *The Man Who Knew Infinity: The Life of the Genius Ramanujan*, New York, Scribner's, 1991.

Keats, John, *The Letters of John Keats*, ed. Maurice Buxton Forman, 4th edn, London, Oxford University Press, 1952, 1960.

McEwan, Ian, *Saturday*, London, Jonathan Cape, 2005.

McNally, Richard J., *Remembering Trauma*, Cambridge, Mass. and London, Belknap Press/Harvard University Press, 2003.

Mahowald, M. W., Woods, S. R. and Schenck, C. H., 'Sleeping Dreams, Waking Hallucinations and the Central Nervous System', *Dreaming. Journal of the Association for the Study of Dreams*, vol. 8, no. 2 (June 1998), pp. 89–103 (published by Human Sciences Press, New York).

Myss, Caroline, *Anatomy of the Spirit*, New York, Three Rivers Press, 1996.

O'Brien, Flann [Brian O'Nolan], *The Third Policeman*, 1967; London, Flamingo, 1993.

Penrose, Roger, *The Emperor's New Mind: Concerning Computers, Minds, and the Laws of Physics*, New York, Oxford University Press, 1989; London, Vintage, 1990.

Radcliffe, A. J. J., *A History of Dreams*, 1923; Random House/ Senate, 1996.

Ramachandran, V. S. and Blakeslee, Sandra, *Phantoms in the Brain: Human Nature and the Architecture of the Mind*, London, Fourth Estate, 1998; paperback edn, 1999.

Roberts, Royston M., *Serendipity: Accidental Discoveries in Science*, New York, John Wiley & Sons, 1989.

Shafton, Anthony, *Dream Reader: Contemporary Approaches to the Understanding of Dreams*, New York, SUNY Press, 1995.

Shanley-Toffolo, Oonagh, *The Voice of Silence: A Life of Love, Healing and Inspiration*, London, Rider, 2002.

Sheldrake, Rupert, *Dogs That Know When Their Owners Are Coming Home and Other Unexplained Powers of Animals*, New York, Crown Publishers, 1999; London, Arrow, 2000.

Sheldrake, Rupert, *The Sense of Being Stared At and Other Aspects of the Extended Mind*, London, Hutchinson, 2003; Arrow, 2004.

Shelley, Mary, *Frankenstein*, 1818; ed. J. M. Smith, Basingstoke, Macmillan; Bedford, St Martin's, 2000.

Shulman, David and Stroumsa, Guy (eds), *Dream Cultures: Explorations in the Comparative History of Dreaming*, Oxford, Oxford University Press, 1999.

Solms, Mark, *The Neuropsychology of Dreams: A Clinico-Anatomical Study*, Mahwah, NJ, Lawrence Erlbaum, 1997.

Something Understood: An Anthology of Poetry and Prose, introduced by Mark Tully; compiled by Beverley McAinsh, London, Sydney and Auckland, Hodder & Stoughton, 2001; paperback edn 2002.

Stevenson, Robert Louis, *The Letters of Robert Louis Stevenson*, ed. Bradford A. Booth and Ernest Mehew, 8 vols, New Haven and London, Yale University Press, 1994–5.

Stoney, Barbara, *Enid Blyton: A Biography*, London, Hodder & Stoughton, 1974, 1992.

Van Eeden, Frederik, 'A Study of Dreams', *Proceedings of the Society for Psychical Research*, vol. 26, part 47 (July 1913), pp. 431–61.

The Victorian Book of Dreams, including signs, auguries, divination by cards and prognostics from the physiognomy and moles, &c., &c., ed. Marion Giordan. n.d.; repr. London, Hugh Evelyn, 1964.

Von Franz, Marie-Louise, *On Dreams and Death: A Jungian Interpretation* (1984 in German); trans. E. Xipolitas Kennedy and Vernon Brooks, Boston and

343

London, Shambhala, 1986, 1987.

Wilhelm, Richard, *The Secret of the Golden Flower: A Chinese Book of Life*, trans. R. Wilhelm with a European commentary by C. G. Jung; trans. from the German by Cary F. Baynes, New York, Harcourt, Brace & World, 1962.

Yeats, W. B., *The Collected Plays of W. B. Yeats*, 1952; London, Macmillan, 1982.

Yeats, W. B., *The Collected Poems of W. B. Yeats*, London, Macmillan, 1933.

INDEX

INDEX

INDEX

INDEX